JOANNE

By

Dlanor Rellim

Copyright © Dlanor Rellim 2024
This book is sold subject to the condition that it shall not, by way of trade or otherwise, be lent, resold, hired out, or otherwise circulated without the publisher's prior consent in any form of binding or cover other than that in which it is published and without a similar condition including this condition being imposed on the subsequent publisher.
The moral right of Dlanor Rellim has been asserted.

This is a work of fiction. Names, characters, businesses, organisations, places, events and incidents either are the product of the author's imagination or are used fictitiously. Any resemblance to actual persons, living or dead, events, or locales is entirely coincidental.

*To my family who have always believed in my ability
and who have been of great support to me on this long road.*

CONTENTS

CHAPTER 1 All Change 1
CHAPTER 2 Defining Meetings 13
CHAPTER 3 Dream Home 24
CHAPTER 4 Building Bridges 38
CHAPTER 5 Joanne's New Job 49
CHAPTER 6 The Company Dinner 64
CHAPTER 7 Tom Opens his Heart 78
CHAPTER 8 Difficult Times 87
CHAPTER 9 Continued Improvements 98
CHAPTER 10 The Morning After 108
CHAPTER 11 Chance Meeting 119
CHAPTER 12 Frosty Exchanges 129
CHAPTER 13 On Reflection 139
CHAPTER 14 Worrying Times 150
CHAPTER 15 Painful Decisions 163
CHAPTER 16 Help is Needed 173
CHAPTER 17 Awkward Times 183
CHAPTER 18 Some Good News 196
CHAPTER 19 Joanne Aids Tom's Recovery 206
CHAPTER 20 Close Times 216
CHAPTER 21 New Developments 227
CHAPTER 22 Broken Ties, Harmful Lies 240
CHAPTER 23 Troubled Emotions 255
CHAPTER 24 A Rushed Plan 269
CHAPTER 25 A Painful Experience 281
CHAPTER 26 Serious Times 294
CHAPTER 27 Disturbing News 308
CHAPTER 28 Loose Ends 321
CHAPTER 29 Waiting Time 336
CHAPTER 30 Coming to Terms 351
CHAPTER 31 Pulling Together 367
ABOUT THE AUTHOR 385

Japeth Banting, who provided the initial hand-drawn cover design which I absolutely love.

CHAPTER ONE

All Change

Joanne replaced the phone's handset and walked towards the French windows which opened onto a small balcony; it was meant to be summer but the scene she surveyed from her room in The Grand Hotel Eastbourne gave quite a different impression. Opening the French windows and stepping momentarily out onto the balcony, she looked past the statue of Spencer Compton, the eighth Duke of Devonshire. The sea was swirling in the wind and the fast-moving clouds were changing colour by the minute. As she continued to look out to sea, she felt a few spots of rain land on her arm and decided it was time to go back into the warmth of her room. She stepped back inside and as she turned to close the doors, she noticed the speed with which the rain was now hitting the windows. Joanne felt totally alone for the first time, and when she thought about it, she was … well, apart from her aunt Matilda.

Joanne had met and married Andrew while she was still studying for her law degree at university. She had always wanted to be a solicitor. They struggled at first: Joanne was always studying, and they had little time for each other. Her mother and father had pleaded with her to wait until she had finished university, but Joanne was so in love with Andrew that she refused; she didn't want to lose him.

Once Joanne had finished her degree, she got a position at a reputable law firm in London. She still found the learning process extremely hard and although they had more time together, Joanne was always tired. Andrew became increasingly distant and blamed it on his position as office manager, but in truth he was becoming bored with the situation and was finding it hard to cope. Although they both tried hard to correct things, Joanne felt that she was always trying harder, which gave her the impression that Andrew didn't want to try at all. It soon became apparent to her that it just wasn't going to work and soon the distance between them became progressively worse.

Andrew spent more time working late, often arriving home after Joanne had already gone to bed. Somehow, they accepted the way things were and that was the way they continued until Joanne's life was turned upside down with the news of her parents' sudden death. They had been on holiday in Greece when they were both killed in a boating accident. Joanne was poleaxed, to put it mildly, and being an only child did not help matters: she had no one to turn to. What made things even worse, if that were possible, was that it was down to her to inform her aunt Matilda of their deaths. She remembered how she felt when she picked up her phone to ring her aunty, immediately cancelling the call. She just could not do it to her, so she quickly left a garbled message for her boss, got in her car, and drove all the way to Eastbourne to Aunt Matilda's. Now whenever she thought of her aunty all she could remember was the absolute look of horror on her face. Having opened the door and unexpectedly seeing her niece standing there in front of her, she let out the loudest scream that Joanne had ever heard from anyone. That evening haunted Joanne; it was full of lots of tears and cuddles and very few words. Even now, as Joanne stood there, the tears started rolling down her cheeks again. She had found it very hard to get over the death of her parents and was still completely devastated. It also appeared to her husband that she had encased herself in a protective shell from which she distanced herself from everyone but her closest friends – and he wasn't one of them. Andrew continued to make extra allowances for her but in the end he found it just too difficult to contemplate. He couldn't understand how eighteen months after the accident she still couldn't fully accept the loss of her parents and was still having frequent panic attacks. He found it increasingly hard to come to terms with her mood swings, which often led to heated rows and caused him to walk out on more than one occasion.

Joanne had come to accept how Andrew reacted and never really questioned him when he disappeared for hours after one of their intense arguments. However, when those hours turned into a day or more, she began to wonder where exactly he was. It was during one such disappearance that Andrew had decided he could not take any more, and, on his return, he asked Joanne for a divorce. Joanne had been having her doubts about her husband's excuses for a while and wondered if he had been having a secret affair with someone in his office, a practice that was forbidden by his company. When Andrew came straight out and asked for a divorce, she felt there may have been some substance to her assumptions, but she needed to find out for sure.

Not wanting to cause a massive scene, Joanne didn't argue with Andrew, but instead hired a private detective to trail her husband for a couple of days. The report she received was damning and completely confirmed her suspicions. Joanne used the information to her advantage, and when she confronted her husband with all the evidence she had obtained, he could not deny anything. She had left him with no alternative but to agree to her demands and the terms of the divorce, which she would grant him without question. Andrew was shocked by Joanne's proposal but if he wanted to keep his job and protect the job of his new partner too, he had no other option than to accept the terms of the settlement his wife had laid out before him.

Using the situation in her favour, Joanne kept all the money her parents had left her. They sold their house and Andrew gave her eighty per cent of the value, seeing that she had paid off their mortgage from the sale of her parents' house. This left her with the means to start a new life – simple, or at least that was what she thought. However, as is very often the case, things are not as simple as they are expected to be, something that Joanne very quickly found out.

At first, Joanne wasn't sure what she wanted, but what she did know was that she had to restart her life and she had to do it quickly, without it affecting her work too much. After speaking to her boss and explaining everything, he arranged for her to move into one of the company flats that they kept for emergencies – a temporary solution to her homelessness – for which she was incredibly grateful. That gave Joanne the breathing space she needed to find herself a flat of her own, something not too far away from the office. Property there was not cheap and although money was not an immediate problem for her, she didn't want to waste copious amounts of it on something that she was only ever going to rent. It took her a few weeks to find the perfect place, a bedsit which had all that she needed. It also gave her the freedom of complete independence as she no longer felt an obligation to be tied to her position at work.

Things were okay for a while, but as the months passed, Joanne shut herself away and threw herself into her work. As good as it seemed, she knew that she could not keep up the pace forever. After living as a virtual recluse for almost six months, she decided it was time to let her hair down. She felt that she had weathered the storm of her divorce, albeit with help from her work colleagues, but now the time was right for her to re-integrate with the outside world. That decision alone was the one that would shape what was to happen next and would almost lead her to the brink of complete exhaustion.

Joanne allowed herself the odd meeting with friends from the past and to start with everything was fine. However, it was not long before the odd one-off meeting became the norm as she began to realise just how much she had missed her friends. Then she realised too that what had been her new life as a single woman was often becoming an upsetting experience for her. The problem was she just could not get away from Andrew. It wasn't that he was harassing her or anything like that, it was more that they had the same circle of friends; wherever she went, he was there. Friends' get-togethers, birthdays, weddings, funerals – you name it, whatever the occasion they would both be invited.

Joanne hadn't been sure what to do, but she knew that she couldn't just sit around and do nothing. She had a choice to make: either continue meeting in the social circle that she was in or return to being a recluse. She knew that neither was acceptable and that both would see her mental health deteriorate.

As she sat alone in her bedsit, casting her mind over the latest celebration, if that was the correct definition, which had left her completely shattered, she decided to act. She went to work on the Monday and asked if she could take a week's annual leave. Once her request had been accepted, she rushed back to her flat, threw some clothes in a case and was soon on her way down to Eastbourne. She booked herself into a room at the Best Western Lansdowne Hotel. Remembering her last visit to her aunt, this time she rang her first to let her know she was in Eastbourne, before visiting her. They spent the whole week together, shopping, and eating out, they watched a couple of films at the local cinema and even went on a day trip to Brighton. As a special treat, Maria also managed to purchase two tickets for the Eastbourne Tennis Event, a sport she knew her aunt loved to watch. The week went too quickly but the break was exactly what she needed. The confusion in her head had cleared, her body had started to feel stronger, and she found that she was enjoying being able to breathe in fresh sea air rather than the fumes from London's incessant traffic.

When the week was over, Joanne headed back to London, to her flat and, ultimately, to work on Monday morning. As she entered the office that morning, everyone noticed a spring in her step and the look of joy on her face. She went straight into her boss's office and asked to be released from her contract. He was shocked at her request; he certainly hadn't seen it coming. He sat there for a minute, not speaking, staring at the painting on his office wall while playing with the paperweight on his desk.

"Close the door and take a seat," he said as he turned to look at her.

"Joanne, do you know what that painting is of?" he asked her.

Joanne looked at the painting on the wall.

"It's a painting of a boat at sea, in a storm," she replied.

"It's a little bit more than that," he replied as he glanced back to look at the painting. "It's a painting of Christ in the storm of Galilee, by Rembrandt. You know you may feel as though you are in the middle of that storm right now, Joanne, but storms do not last forever. Your storm will be over, and you will gain strength from your experience. You have friends around you here to help you. To be honest, you have a wonderful opportunity here and I don't want to see your talent go to waste."

"With all due respect, I do not think you realise the pressure I have been under. To lose my parents the way I did, and then to lose my husband whom I trusted, has all been too much. Right now, my life feels worse than being in a storm: it feels as though I have been in a shipwreck. You say I have friends here and yes, I do, but most of my friends are also Andrew's friends and he has made it clear that he has no intention of changing those friends to satisfy me. Apart from that, my aunt Matilda lives in Eastbourne and right now she needs me. She's struggling the same as I am. I lost my mother and father and my aunt lost her only sister, a sister whom she loved and adored. She is now my only living relative, as I am hers, and she loves me dearly like the daughter she never had. I have enjoyed my time here, learning from you and those around me, but if I stay my life will never change. I will always be living in a perpetual shipwreck. I will become a burden to you and I do not want that to happen. Please, I ask you to accept my notice," she concluded as she slid an envelope across his desk towards him. Her boss picked up the envelope and looked at it.

After he had read it, she reiterated that she needed a complete break from her previous life and circle of friends before she could finally rebuild her life. She still had four weeks holiday left to take, which he allowed her to take as her period of notice. Joanne walked out of the office, cleared her flat and in no time at all she was driving back down to Eastbourne and freedom.

Joanne had always got on well with her aunt whom she visited regularly, and it was during one such visit that she had noticed a small house nestled halfway up a hillside; she fell in love with the property almost immediately and had always said that one day she would like to buy it. She had phoned her aunt and asked her to get details of all the properties available for sale in and around the Eastbourne area. Joanne couldn't believe her eyes as she sifted through the information and saw a photograph of the house she had set her heart on. It may have been that her life was in turmoil, but something was finally going right for her! She had immediately contacted the estate agents to set the ball rolling in what she hoped would end in the purchase of her dream home but a process that would eventually mean so much more to her than just a house.

As Joanne moved away from the window to start dressing, her phone rang, it was her aunt.

"Joanne, dear, it's Aunty. What time did you say that you would be visiting me today?"

"I'm still not sure, it just depends on how long it takes to look over the house. Why, Aunty? Is there a problem?"

"No, dear, not really, it's just that I have to go out to get some shopping and didn't know if I would have time before you arrived or whether to leave it till after you dropped me back home."

"I was about to ring you anyway, Aunty. I thought that if you had time to spare today then perhaps I could come round and pick you up. First, we could both look at the house. After that, we could have lunch, then you can do your shopping and I'll drop you back home when we've finished. That way we could do all the things we need to and spend time together as well."

"That would be lovely, Joanne, thank you; what time should I expect you then?"

"Breakfast is in twenty minutes, so shall we say nine to nine-fifteen? I need to be at the house by nine-forty-five."

"That'll be fine, dear. I'll let you go and have your breakfast then. See you later. Bye."

"Goodbye, Aunty," replied Joanne as she ended the call placing her phone on the table.

Joanne hurried to get dressed before making her way down to the hotel restaurant for breakfast. As soon as she had finished, she went straight to her car and drove to the apartment building where her Aunty lived. As she drove into the car park, she saw Matilda was already waiting by the main entrance door. Joanne pulled up, got out of her car and walked round to her Aunty, kissing her on the cheek.

"Good morning, Aunty. Shall I put your shopping trolley in the boot?" she asked.

"Yes, please," replied Matilda.

Joanne put the shopping trolley in the boot and got back in her car.

"Are you ready for this, dear?"

"I think so, Aunty, I think so," replied Joanne, looking at the time on the dashboard clock. "But I think we need to get moving as it's nine-thirty already," added Joanne as she started the engine and drove out of the car park.

Joanne was now beginning to feel quite nervous as she realised just how close she was to being able to complete one of her dreams: the purchase of her favourite house. It was almost nine forty-five as they drove up the hillside towards the property. She could see a car already parked outside, so she knew that the estate agent was waiting for her.

"Joanne, I'm so happy for you! This is such a lovely house and I'm sure that you are going to make it look really beautiful inside. I can picture it now," remarked her aunt as they got out of the car.

"Aunty, I haven't bought it yet! There are a lot of things to be ironed out," replied Joanne as they walked towards the door. Before Joanne could knock, it was opened by a stern-looking man in a suit, which she thought had seen better days.

"Miss Webster, I'm Johnson. You spoke to my colleague on the phone. Unfortunately, he was called away to the hospital unexpectedly this morning. His wife is pregnant, so I've been left holding the baby, if you'll pardon the expression."

"I do hope everything will be alright," replied Joanne.

"I'm sure it will, Miss Webster. Anyway, let's do what we're both here for, shall we? If you would like to follow me, I'll show you around."

Joanne was a little perturbed by the estate agent's manner. He was completely different from John Hales with whom she had been dealing. She followed him around, looking closely at the property she was hoping to buy but taking little notice of the spiel given by the agent. As they made their way from room to room, looking out of the windows Joanne couldn't but help notice the figure of a man who appeared to be mending the perimeter fence at the far end of the property. She was sure that her Aunty had spotted him too, as she stood by the window looking in the direction of the man for some time while Joanne asked the estate agent questions about the house.

"Well, Miss Webster, do you think you would like it here?" asked Johnson.

"It is certainly what I'm looking for, I must admit; however, I shall have to think about it for a day or two. There are a couple of points that I would like to clarify with Mr Hales," replied Joanne.

"Well, I can answer your questions, Miss Webster, and of course, you can sign a contract with me should you decide to proceed," replied Johnson.

"I see you have employed someone to mend the boundary fence," she added.

"Excuse me?" he asked, sounding a little bemused by her statement.

"I noticed from the bedroom window that there was a man at the end of the property fixing the fence," replied Joanne.

"Oh no, that'll be Tom, Miss Webster," he replied.

"Tom?" questioned Joanne.

"Oh, so Hales didn't tell you about him? Now, that does surprise me," replied Johnson.

"Well, then perhaps you could enlighten me as to who exactly Tom is!" said Joanne.

Johnson walked over to the window and looked out towards where Tom was working. As he turned back towards Joanne, he said, "He's a sort of odd-job man. He used to carry out a lot of repairs on the property for Miss Wheeler, the previous owner. In return, she let him live in the old barn; he is a strange chap, lived in Eastbourne all his life, used to be quite clever, then just fell apart when his wife and child died in a car crash. He seems a bit on the simple side now, probably because he never speaks to anyone."

"Well, I don't want to seem harsh, but surely someone should have told him he can no longer live here now the old lady is dead?"

"Unfortunately, it is not that simple Miss Webster. You see, in her will, Miss Wheeler gave him the right to stay on the land until the property has been sold. No one has been prepared to challenge that as it meant there was always someone here looking after the place while it remained empty."

"Well, that might be so, but if I do decide to buy this house, then I want you to make sure he is gone, long before I move in. Do I make myself clear, Mr Johnson?"

"Explicitly clear, Miss Webster, explicitly," replied Johnson.

"Come on, Aunty, we're going now. I have seen and heard enough," said Joanne as she walked towards the front door.

Johnson followed the two of them out of the house and watched as they got in the car. Joanne opened the car window as she was about to drive away.

"Mr Hales knows where I am staying if he should want to contact me to explain," she said then drove off at high speed.

Joanne's Aunt Matilda sat quietly, looking out of the passenger seat window as Joanne drove towards the town centre. Matilda sensed that her niece was annoyed and thought it best not to say anything until she was asked to. They were almost halfway through the town and she began to think her niece had forgotten she was going shopping, so she decided to break the silence.

"You can drop me here, dear; I haven't got a lot of shopping to do.

I'll catch the bus home."

"It's not right, Aunty. It would never happen in London," said Joanne as she turned sharply into the car park.

Matilda turned towards Joanne.

"But I thought that was why you wanted to move down here – because of the relaxed atmosphere and the friendly approach."

"It is, and I do, but that doesn't excuse protocol! There are ways to do things and to have someone living in an outhouse on the property I want to buy is not right."

"Well, you're not staying in that hotel much longer, my dear; it must be costing you a small fortune. You'll have to come and stay with me."

That was an idea that Joanne hadn't even dared to think about. She loved her aunt Matilda dearly, but she knew that if she lived with her, even for a few weeks, then Matilda would try to organise her whole life for her.

"Thanks for the offer, Aunty, but I'm sure that everything will be sorted out very soon. You see they want to sell that property; it's been empty for a couple of months now and what's more, they know that I can pay cash for it. You know what they say about never looking a gift horse in the mouth."

Matilda laughed.

"You seem very confident, dear. I know how much you like that house and I'd hate to see you disappointed, but don't build your hopes up too high," she replied.

They were in the supermarket when Joanne's phone rang.

"Hello. Joanne Webster."

"Miss Webster, it's John Hales. I've just arrived at the office, and I believe that we have a small problem."

"Well, not such a *small* one, Mr. Hales. I would say he looked at least six feet tall from where I was standing."

"Look, Miss Webster, I know this is very short notice, but can I meet you for lunch and talk things over?"

Joanne thought for a minute before answering.

"I'd love to, but I have already promised to take my aunt for lunch, and she's here with me now."

"That's not a problem, Miss Webster; I'll take both of you out to lunch."

"It's a deal then. What time and where?" she asked.

"Well, I have a few calls to make first, so maybe in about an hour. Will that suit you?"

Joanne looked at her aunt.

"Fancy lunch?" she mouthed. Matilda nodded.

"I still have some shopping to do, so shall we say one o'clock then, Mr Hales?" asked Joanne.

"That's fine with me. We'll meet at Bill's if that's okay with you both?" asked Hales.

"That's fine with us. See you there at one o'clock then. Bye." Joanne slipped her phone back into her bag.

"See, what did I say? Now they're frightened of losing the sale. This could work in my favour, Aunty."

"In what way, dear?" she inquired.

"Well, if I let them think that I'm not going to buy, I may be able to get them to reduce the price."

"Do you think they would do that?" asked Matilda.

"It's worth a try, Aunty, it's certainly worth a try," replied Joanne with a huge grin on her face.

Joanne and her aunt finished their shopping and then climbed back into the car.

"Where are we going now, dear?" asked Matilda.

"We are going to drop your shopping off on the way, Aunty, as you have some fridge and frozen items," replied Joanne.

"Oh, are you sure we have time?" asked Matilda.

"Don't worry about that, Aunty, he will wait," remarked Joanne.

They pulled into the car park at her aunt's apartment block and unloaded the shopping. Joanne helped pack the shopping away and then they made the short drive to the restaurant.

CHAPTER TWO

Defining Meetings

Joanne and her aunt managed to park just around the corner from Bill's, where John Hales was already waiting outside.

"Miss Webster, I can't apologise enough for my colleague's attitude. I just don't know what he was thinking of."

"I can tell you I am not too happy about all this, Mr. Hales. I was so looking forward to buying that house, but now I'm not so sure," replied Joanne abruptly.

"Well, let's have lunch, then we can have a chat. I'm sure the problems are not insurmountable," replied Hales.

Joanne waited until the three of them had finished eating before she questioned Hales about the house. She needed to find out exactly what the situation was with the lodger.

"So, Mr Hales, I need to know exactly what the situation is with the lodger at the property."

Hales sat there motionless for a few moments, playing with his glass before replying to Joanne.

"Look, Miss Webster, I do not know what Johnson has told you, but there seems to have been some misunderstanding, created by him," he replied.

Joanne shook her head as she responded to Hales's suggestion.

"Is that so, Mr Hales? I think the only misunderstanding here is the one that has been created by you not informing me about the occupant of the barn," said Joanne rather forcefully.

"Let me explain, Miss Webster. So, Johnson told me that you saw Tom while you were viewing the property and –"

Joanne was becoming impatient; she wanted the house but needed to be clear about the implications of the arrangement as set out in the will; she interrupted Hales mid-sentence.

"Mr Johnson explained well enough, thank you. The chap, Tom, I think Mr Johnson called him, was permitted to stay on the land and live in the barn until the property was sold. Is that correct, Mr Hales?" asked Joanne.

"Yes, that's correct, but –"

"I am not interested in buts, Mr Hales. Tell me, just how long has this Tom been living in that barn?"

John Hales was stumped; he didn't know the answer to that and he knew he was going to have to try to bluff his way out of this one.

"Oh, not very long at all, Miss Webster, but that's not your concern. All you need to concern yourself with is whether you are still interested in the property or not."

"I see, and who is going to pay for the court order?" she asked.

Hales sat there expressionless; he didn't know what to say. He was in a corner and couldn't see any way out.

"Um, well, I suppose –" he started to reply.

Joanne didn't let him finish; she didn't see any sense in prolonging the agony, so she decided to finish Mr Hales off there and then.

"Just as I thought, you're quite willing to sell me the property but you expect me to pay to get rid of a sitting tenant," she replied.

Without further comment, Joanne turned to her aunt Matilda.

"Come on, Aunty, we're leaving. I've heard enough," she said as she rose from the table.

Hales was flustered; he knew he had messed up and would have to change tack.

"Please, Miss Webster, just wait for one minute," Hales pleaded.

"I'll tell you what Mr. Hales, I'll give you the asking price, less forty thousand, and I'll sort out the business of Tom. Take it or leave it, Mr Hales. I'll be at my hotel until tomorrow night. If I've heard nothing by then, the deal's off and you can find another buyer."

With that, she turned and walked out of the restaurant, followed closely by her aunt, whom Joanne took home first before making her way back to the hotel.

Joanne parked her car in the hotel car park and then walked across the road to the beach. She sat there for a while just looking out to sea and watching the windsurfers. She thought it must be quite exhilarating, riding the waves as they did, but there was no way she could ever imagine herself partaking in such an activity; she thought it far too dangerous. The wind was picking up again, she could feel a chill in the air, and she was sure she felt a few raindrops from the steadily increasing cloud cover; she decided it was time to go back to her hotel room.

After dinner, Joanne spent an hour in the bar before retiring to her room for an early night. After a long soak in the bath, which she felt she deserved to relieve the stress of her harrowing day, she lay on her bed looking through all the information she had received about other properties from various estate agents. As much as she tried, she could not find one that matched her dream home. She was beginning to think that maybe she had been too rash during her meeting with Hales, but she was determined not to give in.

Joanne opened her eyes and saw the sun shining through the curtains. She was still lying on the bed, wrapped only in a bathrobe. She had fallen asleep looking at all the houses. She quickly dressed and went down for breakfast. Once she had eaten, she felt much better and went back to her room to collect a couple of things. She then decided that what she needed to complete her recovery from her feelings of the previous day was a spot of window shopping, a proven remedy for her. She knew it would be the perfect anecdote to take her mind off things, and the walking would also give her valuable exercise, something that had been in short supply since she had arrived back in Eastbourne.

Joanne spent the morning looking around the shops and getting used to where everything was. The one thing she noticed was how different it was from shopping in London. Although the shops were quite busy, it was far more relaxed than shopping in the city, where everything was done at breakneck speed. She was getting over-excited and spent hours mainly looking for things she could buy if she did purchase her dream house. When she stopped to look at her watch, it was already one o'clock and time for something to eat.

It was while she was sitting in the restaurant that Joanne cast her mind back to the previous day. She now felt quite bad about the way she had left the estate agent and even worse about the way she had treated her aunt.

Aunt Matilda was the sweetest woman Joanne had ever met, apart from her mother, and the last thing she meant to do was to upset her. She was after all one of the main reasons for her moving to Eastbourne in the process of re-setting her life. As far back as she could remember, Aunt Matilda had lived here. Joanne didn't know much about Matilda, only that her uncle had died about fifteen years ago. But now she was hoping to find out much more about her aunt. She decided to send her some flowers by way of an apology for her actions. So, when she had finished her meal, she went looking for a florist's shop.

It was while she was in the queue waiting to pay for her flowers that she was disturbed by a voice coming from behind her.

"Five hundred and twenty and it's yours."

Joanne spun round. It was Hales.

"Were you talking to me?" she asked.

"You certainly are a hard lady to track down, Miss Webster. I've been trying to contact you all morning at the hotel. I've tried your mobile, too, but you're not answering your calls. It's just lucky that I had to buy my wife some flowers," answered Hales.

Joanne moved forward in the queue to pay for her flowers and then, looking rather confused, she turned once again to Hales.

"I'm sorry, you've lost me. It was the bit about five hundred and twenty that I was enquiring after, nothing else."

"The house, Miss Webster, it's yours for five hundred and twenty thousand," replied Hales.

"I see maths isn't one of your stronger points, Mr Hales," replied Joanne as she turned and left the shop.

Hales couldn't let her go. He had to complete the house sale, so he quickly paid for the flowers he had selected and ran after her.

"Miss Webster!" he called out, somewhat out of breath as he got close to her.

Joanne appeared not to hear him, or if she did, she chose to ignore him and continued walking.

"Miss Webster," he called again; this time she stopped and turned to face him.

"Mr Hales, do you harass all your female clients in this way?" she shouted so that everyone could hear.

Hales stopped in his tracks as he realised that people were staring at him. He could feel his cheeks going crimson and knew that he had to reply.

"Only if I've got something that they want," he replied.

Joanne knew she was stumped; she also knew that other shoppers had stopped and were watching them.

"And pray do tell me, Mr Hales, what you could have that I want so badly that you chase me through a main shopping area full of people?" she asked him.

"A house, Mis Webster, a house. Or had you forgotten about that?" he asked.

"Five hundred thousand, Mr Hales, and that's my final offer, take it or leave it," she replied.

He smiled.

"Done! I'll take it."

Joanne smiled as she held out her hand.

"Deal then, Mr Hales," she said. "Can we go to your office now and sign the pre-transfer papers?" she asked.

Hales was shocked.

"Yes, of course, but most people usually wait 24 hours before signing the paperwork," he replied.

"I am sure they do, Mr Hales, but I am not like most people and having decided to buy the house, there is no way that I want to lose it, so if we could just sign the papers now secure it and I will transfer the money in the morning," she replied.

"In that case, Miss Webster, please come with me and we can have those papers signed in just a few moments," said Hales as he pointed in the direction of his office.

It was certainly a strange place to conclude such an important business decision, but that didn't worry either of them; they had both got what they wanted. Joanne followed Hales to his office which was only a five-minute walk. Once there, he asked her to take a seat as he went to get the required paperwork for her to sign so that the house could not be sold to anyone else. Hales reappeared within a few minutes with his manager.

"Miss Webster," he said as he approached her. "I am Stuart Finch, the Business Manager here. My colleague has informed me that you wish to sign a declaration of purchase, of which the transfer of funds will be completed tomorrow – is that correct?" he asked.

"Yes, that is correct. Why, is that a problem?" asked Joanne.

"I am sure it won't be, Miss Webster, but I need to be sure that you have sufficient cleared funds available to be able to proceed with the purchase."

Joanne was rather annoyed by the Business Manager's tone.

"Mr Finch, do you honestly think I would be sitting here in your office at this time of day if I didn't have funds available to complete the purchase? If that is what you think, then I am wasting my time and it would appear I am also wasting yours too, but before I leave, I will point out that I doubt your company will be happy to lose a cash sale when the property concerned has been on the market for more than four months. I don't suffer fools gladly and I doubt your company will either. Goodbye."

Turning to Hales, Joanne added, "Mr Hales, all I ever wanted was to buy that property. It has been my dream for many years. I will make sure that your company know you did everything possible to complete the sale, but you were stopped by needless meddling. Thank you for your help. I'm sorry you were stopped from completing the purchase," she said then turned to leave.

"Miss Webster, wait, please." As she turned around, she saw Hales grab a form from Finch and place it on the desk. "All I need is your signature and it's yours," he added, holding out a pen for her.

Joanne walked towards the desk, placed her bag on the chair and, taking the pen from him, signed the document.

"Easy, isn't it?" she said, looking up at Stuart Finch. "I will be in tomorrow as soon as the bank is open to pick up the keys."

Joanne was extremely excited to view her new house again. All she wanted to do now was to drive through the gates and up to the front door of the house, knowing full well that it was about to become her dream home. She was so excited that she didn't feel as though she could wait another day before visiting the property again so she went straight back to the car park and drove out of town.

Joanne pulled up outside the house and got out of her car. She just wanted to have a look around. She found it hard to believe that the house was going to be hers. Walking around the perimeter, she looked at the paintwork and the condition of the windows and doors. The house was situated in extensive grounds, most of which were undeveloped, but it was something that she would address in the future. As she walked back towards the front of the house, she looked down towards the barn and noticed that the doors were open. She hadn't intended to look for Tom while she was there, but seeing the doors open she thought she might as well introduce herself to him.

As she stood in the entrance to the barn, she saw him standing towards the far end of the building and decided that now was as good a time as any to have a word with him.

"Good evening. Tom, isn't it?" she asked as she held out her hand.

"Yeah," was the solemn reply, without any effort to acknowledge Joanne's offer of a handshake.

Joanne withdrew her hand. "I'm Joanne Webster. I've just signed the paperwork to buy this property, and they informed me that you used to do repairs for the previous owner."

Tom looked up and gazed at Joanne without making eye contact. "Yeah," he replied.

Joanne hadn't realised that this was going to be so difficult. "I understand that in return she used to allow you to live in this barn."

"Yeah."

"I'm not sure if anyone has told you, but there was a clause in her will that allowed you to stay on until the place had been sold."

Tom looked at Joanne. "They told me you don't want me here; I'll be gone by the time you move in," he said and turned to walk back inside.

"That's just the point, Tom. Is it alright to call you Tom?" she asked before continuing.

"That's my name," he replied.

"You see, Tom, I've been thinking that maybe I was being a little rash, and perhaps you could stay on here and work for me."

"What made you think that I would want to do that?" he asked, looking straight at her.

"Well, they told me that you had nowhere else to live," she replied.

"I don't want your charity, Miss, and I don't stay where I'm not wanted. I'll be gone in a couple of days," he said and carried on back into the barn.

Joanne didn't know how to take Tom; he was a bit rude and she remembered the estate agents saying that he didn't talk much. However, she decided to give him the benefit of the doubt and followed him into the barn, stopping just inside the doors as she didn't want to infringe on what was after all his territory, as it were, although technically the barn was hers now.

"Tom," she called.

He appeared from out of the shadows at the far end and walked towards her, stopping just short of the area swathed in sunlight.

"I'm sorry, Tom. I didn't mean to insult you; what I was trying to say was that if you have nothing else planned, then I would very much appreciate it if you would consider staying on here and doing some work for me. You see, I'm not particularly good at DIY, but I was told that you are. Even if I was any good at it, I just don't have the time to spare. I could afford to pay you, although not a great deal, and you could continue living in the barn for the time being. Then perhaps we could sort something else out in a couple of months."

Joanne stopped. She knew she wasn't explaining herself very well. She waited for an answer, but it wasn't forthcoming.

"What do you think then, Tom?" she asked.

"The barn is just fine. I don't need anywhere else," he replied.

"They tell me you've made it very cosy in here. Do you mind if I have a look?" she asked.

Tom moved to one side, allowing Joanne to pass, although he didn't reply. She was quite surprised by what she saw; he had a comfortable armchair, a table, a chair, a bed, quite a collection of books, and various other miscellaneous items. She also noticed that he had built a fireplace, above which hung a cooking pot. She turned towards him.

"As long as you are comfortable here?" she asked.

"It suits," was Tom's reply.

"That's great then. I'll get some papers written up to that effect, a sort of contract if you like, and if you agree, then we can both sign it so that we know where we stand," replied Joanne.

"Is there anything you want me to start on, Miss?" he asked.

"Not now. I'll be back tomorrow though, Tom, to look over the whole of the property. If you could do that with me, you may spot things that I miss, and I am sure you are already aware of things that need repairing. I will be picking up the keys to the house in the morning."

Joanne noticed Tom reach out and take something from a small cupboard. Turning towards her, he held it up and said, "I have a key here, Miss. If you would like to have another look around now."

"Tom, that's great. Do you think it would be okay if we started inside?" she asked.

"I don't see why not, Miss. It's yours now anyway, or it will be tomorrow," he replied as he held out the key.

"Would you come with me please, Tom?" she asked. "I'm not sure I like walking around empty old houses on my own, especially as the light is starting to fade a little."

"It's okay, Miss. I have a strong torchlight here," he said, holding it out towards her.

"Please, Tom, I would prefer it if you came with me. After all, you must have the authority to go in and out of the house otherwise you wouldn't have a key. Technically, I do not have the authority until tomorrow, but if I was with you, then I think that would be alright," she said.

They walked up to the house together. Joanne returned the key to Tom and he opened the front door, which was large, heavy and very stiff.

"It's only the hinges, Miss, nothing serious," he added, opening the door wide.

"That's good," she replied. "Is there much that needs replacing?"

"No, Miss, not much, it just needs redecorating to your taste, that's all, unless there are any structural alterations you want carried out," he answered.

Tom followed Joanne as she walked through the ground floor rooms. She stopped by the French windows.

"Do these open, Tom?" she asked.

"Yes, they do. A little stiff but once again, it's just the hinges."

Joanne turned towards him. "Thank you, Tom. I know I am going to like it here. I think we'll leave it for now and have a good look around tomorrow in daylight if that's okay with you?"

"I'm not going anywhere, Miss."

"Good. I'll see you tomorrow then," said Joanne holding out her hand toward him. She was surprised when this time Tom reciprocated the gesture. "If I can call you Tom, I don't see any reason why you shouldn't call me Joanne," she added as they shook hands.

"Whatever you like, Miss," replied Tom as Joanne turned and walked back towards the front door.

Joanne waited for Tom to lock up, then got in her car. Opening her window, she said, "Good night and thank you. I'll see you in the morning, then," before she made her way down the drive and out through the gate.

Tom watched Joanne drive away until she was out of the gate, then turned and walked back down to the barn. Closing the doors behind him to help keep in the warmth of the fire, he made his way to the far end and started to remove some of the things he had been packing when he was interrupted by Joanne. He was pleased to be staying; he liked the house very much although he had never spent that much time in it. But it wasn't just the house: he felt at home here, it *was* home, and he liked the independence that it gave him. He had never recovered from the death of his wife and child in a car accident, and although that was now a few years ago, he still preferred not to talk about it or to talk to people in general. The accident wasn't his fault but that didn't stop him from blaming himself for their deaths. At least now he could get on with his life, knowing that he didn't have to find somewhere else to live.

Although the impromptu meeting with Joanne had helped to ease the situation for him, he still wasn't sure about the new owner of the house. On first impressions, he thought she seemed nice enough, but then city folk always did when they first moved to the country. It was usually when they had been there a few months that they started to show their true colours, and that generally coincided with their desire to try to change the way that things had always been done.

CHAPTER THREE

Dream Home

Joanne didn't sleep well. She was too excited and thinking about completing the purchase of her dream house was all she could think about. She knew it needed a lot of work done to bring it up to scratch but she wasn't too perturbed by that, and she in that respect she was hoping to make use of Tom. Joanne realised now that she had made a mistake in the first instance in demanding that Tom vacate the premises before she moved in, and she now thought it would be extremely useful to have a handyman living in such close proximity to help with the repairs and decorating.

As soon as she had finished breakfast, Joanne drove the short distance to town, parked her car and made her way straight to the bank where the manager was waiting for her. She gave him all the transaction details and the transfer was made without a fuss. Joanne waited for the transaction receipt and then went straight to the estate agents to see Hales. Finch manager was standing at the rear of the office but she went straight to the desk where Mr Hales was sitting, opened her bag and took out the transaction receipts and placed them on the desk, whilst saying in a very loud voice for the benefit of Finch: "As promised, Mr Hales, I have transferred payment for the house to your firm. Here are the details of the transaction."

Hales looked up at her. "Thank you, Miss Webster. I had no doubt whatever that you would be here first thing. Please take a seat for a while – I just have some more paperwork to complete but it will only take a few minutes. Would you like a coffee while you are waiting?" asked Hales.

"Thank you, but no, I have only just finished breakfast at the Grand, so I am fine," replied Joanne.

She had only been waiting a few minutes before Hales came back, and placing the final paperwork on the coffee table, he sat down opposite her.

"All we need now is your signature on this contract of sale and if you are happy with it all, I will co-sign, and the property and associated lands will be yours, Miss Webster."

Joann picked up the papers from the table and read through them, pausing briefly as she looked at the drawing plan and the extent of the lands enclosed by the boundary line.

"Is everything okay?" asked Hales. "You look a little worried."

"No, there is no problem," replied Joanne. "It is just that I hadn't seen the plans in this format before. They show much more detail, and the extent of the land is quite surprising."

Joanne placed the papers back onto the table, picked up a pen and signed the document on each page. She slid the papers across the table to where Hales was sitting and watched as he signed too. When he was finished, he placed the pen back on the table, took two sets of keys from his pocket and slid them across the table to Joanne.

"Congratulations, Miss Webster," he said as he held out his hand towards her.

Joanne accepted his offer of a handshake.

"Thank you very much, Mr Hales," said Joanne.

"The pleasure is all mine, Miss Webster; I am sure you will be very happy in your new home," he said.

Finch had been watching everything. Joanne turned and walked towards him, holding out her hand to him, an offer that he decided to decline.

"Life can be so simple, Mr Finch. Why try to complicate things?" she said and walked towards the door.

Joanne left the estate agents feeling on top of the world. The excitement was boiling over inside her. She rushed back to her car and then drove straight up to the house. She still wasn't quite sure what to make of Tom. During their brief meeting she had found him rather strange but at the same time intriguing. It was difficult for her to understand how he preferred to live in the way that he did. She thought it must be a kind of 'half-life'. Driving up, she could see that Tom was already waiting for her.

"He's eager," she muttered to herself. "Morning, Tom, I hope you haven't been waiting too long."

"I had nothing else to do, Miss, so I thought that I may as well wait here," he replied.

Joanne couldn't believe the change in him from the previous day when she had found it difficult to get more than two words out of him. She put it down to the fact that he now knew that he didn't have to find somewhere else to live.

"When I was here viewing the property, Tom, I noticed that you were repairing a section of the perimeter fence. Is it okay now?" she asked.

"It'll do for now but it could all do with replacing; I think it's been there since the place was built."

"Well, if you could let me know how much wood you need, I'll see if I can afford it," replied Joanne.

"It will be a long job; maybe it would be best to do it in sections."

"That seems to me to be a perfect solution. I will leave that with you then, Tom. Just let me know when you need to order more wood. I want to look in the house – could you help me measure the rooms?" she asked.

Tom followed Joanne inside.

"What are you measuring?" he asked.

"I'd like to get some new carpets and I think all of the rooms could do with decorating; it's a lovely house but there is such a lot that needs doing to it."

"The decor is not to your taste then?"

"I'd like the rooms to be a little brighter, nice vibrant summery colours rather than the dull autumnal ones that are here at the moment," replied Joanne. "I don't suppose you are any good at decorating, are you, Tom?" she asked enquiringly.

"I'm certainly not professional standard, Miss, but I'll have a go if you want some help."

"Thank you, Tom. That would be great," she replied. "I'll pay you of course."

They went from one room to the next, measuring the floors and walls, and all the time Joanne was making notes about what colour scheme she wanted. She was enjoying herself so much it wasn't until she glanced at her watch that she realised it was almost twelve-thirty. She sat down on the floor waiting for Tom to give her the final measurements.

"Do you have anything planned for today, Tom?" asked Joanne.

"No," he replied.

"I'd like to go and get some paper and paint for a couple of the rooms, and I thought that if you'd like to come with me, perhaps we could have some lunch as well."

"I'm not sure about that, Miss," he replied. "I don't mind coming with you to buy the paper and paint, but I'm not too sure about lunch."

Joanne stood up and looked out of the window, then, making her way to the door, she turned towards him.

"Come on, I'll not take no for an answer. You've been very helpful this morning, so the least I can do is buy you lunch. Look, Tom, as I've said before, I'd prefer it if you were to call me Joanne – you make me feel like an old spinster the way you keep calling me 'Miss'."

That was settled, then. Joanne took Tom out for lunch, and in return, he would help her match the paper and paint that she wanted.

"So, what brings you to these parts then?" asked Tom as they waited for their lunch to be served.

"It's a long story. I wouldn't want to bore you. Anyway, everyone has been telling me that you never talk to anyone," replied Joanne with a smile on her face.

"That's not exactly true," replied Tom.

"How do you mean?" she asked.

Tom stopped fiddling with his fork and looked at Joanne.

"I used to talk to Mrs Wheeler."

"Anyone else?"

"I talk to people if I like them, or if I find them interesting," replied Tom.

Joanne picked up her wine glass and took a sip before replacing it on the table.

"And which of those categories do I come into then?" she asked.

Tom lifted his hand from the table and shook it gently.

"I haven't quite decided yet. Anyway, you still haven't answered my question."

She sat for a while just playing with the wine glass, not knowing how best to answer him.

"I just fancied a change really," she eventually replied.

"Why Eastbourne?" asked Tom inquisitively.

"Mainly because my aunt lives here and because I've always loved that house. Whenever I've visited, I've always said that one day I would buy it, and now I have. Anyway, that's enough about me. Why do you choose to live in that barn?" she asked him.

"It suits me at the moment, and it'll give me time to sort my life out," replied Tom.

"You seem to have made it very comfortable. How long have you lived there?"

"A couple of years maybe," he replied.

"But why? You seem to me to be quite educated, Tom. There must be somewhere else you could live."

"That may be so, and when you can tell me the real reason why you've moved down here from London, then perhaps I'll tell you the real reason why I choose to live in a barn."

"Touché!" replied Joanne.

That seemed to kill the conversation a bit; they ate lunch and then visited a couple of DIY stores to get the paper and paint that Joanne wanted for the house. She was incredibly pleased that she had asked Tom to accompany her; he was extremely useful and had quite a good knowledge of colour schemes. It was obvious to her that he had had plenty of experience at home-decorating in the past, although he wasn't letting on. It was almost six o'clock when Joanne pulled up outside the house. If she were going to be in time for dinner at the hotel, they would have to hurry up unloading the car.

"I think we'll just put everything in the lounge for now, Tom, and I'll sort it all out tomorrow."

"It's okay. You get going – I'll sort it out; I can remember your colour scheme for each room."

Joanne was amazed. "If you're sure that's alright?" she asked.

"It's no problem, Joanne, you get going, you'll miss dinner otherwise," replied Tom as he shut the boot of the car.

"Thank you, Tom," she said as she smiled at him, starting the engine. "That's the first time you've called me by my name!"

"Just a slip of the tongue, *Miss*," he replied, laughing. "I keep meaning to ask you when all your furniture is being delivered."

"There is no furniture at the moment. I'm going out with my aunt tomorrow to sort that out."

"You believe in travelling light then! I'm intrigued," he said and turned towards the house.

"I'll probably drop by sometime tomorrow, Tom, but if not I'll see you Thursday. I'll leave you to make sure everything is locked up. Bye and thank you so much for all your help today." Then she closed the car window and drove off down the drive.

Tom sorted all the decorating materials out and placed the wallpaper and paints in the rooms where Joanne wanted them, according to her colour scheme. He found it hard to admit it to himself, but he had enjoyed the day, and that feeling included Joanne's company. It had been such a long time since he had spent that amount of time with anyone that he had almost forgotten what it was like. He remembered that he still had a key to the house, the one that the old lady had given him, so he pulled the door to while he walked down to the barn to make himself something to eat before returning to the house to make sure everywhere was securely locked up.

Joanne arrived back at the hotel and went straight in for dinner. She didn't even have time to go to her room to change. Back in her room, she took a shower, following which she picked up her phone and rang her aunt.

"Hello, Aunty. Sorry it's a little late but I just thought I would ring you to make sure that you still want to come shopping with me tomorrow while I search for the items of furniture that I need for the house?" said Joanne.

"Oh yes please, dear. I can't wait to see what you are going to buy for your new home; I know you will make it look beautiful," replied Matilda.

"I will pick you up straight after breakfast. Will that be okay for you?" asked Joanne.

"Yes, dear, I will make sure that I am ready."

"Yes, I think it's going to be a busy day as I have a lot to do. I'll see you in the morning then. Good night."

"Good night, dear," replied Matilda.

Joanne lay down on the queen-size bed and decided that was the same size she wanted for her main bedroom, which was large. As she lay there, becoming more tired by the minute, she tried to keep her eyes open and to search for items of furniture that she intended to look for when out shopping with Aunt Matilda. The events of the day had taken their toll on her and Joanne could feel herself drifting off, but she just did not have the energy to fight the tiredness.

Practically all the next day the two of them traipsed around furniture shops. Joanne had hoped to get almost everything done in one day, but taking her aunt with her was a hindrance rather than a help. Joanne was now more than a little annoyed, though as much as it pained her to admit it, she knew that it was not her aunt's fault. The stark realisation of the matter was that she should not have invited her aunt in the first place, something she had to remember for the future. In the end, she decided to leave most of the small furniture items until another day, although after looking around she had decided on most of what she was going to buy. She did, however, manage to get the carpets ordered, along with the kitchen essentials, a sofa, and bedroom furniture, and secured delivery dates for all of them.

By the time they had finished their tour of the shops, it was getting rather late. Joanne decided she needed to take her aunt straight back home. However, she did stop on the way to buy a fish and chip supper so that Aunt Matilda did not have to cook. As Joanne drove into the hotel car park, she realised that she just about had time to go to her room to wash and change before dinner, which she was certainly looking forward to as the day's ordeal had left her feeling rather hungry. When dinner was over, she sat in the bar for a while to relax, before retiring to her room. It was while she was sitting there that she suddenly had the feeling of loneliness again. Being in the hotel for any length of time was something that she had not carefully considered, and she was now realising it was not good for her. Her aunt had previously mentioned that she could stay with her until she had sorted out a house, and now she had completed the purchase, she wondered what she was still doing in the hotel?

Joanne felt uncomfortable, not with her existence but with the way she was living; to her it was completely alien. Hotels were okay for holidays, a weekend break, or overnight stays, but they were certainly not meant for living in; that was her feeling anyway. She needed to decide what to do, but she was scared; she needed someone to talk to but who? She had been ready for bed, but she walked across the room to the wardrobe and took out a hooded top and jeans before picking up her car keys and going down to her car.

As she climbed in and started the engine, she had no idea of where to go, or what to do, but she just wanted to drive. She found herself driving up to Beachy Head. She turned off the road and into the car park. She got out and stood looking out to sea, not that there was much to see as it was already nine forty-five. She had only been standing there for a few minutes when she heard another car approaching. Turning around, she noticed it was a police car. It pulled up behind where she had parked, and one of the officers got out of the car and walked towards her.

"Are you okay, Miss?" he asked.

"I'm fine officer, thank you for asking," replied, Joanne.

"Well, it's just that it's quite late and we were concerned in case you should be thinking of jumping,"

"No, honestly, officer, I can assure you it hadn't even entered my mind," she replied.

"I am very pleased to hear that but could I just ask you what you are doing here at this time of night? Have you just driven here from London?" asked the officer.

"Certainly not. I am staying at the Grand Hotel, in Eastbourne. I have been there just over a week. You can check with them if you like. The name is Webster, Joanne Webster."

"Thank you. My colleague will check that if you don't mind; are you on holiday then?" asked the officer.

"No. I have moved here from London. I've just bought a house, but it is being re-decorated which is why I am staying at the Grand," replied Joanne.

"Thank you, Miss Webster. However, could I just ask you to leave the area? I don't think you should be out here on your own at this time of night."

"I just wanted to get some fresh air, officer; it was too stuffy in my hotel room."

"I can understand that, Miss Webster. But could you not have just crossed the road from your hotel and walked along the beach?" he asked. "You see, if I leave you here and anything should happen to you, I would be in trouble. It's all on my body cam."

"Okay, officer, I will leave, but how would that stop me from returning later after you had gone?" asked Joanne as she opened the door of her car and climbed in. She started the engine and as soon as the police car had moved forward, she reversed out and drove off.

Joanne turned left onto the main road, which she soon realised was a mistake as that direction took her away from Eastbourne and towards Brighton. She knew that she needed to turn around and she was looking for somewhere safe to do that when she saw in her rear-view mirror that she was being followed by the police officer.

"What a bloody cheek," she muttered to herself. "What are they doing?" She pulled off the road onto a small lay-by and sure enough the police car pulled in behind her. Joanne got out of her car and walked back towards it. She was almost there when the car suddenly started and drove off at speed, its blue light flashing and siren wailing.

"Typical," she muttered. "When you don't want them, they turn up, but when you want to speak to them, they are always going somewhere else."

Joanne turned and walked back to her car. She still didn't want to go back to the hotel and spend another long night on her own, so she continued along the road and took the first right turn; she now knew what she had to do and where to go – and it wasn't going to be Aunt Matilda's.

She had been driving for about ten minutes. Speed and dark country lanes at night were not something she was accustomed to, so she went slowly and carefully. Finally, she was there; she turned off the road and up the driveway, stopping outside the house, which was in darkness. She got out of her car and looked in the direction of the barn. She thought she could see a dim light from within, so she walked along the pathway, stopping outside the barn doors where she banged on the door.

"Tom, Tom? Are you in there? It's me, Joanne." She waited but there was no answer, so she banged on the doors again.

"Tom, it's Joanne, are you there?" she asked but still no answer.

She was about to knock again when she heard a noise from behind her.

"You're wasting your time. I'm here," said the voice.

Quickly turning around, Joanne saw Tom approaching from out of the shadows.

"Tom, don't do that, you frightened me!" she exclaimed.

"Sorry, but what are you doing here at this time of night?" he asked.

Joanne gave a snigger before replying.

"You know, Tom, I have no idea! I was in my hotel room after dinner and I was ready for bed, but then I felt I just needed to get out. I drove up to Beachy Head where I was stopped by the police, wanting to know what I was doing there. They seemed to be worried that I might be contemplating jumping off the cliff. Although I assured them I had no intention of doing anything like that, they still insisted that I leave so I did. I just drove and ended up here."

"I see," replied Tom thoughtfully, "and is that the only reason you are here?"

"I'm not sure, Tom," replied Joanne as she looked at him. "I just felt while I was driving that I had to come. I *needed* to be here – does that make sense to you?"

"I guess," replied Tom, "and now that you are here, what do you intend doing?"

"Forgive me, Tom" she replied. "Maybe I shouldn't have come. It's getting chilly and I don't have a coat with me, so maybe I should go."

Tom stood there looking at her; he could see the sadness on her face and in her eyes.

"You have every right to be here; it's your house, your property. But if you are feeling cold, we can sit in the barn and chat. It will be warmer in there."

Joanne looked at him and she could hear the sincerity in his voice;

his offer was too good to refuse.

"Thank you, Tom, I would like that very much," she eventually replied.

Tom walked towards the barn and, opening the door, he beckoned to Joanne to enter, which she gratefully acknowledged, feeling the warmth as soon as she stepped inside. Tom followed her and stopped just inside the barn doors.

"Are you happy for me to close the doors, just to keep the warmth in?" he asked.

"But of course, Tom," she replied.

"Take a seat. Would you like a cup of tea? Sorry but I don't have anything stronger," he asked.

"Tea would be lovely, Tom, thank you," replied Joanne as she sat there looking around the barn, trying to take everything in. "This really is very cosy; I could never have imagined how nice a barn could be."

He walked over to Joanne and handed her the tea.

"Thank you. I have tried hard to make it as comfortable as possible, not only for me but for Mrs Wheeler too. I wanted her to see how much I appreciated her kind offer of allowing me to live here when I needed it," explained Tom.

"Well, I am sure she must have been as amazed as I am, Tom. It's very nice in here."

They both sat there drinking tea. The effect was quite opposite to the tea: on the one hand, it was obviously warming them up and quenching their thirst, but on the other hand their conversation had gone cold and dried up. Joanne sat there, occasionally looking towards Tom, wondering if he would say something, but it wasn't to be. There was so much she wanted to say to him, but she didn't know how or where to start, so in the end, she just opened her mouth and let the words flow.

"You know, Tom, earlier this evening while I was sitting in my hotel room, I was faced with the stark reality that there are only two people in Eastbourne whom I knew and with whom I could chat to if I needed to. The first one is my Aunty and the second one is you, and that I guess is why I am here. I just had this urge that I needed to chat with you. Don't ask me why, but that is how I felt. I sat looking at my phone and just wanted to speak to someone, but you don't have a phone, or if you have, I am not aware of it, so that's why I am here."

Joanne stopped and looked up at Tom. She was still cradling the cup in her hands, waiting for an answer. He was looking blankly into his cup of tea.

Joanne sat there looking at him.

"Tom, we must get used to being around one another. I know I was horrible to you when we first met, and I am sorry for that. I promise I will make it up to you. When you were with me the other day, when I was shopping for paint and wallpaper, you were fantastic; not only didn't you moan about shopping, but you were a great help too, and I don't know what I would have done without you."

Tom wasn't sure where this was leading to, but he felt as though he had to make light of it. He soon realised that Joanne was not making any sense, he guessed only too well what she was intending, but he wasn't ready and had no intention of, letting things get out of hand. Apart from Mrs Wheeler, the previous owner he hadn't spoken one-on-one with any woman since the death of his wife, that was his choice and one which he was now struggling with. He was happy to chat with Joanne, it was his job. However, he got the impression she was looking for something more, which he felt he could not cope with.

"You'd have managed. I am sure you could have got someone else to help you," he replied as he shifted uncomfortably in his chair while trying not to make eye contact with Joanne.

"No, Tom, there is no one else. Look, I don't know how you feel about me, but I can assure you that when you get to know me, I am not a bad person. Just give me a chance, please, that is all I am asking."

Tom sat there motionless, still looking into his cup. He was shocked by Joanne's outburst and didn't quite know how to respond.

Joanne guessed that she had probably gone too far, but she said what she came to say and now it was time for her to leave. She stood up and walked towards him, placing her cup on the small table, and continued past him towards the barn doors, at which point she turned towards him.

"I'm sorry, Tom, I shouldn't have blurted out like that. You know, my father always used to tell me my mouth would get me in trouble one day. I guess I know now how right he was."

Tom stood and walked towards her.

"I'll open the doors for you."

Tom watched as Joanne walked towards her car. When she got halfway, she stopped and turned back towards him.

"I meant what I said, Tom, but I am sorry if you found my comments hard to accept. Please forgive me," she said.

Joanne hadn't wanted to leave, she could feel the tears welling up in her eyes, her throat was dry, and she was shivering, although it was not that cold. She was looking for some sign from him, some movement, but there was none. Standing there she wanted to rush up to him and hold him tightly, but the voice in her head was telling her No! Don't ruin what you have, with that she turned slowly and continued to her car. She sat there momentarily before starting the engine, then winding down her window she called out to him, "Good night, Tom," her voice breaking up as she did so.

"Good night and drive safely. I'll see you in the morning," he replied.

Tom sat back down in his chair, trying to piece together what Joanne had just said and, what was more important, he was trying to understand what she meant, wondering if he had misinterpreted her meaning.

CHAPTER FOUR

Building Bridges

Joanne woke early. It was still dark outside. She had hardly slept and was still troubled by her actions of the previous evening. It was so out of character of her, and she knew she had overstepped the mark. Her thoughts turned to Tom. She was wondering what he must be thinking of her, hoping he wouldn't take her impromptu speech too badly.

Joanne walked across the room, opened the double windows, and placed a chair just between them inside the room, then went to make herself a strong coffee. She sat on the chair drinking her coffee, trying to collect her thoughts while watching the sunrise above the horizon. Joanne wished she could ring Tom to apologise; she thought it might be easier speaking to him on the phone rather than face to face. She knew that she would have to try to explain her outburst and apologise in person when she saw him later. Having finished her coffee, she went to take a shower before laying her clothes out on the bed and getting dressed.

Joanne had intended to skip the hotel breakfast and stop off at McDonald's on the way to buy two breakfasts, but she was not sure about that now as she had no idea how Tom would be feeling. She took her time getting ready, trying to delay the inevitable, but she knew that she was going to have to make a move. There was a lot to be done and she just wanted to get to the house and get started. Joanne decided to stick with her original plan, so on the way to the house she stopped at McDonald's to pick up a couple of breakfasts. She wasn't even sure if Tom would eat it, but she wasn't unduly worried as she felt hungry enough that she would be able to devour both should the need arise. As she got out of the car outside her front door, she smelt the distinct aroma of fresh paint.

"Painting already," she muttered to herself as she pushed the front door, expecting it to be open.

"Tom, are you in there?" she called as she fumbled in her bag for the door keys.

"I'm here," came the reply.

"Oh Tom, there you are! Could you hold these for me, please?" she said, handing him the two MacDonald's bags. "Have you eaten yet?" she asked as she opened the front door.

"Not yet, I've just been for a walk. I have one every morning – gives me an appetite," he replied.

"Well, I'm glad about that. I bought you breakfast."

"You didn't fancy the hotel breakfast this morning, then?" he asked.

"I just wanted to get an early start. I couldn't afford to hang around, so I thought this would make a change. You do eat at MacDonald's, don't you?" she asked.

"I'll eat it, Miss," he replied.

Joanne sat on the stairs, while Tom sat in the passage just in front of her.

"I meant what I said, Tom. I would rather you call me Joanne. You make me feel so old, the way you keep calling me 'Miss'."

Tom didn't answer; he nodded and continued to eat his breakfast.

"Tom, about last night. I owe you an apology. I am so sorry, it was very insensitive of me, and I was completely out of order. Will you please forgive me?" said Joanne.

"Sorry? Forgive you? What for? Did I miss something?" he asked in an inquiring manner.

"Oh, come on, Tom, you know exactly what I am talking about! But thank you for trying to make this easier for me. I appreciate that, and I am hoping that we can be friends?"

"Friends?" he asked inquiringly. "I'm not sure that would work. Wherever I have worked before, being friends with an employer just didn't work," he replied.

"Tom, I promise you it will work with me," she replied.

"In that case, I'll give it my best shot."

"Thank you, Tom. I hope I don't let you down."

Joanne looked around as she sat on the stairs and realised that it would take her years to get the place looking just as she wanted it.

"So, what have you been up to, Tom? I can smell fresh paint."

"Not much," he replied with a snigger. "I had some spare time yesterday so I thought I may as well make a start for you."

"Come on then, show me what you've been doing!" she asked excitedly.

Tom led the way up to the main bedroom and as they entered the room, Joanne couldn't believe what she saw.

"Tom! You're marvellous! It's almost finished!"

"Well, I thought that you'd want your room done first, so I just made a start and got as much done as I could," he replied.

"Oh, come on, Tom, this is more than a start. You must have been working all evening and all night! I just don't know what to say,"

Joanne walked towards him. She knew that he had put a great amount of time and effort into decorating her bedroom and she didn't know how to thank him. She felt so comfortable with him; he reminded her somewhat of her ex-husband when she'd first met him. She was about to lean forward to kiss him on the cheek when he turned away from her.

"If you want me to help, I haven't got time to stand about here gawping, I've got work to do," he said as he walked towards the door.

"Well, I *am* here to help, Tom, so just let me know what you want me to do," replied Joanne.

By the end of that first day, Joanne was sorry that she mentioned she was there to help; every muscle in her body was aching and she felt absolutely shattered. She wondered where Tom got his energy from. He had hardly stopped all day, but he still wanted to keep going, whereas she just wanted to sit down and rest.

Tom could see that Joanne was wilting.

"Come on, take a seat. I'll make you a drink and you can rest for a while before going back to the hotel for your dinner," he said, watching her face light up at the thought.

"Thank you, Tom," said Joanne as he placed the cup of tea in front of her. "I know you've accepted my apology for my outburst last night, but it is still worrying me. Will you let me explain the reason for it?"

Tom sat on the floor holding his cup of tea.

"If you think you need to," he replied.

"It's a strange situation, living in a hotel. It's not something I am used to or something that I would want to get used to. It is completely alien to me, but what can I do? It is all I have at this moment in time. Yes, I have this house and it is mine, but I can't live here, not yet anyway, and that is the problem. I want to be here, I don't want to stay in the hotel any longer, but it could be weeks before I can move in and it is making me depressed. I guess last night I just boiled over," she explained.

"Is that all?" asked Tom.

Joanne looked puzzled. "What do you mean, is that all? Don't you think my outburst was enough?" she asked.

"You had me worried for a minute. I thought you were trying to make a pass at me last night, so that's a relief," replied Tom with a straight face.

"I hope you are joking, Tom," remarked Joanne.

"Why would I joke about something as serious as that? But tell me, why will it be weeks before you can move in?" he asked inquiringly.

"Oh, come on, Tom, look around you – there is so much to do and there is only you to do it. I am not much help at all, apart from keeping you supplied with copious amounts of tea," she replied.

"Look, if you wanted to move in now, you should have told me, but not to worry, we can still do it. We just need to implement a change of plan. If you want to leave the hotel, this place can be ready for you by the end of the week. Not every room, obviously, but enough rooms for you to live here," replied Tom with a firmness that made Joanne believe in what he was proposing.

"If you are sure, I would be so grateful. Do you honestly think it is possible?" asked Joanne.

"Leave it to me, it will be ready for you," he replied. "I will make sure your bedroom is finished, along with the kitchen and the lounge. The stairs, entrance hall and passageway will also be completed by then."

That paved the way for a week of extremely demanding work. Joanne returned to the hotel that evening and told them she would check out at the end of the week. She was surprised how one day could make such a difference to her feelings. The transformation in her and her attitude was quite amazing. She was up at the crack of dawn every day and then made the obligatory stop at McDonald's on the way to the house. Each day when she arrived, Tom was already up and working.

Joanne just could not believe how hard Tom worked. Anyone who didn't know differently would have thought it was his own house as he was working so hard to get each room finished. Joanne did help where she could but most of the demanding work was completed by Tom. She didn't feel guilty, though, as she was paying him, although they had never sat down and agreed on a figure. Anyway, she guessed that he was in his element, and quickly realised that he knew what he was doing – it showed. As he had promised, Joanne was able to move into the house at the end of the first week. He had redecorated her bedroom, the stairs, the kitchen and the lounge. He was like a dynamo, starting at seven in the morning and still working at nine in the evening, seven days a week, and not once did Joanne hear him moan, apart from when he did something wrong, and then the air would turn blue for a few minutes. She always took that as her cue to make yet another cup of tea.

Joanne worked alongside Tom the whole of the first week and she was surprised at how well they got on together. She found out a lot about him during that time, like how much tea he could drink in a day, and that he appeared to have a cast-iron throat. No sooner had she placed a cup of tea in front of him than it was gone. She wondered if he had ever had a job as a fire-eater. What surprised her though was the fact he seemed to be able to go all day, sometimes twelve hours or more, without stopping for something to eat. Where the decorating was concerned, he was like a robot; he started something and wouldn't stop until it was finished.

Joanne could hardly believe it when, at the end of that week, she was able to leave her room at the hotel and move into the house. Tom had completed everything that he said he would. It was also an immense help that all the items of furniture she had ordered were delivered on time, too. The only room that wasn't completed was the bathroom next to her bedroom, but Tom had already told her that would not be finished in time, but she was able to use the smaller bathroom further down the landing.

Tom had worked so hard and he made her feel unbelievably comfortable just being around him that she knew she had to repay him. She was becoming inextricably attached to him, but she also knew that there was no way now that Tom would succumb to her advances, so she had to take things slowly and bide her time. The more time she spent in Tom's company, the more she was unable to control her feelings for him.

"Tom, where are you? Have you nearly finished?" she called to him from the kitchen.
"I'm done here now, just coming down. What do you want?" he asked in a loud voice as he closed the bathroom door behind him and replaced the 'not-in-use' sign on the door.
"I want you to get cleaned up and changed. Tom, I'm taking you out for dinner," she replied.

"Dinner? Why?" he asked as he walked into the kitchen.

Joanne was sitting at the breakfast bar, drinking a coffee.

"There's a tea there for you, Tom," she said, pointing to the pot as he sat down opposite her.

"So why the meal? Is it your birthday?" he asked with a chuckle in his voice.

"No, it is not my birthday; I just want to say thank you for all your hard work this week, so I am taking you out to dinner. Is that okay with you?" she asked.

"I won't argue with you, if that is what you want. As it happens, I do feel a little hungry," he replied.

"Great," replied Joanne. "Let me throw some clothes on and I'll be ready."

Tom went back to the barn, cleaned himself up, changed his clothes and was back waiting at the house before Joanne came down.

They went to the restaurant at the hotel where Joanne had been staying and then, after dinner, Joanne drove them to Brighton where they spent an enjoyable evening. They sat for a while on the pier just watching the world go by, but it had been a long day and Joanne felt she was getting tired.

"Tom, do you mind if we go now?" she asked. "I am feeling a little tired."

"No, that's fine, it has been a long day for you and with work that you are not used to doing," he replied.

They walked back to the car, Joanne airing her plans for the other rooms that were still to be decorated.

"Tom, do you know how long it will be before the main bathroom can be used?" she asked.

"Only another week or two. I have to get the electrics checked as there is something wrong with them," he replied.

As they approached her car, Joanne stopped.

"Do you have insurance to drive, Tom?"

"Why do you ask?" he inquired.

"I was hoping you would say yes as I'm feeling very tired now and I was going to ask you if you felt okay to drive," she replied.

"That's okay, yes, I can drive. I have insurance which allowed me to drive Mrs Wheeler's car and any other car, and it's still valid for another six months yet."

"That's great," replied Joanne. "I will leave it up to you to get me home safely then."

"No problem. You just relax, close your eyes if you want to. You'll be safe with me."

"I know – that's the problem," said Joanne, turning to look at him as he started the car.

The rest of the journey was in silence until they were almost back at The Cottage. Tom never could understand why it was called The Cottage because to him it was a house and quite a large one at that.

"We are nearly home, only another five minutes," he said.

When there was no answer, he turned his head briefly to look at her; she was asleep. He decided not to wake her until he pulled up outside the house; he placed his hand on her shoulder and gently shook her.

"We're home now, Joanne," he said as he shook her.

Tom got out of the car and walked around to the passenger door; she was still asleep, so he opened the door and gently shook her shoulder again.

"Come on, we're home now, you need to wake up," he said as he shook her again but a little more forcefully. That did the trick – Joanne stirred and turned to look at him.

"Sorry, Tom, I must have dozed off," she said looking at him.

"I think you could say that, but that's okay, you were obviously very tired, but you can get to bed now," he replied.

"Thank you, Tom. Would you like a drink before you go?" she asked.

"I think a cup of tea would work wonders, but I can make it while you get yourself ready for bed," he replied.

"Would you make me a hot chocolate please?" she asked him as she opened the front door of the house.

Tom went straight into the kitchen and made the drinks, then sat waiting for Joanne to reappear, after getting herself ready for bed.

Tom tried not to stare when Joanne walked into the kitchen, but he had to admit to himself that she was quite special in many ways. He did look up though, took a sly glance and then another quick look at her.

"Thank you, Joanne," he said as she sat down opposite him and picked up her hot chocolate.

"Thank you for what, Tom?" she asked.

"For this evening: the meal, the trip to Brighton, everything. It made quite a change for me. Thank you," he replied.

"Don't mention it, Tom, I'm the one who should be thanking you. If it had not been for all your hard work this week I would not be sitting here now. I would still be feeling awkward and lonely in that hotel room," she replied.

"You didn't like it there, then?" he asked.

Joanne looked across the breakfast bar at him.

"Don't get me wrong, it's a very nice hotel, but that life is not for me, especially since I was on my own; I always felt very lonely there."

"Yes, I know how you feel. My circumstances have been similar although not for the same reasons," he replied.

Tom swallowed the last mouthful of tea and then got up and placed the cup in the sink.

"It's late. I had better be going," he said as he walked towards the kitchen door.

"I'm not feeling tired now Tom, if you want to chat," she said.

"Maybe another time," replied Tom. "I still have a lot of work to do here."

Joanne stood up and followed him. He turned towards her as he reached the front door.

"Good night and thank you once again for this evening," he said as he opened the door and started to walk down towards the barn.

"Tom! Wait!" she called after him.

He stopped and turned around. "Yes, Joanne?"

"Please don't take this the wrong way but I was hoping that you might agree to stay in the house tonight," she said.

"I'm sorry but I don't think that is a good idea," he replied.

Joanne walked down the pathway towards him.

"Tom, please reconsider. It is just that it feels so strange to me, I feel strange, my first night here, in this big house and I will be alone. I will feel much more comfortable if I know you are also in the house with me. Please will you stay?" she pleaded.

He stood there for a while, not knowing what to say. He felt as though he was being placed in a no-win situation; he didn't want to say yes but at the same time he felt there was no way he could say no.

Joanne stood waiting for Tom to answer.

"Please?" she asked again.

"Let me gather a few things together," he replied and turned towards the barn.

Joanne watched as Tom continued down the pathway into the barn; she could feel the chill in the air but rather than go inside, she stood just inside the doorway from where she could see Tom at the back of the barn, taking some clothes out of boxes.

"Do you need a hand?" she asked.

Tom glanced up at her, not realising that she had followed him down there; the large bright light hanging down from the ceiling was directly behind her. Although she was wearing what appeared to be a nightdress or dressing gown, it was very thin and the light shone through her clothing, exposing the contours of her body, leaving little to the imagination.

Tom walked towards her, picking up a blanket that was lying on the table.

"Here," he said as he handed her the blanket, "put that around you. I can see you are very cold."

"Thank you, Tom," she replied as she wrapped the blanket around her shoulders, covering her chest. "Always the gentleman."

Tom picked up the things he had been sorting out and walked back towards her.

"Can I carry anything for you?" she asked.

"No, only the blanket," he replied.

They walked together back up to the house and once inside, Tom turned to her and asked, "Shall I sleep on the sofa?"

"Yes, Tom, yes, and thank you," said Joanne. "I hope that will be comfortable enough for you."

"It will be just fine. Goodnight, Joanne."

"Goodnight, Tom, and thanks again."

CHAPTER FIVE

Joanne's New Job

When Joanne woke, the sun was already shining through her bedroom window. She got out of bed, walked towards the window and opened the curtains. Standing there she could feel the heat of the sun through the glass, and, opening the window, she could smell the freshness of the country air. She took a deep breath and knew straight away that she had made the right decision, not only in buying the house but also by moving out of London to Eastbourne.

She picked up her dressing gown from the bed and walked towards the small bathroom at the far end of the passageway. As she passed the top of the stairs, she caught the distinct smell of cooking coming from the kitchen. She quickly made herself presentable and then headed straight down the stairs towards the kitchen. As she passed the lounge, she noticed Tom had placed his blanket and his clothes neatly in a pile on one of the chairs. Joanne continued into the kitchen where she was expecting to see Tom but he was not there. Noticing the kitchen door open, she hastily walked towards it and looked outside. At first, she didn't see him and she suspected that he was at the back of the house. She looked down at her bare feet and then out onto the paved area at the side of the kitchen; it looked reasonably clean, so she stepped out and walked around to the back of the house. Tom was sitting at a small table, drinking from a cup, probably tea, and noticing steam coming from another cup placed on the table, she continued towards him.

"Good morning, Tom," she said as she approached the table and the empty chair. "Is this for me?" she added, pointing towards the cup on the table.

"Yes. I heard you go into the bathroom, so I made you a coffee and brought it out here. I hope you don't mind," he said.

"Do I mind? No, of course not, Tom. Are you cooking something too?" she replied.

"Yes, breakfast. I hope that is okay. I looked in the fridge to see what you had there and just started cooking."

"Thanks – you're wonderful, and I'm extremely pleased that you are making yourself feel at home," replied Joanne.

"Sorry, it wasn't my intention to encroach in your house. I just thought I'd thank you for last night," he replied.

"There is no need for you to thank me. I told you before I am the one that should be thanking you. I had a very peaceful sleep. I had been worrying all week about how I would feel sleeping in such a big house on my own but knowing that you were here gave me a sense of security, so thank you," said Joanne.

"I have to check on the breakfast. I'll call you when it's ready," he said as he got up from the chair and walked towards the kitchen door.

Joanne sat there, finishing her coffee and breathing in the fabulous fresh air. She could feel it go straight to her lungs. It was such a lovely feeling and one which she hoped to experience many times again.

Tom was busying himself in the kitchen. He took out two trays and placed a plate of food on each one: bacon, egg, sausage, tomato, mushrooms and hash browns, along with toast and a glass of orange juice. He picked up one of the trays and took it out to Joanne.

"Breakfast is served," he said as he placed the tray on the table in front of her.

"Wow, thank you! This looks extremely nice. Where's yours?" she asked.

"Don't worry, I'm just going to go and get mine," he replied.

Joanne finished her breakfast and picked up her glass of orange juice.

"That was lovely, thank you. Where did you find the table and chairs?" she asked.

"I had them in the barn," replied Tom. "So I went down there this morning and brought them up here; at least they will get some use here."

"So, what are your plans for this week?" asked Joanne.

"Pretty much the same as last week: more decorating, although this week I thought I would start on the back lounge and then move up to the second bedroom if that's okay with you?"

"That's fine. You are doing a grand job! Will you be doing any more to the bathroom this week?" she asked.

"Yes, that and hopefully it will be finished soon," replied Tom.

"I can't wait to see what you have been doing – can I have a sneak preview?" she asked.

"That would ruin the surprise, so certainly not!" he replied.

"Sorry, but I am not going to be much help to you this week as I have a few interviews to go to."

"No problem. Everything I have planned for this week I can do on my own although I will miss your constant supply of tea," he replied.

"If I'm here, I will do whatever I can to help," she said.

"Good luck with your interviews. How many do you have this week?"

"I have five booked but hopefully, if I get lucky, I won't need to attend all of them," she replied. "The first one is lunchtime today so I'd better get ready after I've cleared up in the kitchen."

"No, you go and get yourself ready, I can sort the kitchen out. After all, I was the one who made the mess," replied Tom.

"Thank you, Tom, I won't be long," replied Joanne as she went up to the bathroom to get ready.

Tom cleared up in the kitchen and then thinking again of his plans for the week, he decided to switch rooms and start on the second bedroom instead. On closer inspection of the room, he decided that the paintwork didn't need a lot of rubbing down, so he had already completed that and started painting by the time Joanne came out of the bathroom, something that wasn't missed by Joanne as she walked past the room.

"Hey, are you painting already?" she asked.

"I sure am," he replied.

"Is it safe to come in and look?" she asked.

"You can come in but stay away from the walls."

Joanne opened the door cautiously and entered the room.

"Wow! You work so fast! You've nearly finished the painting in here. Maybe I took too long in the bathroom," she commented.

"The skirting boards were easy; the window frame will take a little longer and then the door. With any luck, I can get half the room papered by tonight. I just need to make sure that all the paintwork is dry before I start hanging any paper, but in any case, I can start on the paintwork in the back lounge while I am waiting," he explained.

"Thank you very much, Tom. You are marvellous!"

"I think you need to go and get dressed or you will end up being late for your interview," said Tom.

"Okay, I'm going."

By the time Joanne had dressed and was ready to leave, Tom had finished painting the window frame and was about to start on the door; he heard a faint tap, followed by her call.

"I am going now Tom. I'm not sure what time I will be home, but I hope the interview won't take too long," she said.

Tom was shocked when he opened the door and saw her standing there in her work suit. She looked amazing – very professional – and all he could do was stare at the vision in front of him.

"Is something wrong?" she asked.

"No, no, I didn't mean to stare, you just look so different in your work suit, totally different, and very professional. Good luck! Just stay calm. You certainly look the part. Very elegant," he said.

"Thank you, Tom," she replied. "It's nice of you to notice, and even nicer of you to say so. Don't work too hard. I'll see you later."

Tom stood in the doorway and watched as she turned and walked along the landing towards the stairs.

Joanne arrived early for her interview which was what she had planned. She felt it went well but she wasn't sure it was what she was looking for. It was a small practice and from what she could tell most of the staff appeared to be well into their fifties, not that she had anything against quinquagenarians, but she wasn't quite sure how she would fit in. However, she did feel that if she were offered the position there she would accept it, if only for a new experience.

Seeing that she was on her own, Joanne thought she would have a look around the shops to see if there was anything else she could buy for the house. She realised that if Tom were to stay in the house from time to time, she would be short of towels, so she looked around and bought another couple of sets amongst a few smaller items she needed.

Joanne had only just finished putting her shopping in the car when her phone rang.

"Hello, Joanne Webster," she said in answer.

"Miss Webster, this is Warren Fredericks. You are meant to be coming for an interview tomorrow at 10 am?"

"Yes, that is correct Mr Fredericks. Is there a problem?" she asked.

"I am so sorry Miss Webster, but something unexpected has come up and I will not now be available, so I am just ringing to let you know that I will have to cancel your interview. I'm very sorry for the short notice," explained Fredericks.

"That's very disappointing. I was very much looking forward to meeting you and to attending the interview, however, if as you say something has cropped up unexpectedly then no problem," replied Joanne, trying to keep her cool and not letting her voice break up.

"Yes, I am sorry Miss Webster. Apart from tomorrow, I already have a very busy week, so I am not sure that we will be able to re-schedule," Fredericks explained.

"That is extremely disappointing, Mr Fredericks. I don't suppose you would be available now?" she asked.

"I am in the office, yes, but I planned to leave in about an hour as I have some work to do at home for tomorrow," he replied.

"I don't want to sound too pushy, but I am in town at the moment. I could be with you in about ten minutes if you feel you would like to conduct my interview now?" she asked.

"Miss Webster, yes, you are being a bit pushy but I like that in a person, just so long as it is controlled! Okay, if you are here in ten minutes, you have a deal. The clock is ticking," he replied.

"Thank you! I am on my way now."

Joanne set the timer on her phone to ten minutes and quickly made her way to Fredericks' office. She knew she could make it in time, but she didn't want to be early. As she approached the entrance to the offices, she still had two minutes to spare. She waited outside until she had one minute left then she pushed the entrance bell.

"Fredericks. How can I help?" said the voice on the other end.

"Joanne Webster to see Mr Fredericks," she replied.

"Come on up, Miss Webster, Mr Fredericks is expecting you."

Joanne walked up the stairs to the first floor and opened the door to the reception.

"Miss Webster, I presume," said the man standing in front of her.

"Mr Fredericks," replied Joanne, holding out her hand towards him.

"Spot on with your timing," he said as he shook her hand. "Please, follow me."

Joanne followed him into his office.

"Please take a seat, Miss Webster. So, can you tell me what brings you to Eastbourne?" he asked.

"Yes. After a broken marriage, a painful divorce and struggling to fit into society again, I needed a complete change," she replied.

"You weren't worried or frightened by the total change?" he asked.

"Not really. My aunt lives in Eastbourne. She is my only living relative, so I am not completely alone."

"On your application, you gave your contact address as The Grand

Hotel."

"Yes, but I've bought a house now. I moved in at the weekend," she replied.

"That's good then. So you are single again? Boyfriend, girlfriend, partner?" he asked.

"No distractions, although there is the possibility of a male partner in the future," replied Joanne.

"Well, your previous chambers were sad to see you leave, I have an extensive report in front of me, it is plain to see that they were aggrieved at your decision, why do you think that is?" asked Warren Fredericks.

"I will be the first to admit, it was not a decision I took without serious thought. Everyone there had been extremely helpful to me and was always willing to offer their support in my continued learning. I feel they were hoping I would stay and had it not been for my marriage breaking down I would have, I enjoyed working there," she replied.

Warren glanced back at the report in front of him and then looked up at her, "Miss Webster, Joanne, I know exactly why they wanted to keep you, this is not a reference I have from them, it is a report, of everything you did, every case you were involved with, you did not lose one case that you were involved with. The leg work you did on your first few cases was they tell me, exemplary, as it needed to be to get a result. You do not need to minimize your input, you should be proud of yourself and the way you covered your work, treating colleagues and clients with the same respect," he replied.

"Tell me, what do you think you could bring to my practice that would improve the quality of service to the client?" he asked.

"Sir, I think some visual changes would relax a client more. The reception area is too small, there are only two seats both of which are uncomfortable, and no coffee or tea machine. The offices are too open, more privacy is required and maybe some re-decoration. And when looking through your spiel on your web page, there was no mention of staff appraisal; an in-house system of staff appraisal would increase your client base," she replied.

"Well, Miss Webster, you have pretty much trashed my business there! Do you feel comfortable with that?" he asked.

"You asked me a question and all I could do was to give you a reply based on my first impressions. There would be no point in lying to you."

"So, tell me what makes you think you could facilitate the improvement of all those things and more?"

"I don't *think* I could make the change; I *know* I could. Some things would require a cash investment but that would be tax-deductible. When completed, I guarantee you will see a client base increase," replied Joanne.

"Okay, Miss Webster. I think that concludes everything I need to know about you; is there anything you would like to ask me?" he said.

"I have only one question – when do I start?" she asked.

"Miss Webster, as I explained I am unavailable tomorrow, but should you be the person we are looking for to progress our company further then we will be in touch with you. Thank you for coming," said Fredericks in closing.

Joanne left the office feeling rather downbeat; she got the impression from Mr Fredericks' last statement that she had messed up. She had been too open about her true feelings but then that had always been her problem. All she could think about now was how she was going to tell Tom that she had completely trashed her interview. On the way home, she stopped by the supermarket to pick up a few things for dinner; she would cook a meal for him as she imagined he would be exhausted after his day's work and she would be able to break the news about her interview over dinner.

Pulling up outside the house, she noticed that one of the doors to the barn was slightly open. She walked slowly down the pathway and stopping outside the barn, she gently pulled the door that was already partly opened and called out to him.

"Tom, are you in there?"

He was at the far end of the barn and, caught unaware by Joanne's return, he quickly turned, grabbing a towel from the cabinet to the side of where he was standing and wrapped it around himself.

"Sorry! I didn't hear your car pull up," he said.

"Maybe because your radio is so loud, but don't apologise, Tom, I should have knocked first, but I hadn't expected that you would be naked in here at this time of day," she replied.

"I wanted to wash before you got home."

"Why didn't you use the bathroom, Tom? I put an extra towel in there in case you wanted to use it."

"Well, you weren't there to ask and I didn't want to use the shower without asking your permission first," he replied.

"Well, I'm here now and there's no need for you to ask me in future. Anyway, I have bought a few things from the shops. I'm going to cook dinner for you, so when you are ready, please come back up to the house, won't you?"

"Okay. I won't be long."

Joanne was just placing the food on the breakfast bar in the kitchen when Tom walked in.

"That looks very nice," he said.

"Hopefully it will taste as good as it looks," remarked Joanne, "but I'll warn you now, cooking is not my forte'," she added.

"I'm sure it will taste simply fine," he replied. "So, how did the interview go today?"

"I was wondering if you would ask me, but I was trying not to mention it – or them," she replied.

"*Them?*" questioned Tom. "I thought you only had one interview today?"

"Well, I did and that went sort of okay, but I wasn't impressed with the firm. I'll wait to see what happens and if I hear back from them. I would take the position if it were offered to me," she replied.

"So, was there another one then?" he asked.

"Yes. I was meant to be having that one tomorrow, but they rang me while I was in town, explaining that they would have to cancel owing to unforeseen circumstances. So, seeing that I was in town I asked them if they could see me today, and they said yes, but that was a big mistake on my part," she replied.

"Why – what happened?"

"Oh, I completely messed up, Tom. I wasn't prepared and he asked me some really strange questions which didn't have much to do with the actual job," replied Joanne.

"Okay, so not good then," he remarked.

"*Dreadful*, I think would be the word, Tom, but as if that wasn't bad enough, at the end of the interview he asked me if I had any questions, so I asked him when I could start – big mistake. My dad's words were ringing loudly in my ears."

"I'm sure you will find something but you have to try not to let your feelings overtake the situation," replied Tom. "Dinner was very nice, by the way. In fact, I'd say excellent."

"You're too kind – are you sure you're not just trying to cheer me up?" she asked.

"Honestly, it was perfect," he replied.

Tom cleared the plates away, then he rinsed them and placed them in the dishwasher. He did likewise with the pots and pans that had been used.

"Would you like a drink?" Tom asked.

"Just water please, Tom," she replied.

Just then Joanne's phone rang.

"Hello. Joanne Webster," she said as she answered it.

"Miss Webster, Warren Fredericks," replied the voice at the other end of the call.

"Oh, good evening," she replied.

"In answer to your question, Miss Webster, Wednesday," replied Fredericks.

"Excuse me, but what does that mean exactly?" she inquired.

"Have you forgotten your question already, Miss Webster? Now that does surprise me," replied Fredericks.

"No, I haven't forgotten! I was just shocked, but at the same time I am absolutely delighted; I will not let you down," replied Joanne.

"Miss Webster, I am a fair man, but I do not suffer fools lightly; words mean nothing without actions. You will start on Wednesday and you have eighteen days to prove to me that I have not made the biggest mistake of my life," replied Fredericks sternly.

"Thank you, Mr Fredericks. Thank you very much," she replied.

"Goodnight, Miss Webster. I expect to see you early on Wednesday."

The phone went dead. Joanne placed her phone down on the breakfast bar and let out a scream.

"Joanne, what's wrong, what's happened?" Tom asked.

"I don't believe it, Tom! I just do not believe it," she said.

"Believe what? What on earth are you talking about?" asked Tom.

"My interview, Tom. The one that I thought I had messed up! I got it, I got the job! I start on Wednesday!" replied Joanne.

Without saying more, she moved quickly around to the other side of the breakfast bar towards Tom, who was still standing by the sink. Joanne slowed as she approached him.

"Tom, I'm so excited! I've got the job I wanted all along. I cannot believe this is happening. It's a whole new beginning for me."

"Well done," he said. "I am so happy for you, but it's no more than you deserve," he added.

"I only need one more thing now to make it complete," she replied.

"What's that?" asked Tom.

"You, Tom, you," she replied.

At that point, Joanne lost control of her emotions. She had tried self-control but maybe it was her excitement about the job; she wasn't sure, but she could not contain herself any longer. She leapt forward and flung her arms around him, kissing him fully on his lips. Tom pulled back and gently pushed her away.

"Please, Joanne, this is not right, please don't do that," said Tom as he moved away and walked towards the kitchen door.

"Tom! Where are you going?" she asked.

"Home," he replied.

Joanne didn't follow him; she sat back down at the breakfast bar, holding her head in her hands and wondering when she was going to learn to keep her emotions in check. She appeared to be making the same mistake again that she had made with her ex-husband. She was beginning to think that there was something wrong with her, but for now, she knew that once again she had upset the one person who meant something to her, and she was not sure what she could do about it. She walked towards the hallway, turned off the kitchen lights and went upstairs to take a shower.

Joanne came out of the bathroom and walked along the hallway, clutching her towel around her. As she approached the bedroom where Tom had been working, she realised that she hadn't even checked it to see how much he had done. Joanne noticed that Tom had left the door slightly ajar, maybe to let the smell of new paint disperse. She gently pushed the door open and was stunned by what she saw in front of her: the room was finished, well, apart from any furniture of course. The painting, the wallpapering – he'd even laid the carpet and put up the blinds. She just could not believe it but she was thinking once again about how badly she had treated him. It appeared to her now that she just could not be close to him without letting her emotions get the better of her.

Joanne turned and went into her bedroom. She was now feeling saddened by what she had just seen, not because she didn't like it – it was beautiful – but because she had forced Tom away from her. It was late and she felt tired; it had been a long day and the events had taxed her brain. She took a nightdress out of the wardrobe, turned down the duvet and climbed into bed. Joanne picked up her phone and checked to see if there were any messages but there were none. She replaced her phone on the bedside cabinet and lay down.

Almost an hour later and Joanne was still awake. She found it difficult to relax and clear her head. Lying there, she began to wonder if the kitchen door was locked; she hadn't wanted to go and check, but she knew she would have to, otherwise there was no way she was ever going to get to sleep. She walked down into the kitchen and was disturbed to find the lights on, though she knew that she had turned them off. She entered the kitchen with some trepidation. There was no one there so she quickly checked the door – it was locked. She was confused and concerned about why the lights were on. As she turned to walk back to the hallway, she noticed a note on the breakfast bar. It was from Tom.

'It may be a good idea to check everything is locked before you go to bed, especially as you are living here on your own. Goodnight.'

She made her way along the hall to the stairs and glanced into the lounge. Continuing up the stairs, she stopped and headed back down to the lounge. Standing in the doorway, she noticed a figure lying on the sofa: it was Tom. She noticed that his cover had fallen off him and lay on the floor. He was lying there in just a pair of shorts; she picked up the cover and gently placed it over him as she thought he might get cold in the night.

Joanne left Tom there and went up to her bedroom, lying down again on her be. She still couldn't sleep, even though she felt more at ease now knowing that she wasn't alone in the house, but all she could think of now was Tom lying there on the sofa. Getting up, she walked over to the set of drawers and took out a pair of jogging bottoms and a T-shirt, took off her nightdress and replaced it with the top and bottoms. Picking up the duvet cover from her bed, she folded it, picked up a pillow and carried them both downstairs to the lounge. She placed the duvet cover and pillow on the floor a little way from the sofa, then lay down and wrapped the duvet cover around her and that was where she slept.

Joanne opened her eyes. Tom was still lying there on the sofa. She got up and went into the kitchen to make him a cup of tea and herself a coffee. She placed the two cups on a tray and carried them into the lounge, placing the tray on the small coffee table. She sat there on the floor watching Tom while drinking her coffee. It was still early – six-fifteen – but it wasn't long before he stirred.

Joanne waited for Tom to open his eyes.

"Thank you," she said.

"What for?" he asked.

"You know very well what for Tom," she replied. "Thank you for the bedroom. It's lovely. And thank you for coming back, for being here. Thank you for everything."

"I had to come back. I left my things here from Sunday night," he replied.

"Is that the only reason you came back, Tom?" asked Joanne.

"I can't sit about here talking, Joanne. I have work to do, and you won't be thanking me if I don't finish re-decorating your house, will you?" he said as he got up from the sofa and folded his blanket.

Joanne left it at that; she knew there would be no point in pressing him for an answer to her question.

"Where are you going to be working today?" she asked.

"I thought I would start in the back lounge if that's okay with you?" he asked.

"That's fine. Do you need my help?" asked Joanne.

"No, I can manage, thanks," he replied.

"Okay. I need to go into town to get a few bits, and I will pop in to see my aunt as I am going to be somewhat busy for the next couple of weeks," she replied.

Joanne was so right about the next two weeks being busy; it was almost as though her feet didn't touch the ground. She was exhausted every night and at weekends, too. Her life revolved around work, trying to catch up on the cases they'd been working on and getting to know her new colleagues. As in all workplaces, some people are easier to get on with than others, but what she had very quickly noticed was that one of her new colleagues seemed to be everywhere she turned; she just could not shake him off. It had also meant a cooldown on her affection for Tom, not because her opinion of him was changing, it was simply because she was just so tired. Tom always tried hard to converse with her; he was there at night when she got home and there in the morning when she went to work. The first two weeks went by in a flash, but she felt she had weathered the storm and in no time at all it was the company dinner dance. She didn't want to go on her own, but she still hadn't found the right moment to ask Tom to accompany her.

CHAPTER SIX

The Company Dinner

Joanne had so looked forward to the weekend and hoped to have a lie-in but that was not on the cards – she had far too much to do. Tom had still been sleeping downstairs, which she was extremely grateful for, and he had worked wonders with his decorating, including finishing the bathroom next to her bedroom, although he did explain to her that he wanted to make some alterations so that it would become an ensuite. She felt bad; she knew that she had neglected him the past couple of weeks. She waited until she heard him go out and then got up and went down to the kitchen. She cooked a huge breakfast and had just placed it on the table when Tom opened the front door after his morning walk.

"Timed to perfection, young man. In the kitchen if you please," she said as he walked through the door.

"Excuse me?" replied Tom.

Joanne looked at him.

"Breakfast – it's on the table in the kitchen. Don't let it get cold."

"What's this in aid of then?" he asked.

"I've decided you need a day off, Tom, so there'll be no decorating done today. After we've had breakfast, you can go and change and then we'll both go into town," replied Joanne.

Tom looked across the table towards her.

"I'm sorry, but have I missed something?" he asked with a puzzled expression on his face.

"Like what?" she replied.

Tom continued cutting a sausage and lifting it towards his mouth he replied, "The wedding."

"What are you going on about, Tom?" she asked.

"Well, most women usually wait until after the wedding before they start giving out orders," he replied.

"I just thought you've been working so hard you could do with a day off; I haven't been here to help you and what is even worse is that I have been totally ignoring you."

"And you call shopping a day off? I'd rather continue decorating," he replied.

"Well, you know what they say, don't you? A change is as good as a rest, so shopping it is. At least we will be together, which is something that I have greatly missed the last two weeks."

Tom didn't mind going shopping; after all, he had been doing it for years, both for himself and the old lady, but this was different. Joanne had omitted to tell him one particularly crucial factor: she was shopping for clothes, and that he hated. One store after another, one outfit then another and another, and he was meant to give some indication of whether it suited her or not! He didn't even know what style she liked. It seemed to him as though they had been out for hours, and then he heard those magical words:

"That's it, I'm finished."

"Great," replied Tom. "Time for something to eat now."

"Hey, not so fast if you don't mind!" replied Joanne as she took hold of his arm, gently pulling him towards a men's outfitters.

"And what could you possibly want in here?" he asked.

"Me? I don't want anything, but you do."

"I'm not with you. What could I possibly want in here?" he asked.

"A suit, perhaps?" replied Joanne sarcastically.

"I don't think so, no way."

"Tom, you're not going to the dinner tonight unless you are wearing a suit," said Joanne quietly, half turning away from him.

"I wasn't planning on going to a dinner in the first place. Let's go."

Joanne stood in front of him as he turned to leave.

"Tom, you have to. I can't go on my own."

"Aha, I think I get the picture now. You want me to accompany you to a dinner?"

"I told you I was going to a dinner tonight – don't you remember?"

"I remember alright, you just omitted to tell me that I was supposed to be going with you."

"Well, who did you think I was planning on taking? I don't know anyone else," she answered as she pointed him towards a sales assistant.

Joanne felt quite pleased with herself. She had guessed that Tom refuse had she mentioned the dinner before, but this way he would have felt very embarrassed had he done so. He looked a bit of a scruff in his everyday clothes, but as he stood in front of her in the suit, he looked quite smart; so much so that she was beginning to like the idea that he was going to be with her that evening.

Tom couldn't get out of the shop quick enough; he hadn't worn a suit for years and was a little annoyed at the prospect of having to wear one in front of people he didn't even know. He had allowed Joanne to trick him into going with her to the dinner, he knew that, but he didn't want to make things worse by refusing to go at this late hour. They didn't speak much on the way back to the house. Tom felt that Joanne had pushed things too far and Joanne guessed that Tom was less than happy with her.

As they got out of the car back at the house, Joanne turned to Tom.

"I'm sorry, Tom, I should have asked you, but I was sure you would have said no. Please forgive me. Will you please escort me to the dinner tonight?"

Tom looked at her; how could he refuse, especially when she gave him that look she was giving him now? There was nothing he could do; he was putty in her hands.

"Of course, you're right, I would have refused, but seeing that it means so much to you, then I accept," he replied.

"Thank you, Tom," said Joanne as she turned and walked towards her front door.

But Tom hadn't quite finished.

"On one condition, that is," he continued.

Joanne turned and looked at him, wondering what was coming next.

"Which is?" she asked.

"That I can use your bathroom," replied Tom with a smile on his face.

"But of course you can Tom! It goes without saying. I told you before; you don't need to ask me if you want to shower," she replied.

"If you can take my suit in then, I'll go and get some things from the barn; I'm sure you don't want to be late."

Tom was ready first; he was waiting in the lounge when he heard Joanne coming down the stairs. He got up and walked into the hallway to meet her. When he looked up and saw her, he couldn't believe what he saw – Joanne looked stunning, and, although different in looks, the way she moved it might just have been his wife he was looking at. Her hair colour was the same, she was the same size, the same height, and seeing her in her evening gown made his face drop. All he could think of was his wife; she was perfect in every way.

Joanne noticed the look on Tom's face.

"Tom! Is something wrong? Doesn't this dress suit me?" she asked him worryingly.

Tom glanced towards her.

"No, you are fine, the dress is fine."

"Well, you could be a little more encouraging! Or maybe offer a glimpse of a smile," replied Joanne.

Tom was trying to keep his thoughts to himself, but it was hard. His emotions were running high and he was about to answer when he glanced towards the window.

"Ah, here comes the taxi. Are you ready?" he asked, glancing back towards Joanne.

She sensed Tom's relief that he was able to change the subject.

"Umm, right on cue, it would appear," she replied.

The ten-minute journey passed in silence, leaving both to reflect on their conversation and wonder had they made the right choices.

At the hotel, Tom walked around and opened the door for Joanne.

"You look beautiful," he said as he took her hand and walked up the carpeted stairs leading towards the hotel entrance.

Joanne looked at him.

"It took you long enough to decide on that! Are you sure?"

Tom smiled and hinted at a laugh as he replied.

"You know me – never one to make a rash decision."

That seemed to break the ice as they joined the queue entering the ballroom.

Although Tom had reluctantly agreed to accompany Joanne to the dinner dance, he wasn't looking forward to the evening and that didn't help the way he was feeling. Apart from Joanne, he wouldn't know anyone else there, and he expected that they would all end up talking business to each other and Tom was no solicitor. He knew that he could hold his own on many topics of conversation, but on the law, he was completely lost and out of his depth. However, he knew that the evening meant everything to Joanne, and having recently moved from London, she needed to connect socially not only with her colleagues but with other solicitors in the area, too. Tom was also aware of the situation that he was in: Joanne was his proprietor, although he was only living in an adapted barn. It was where he had lived for a while, and he was quite happy there and didn't want to live anywhere else. He had money, but that didn't mean anything to him; what he wanted was to have his wife and son back, but that was not possible.

It quickly became apparent to Tom that the night was a big mistake for him. He tried to join in the conversations but as soon as Joanne's colleagues found out he wasn't a solicitor, they blanked him. Well, all except for one of her colleagues. Tom couldn't even remember his name although Joanne had introduced them to each other when they first arrived.

Tom was standing on his own, looking down at his empty glass.

"You can help yourself, you know, it's all free."

Tom looked up and saw Joanne's colleague standing in front of him.

"Thanks," he replied, "but I'm okay for now."

The man held out his hand.

"I'm Jefferey, by the way. Joanne introduced us when you first arrived."

Tom looked towards him.

"Yes, thank you. I remember now. Jefferey, I'm Tom."

"So, what do you do then, Tom, if you are not into law?"

"This and that, you know, odd jobs, decorating," replied Tom.

"Interesting. And is your girlfriend happy with that?" asked Jefferey.

Tom looked enquiringly at him.

"Excuse me?" he asked.

"Well, you know, Joanne, your girlfriend – is she happy with you doing odd jobs? I mean, what do you earn doing that?"

"Is that what she told you then, Jefferey? That she is my girlfriend?"

"Well, no, but you are here with her, aren't you? I assumed that you were her partner or something."

Tom looked at him.

"Well, yes, Jefferey I am here with Joanne, but you know what they say about assuming things, don't you?"

"Well, no, but I am sure you are going to tell me."

"Never assume anything, Jefferey. If you do, you make an ass of you and me."

Jefferey was rather offended by that comment.

"Huh, I suppose you think you're being clever?" he said.

"Not really, just pointing out a fact that you should never assume anything. I thought that in your business that would have been a prerequisite to success," replied Tom.

Jefferey looked at Tom angrily, his face becoming strained.

"Asshole!" he muttered as he turned to walk away.

"Takes one to know one, Jefferey," shouted Tom as Jefferey walked into the gathering.

Tom stood for a few moments, reflecting on how he had let himself be drawn into something that he wasn't interested in and, what's more, something he certainly didn't like. Deciding that he needed fresh air to relieve himself of the stuffy autocratic atmosphere, he turned and made his way out through the French windows into the garden. Looking up at the night sky, he sensed that somewhere among the stars were his wife and son looking down on him, wondering what on earth he was doing there.

Joanne was looking frantically around the room for Tom, but she couldn't see him anywhere. Then she saw Jefferey approaching her.

"Looking for someone, Joanne?" he enquired.

"Yes, I'm looking for Tom. Have you seen him?" she asked.

"Your partner, yes. He was over by the French windows a while ago, totally out of his depth here. None of my business but how on earth did you end up with someone like that? You can do much better. The guy is a total arse and I told him so, too," he replied.

Joanne didn't want to get into an argument, but her response was instantaneous.

"That's very kind of you, Jefferey, and knowing Tom as I do, I imagine he thought the same of you too. However, you are right, of course – it is none of your business."

Joanne left it there. Heading towards the French doors, she walked out into the garden and saw Tom standing by the pond, still gazing up into the night sky.

"I'll give you a penny for them," she quipped, taking hold of his arm as she stood beside him.

"They're worth a lot more than that. No amount of money could ever buy them," replied Tom as he turned to look at her.

Joanne couldn't help but notice his glazed eyes, so she decided to quickly change the subject.

"I hear that you met Jefferey, then," she said.

"What an arsehole! How on earth do you work with people like that?" he asked.

"I'm sorry, Tom. I hope he wasn't too obnoxious," commented Joanne.

"Don't worry about it. Enjoy the rest of your evening. I'll be here when you are ready to go," he replied.

Joanne was upset, firstly because she knew she was wrong in expecting Tom to accompany her to the dinner, and secondly because she had the feeling that the confrontation between Jefferey and Tom was not without incident.

Joanne took Tom by the arm.

"Tom, please will you come back in with me now? The boss wants to meet you, and he said he has an important announcement to make."

"Come on, then, let's not keep them waiting," replied Tom, looking at Joanne.

As they entered the room, Tom took Joanne's hand and followed her lead towards her boss. As they approached Warren Fredericks, he held out a hand to Tom.

"And you must be Tom, the amazing decorator! Joanne has been telling me such a lot about you. She is extremely lucky to have found a man like you."

Tom was taken back by the comments; he had no idea that Joanne had been lauding his ability as a decorator, but he didn't want to let her down.

"I think I am the lucky one, Mr Fredericks," replied Tom.

Warren looked straight at Tom and, cupping his hand in his, he said, "You could well be right, young man, and from what I have been hearing about Miss Webster's skills I think you and me both."

Warren placed his arm around Tom's shoulder, quite to the amazement of Joanne and a few of her work colleagues too.

"Tell me, Tom, when you have finished the house, do you have another contract waiting?"

"I didn't, but I guess I will have now," remarked Tom.

Warren gave a little chuckle and turning to Joanne, he said, "Joanne, you've found an ace here! Not only an amazing decorator it seems, but an intelligent one at that!"

Then, looking back at Tom, he continued.

"Well, when you have finished Joanne's house, come and see me. I'll have a couple of contracts for you to keep you busy."

With that, Warren Fredericks turned to his staff and their partners.

"Please, everyone, take your seats and enjoy your dinner."

Tom looked at Joanne and, leaning towards her as they took their seats, he whispered in her ear, "Thank you."

"For what? she asked.

"For everything," replied Tom.

Instinctively, Joanne leaned forward and kissed Tom gently on the cheek.

"It's not what you know, it's *who* you know, and I happened to know that Warren was looking to employ someone to spruce up the office a bit. It's incredibly old-fashioned and drab. I just elaborated on your decorating skills in our conversation earlier, but I don't know what the other project is."

Tom waited until Joanne was comfortably seated and then he took his position at the table by her side. Turning to her, he said, "Thank you anyway, whatever it is. I think it may just be what I need to bring me out of my shell and your boss seems quite a nice guy."

"From what I have heard, he is; in fact, very nice, but I have yet to find out for myself," replied Joanne.

When the dinner was over and the guests were chatting amongst themselves, Warren Fredericks tapped his spoon against the glass and rose to his feet to make his speech.

"Thank you all very much for attending tonight. It pleases me so much to see everyone here. You have all worked so hard. It has been a good year and the least I can do to repay you all is to treat you to this evening. I do hope you have enjoyed the meal and the company; I know I certainly have. For those of you who have not experienced one of these nights before, it is at this point when I make company announcements. Thankfully there are only a couple this year but there is one particularly important one.

"However, firstly, to Miss Taylor. I am sure you all know by now that Linda will be leaving us in a few weeks and of course we all hope to see her back after her parental leave, but that is something that only Linda can decide, so we all wish her well and await the outcome. I am sure you all know too that Terrence will be leaving us to test out his skills in Germany. A man of many languages so he shouldn't have too many problems. We will miss him greatly, but he, too, goes with our best wishes. As one leaves so another one joins, and we are indeed lucky to have acquired the skills of Joanne who joins us from a top firm in London. I also said that I would be appointing an executive and I have looked everywhere to find a suitable person. However, the skills I have been looking for are just not around. It is for that reason that I have decided to appoint from within the company, something I previously said I didn't want to do. I know this will come as a total surprise to you all, not least to the person I have chosen, who by the way still has no idea that they are that person. You have all worked hard and you all do a remarkable job. The outcome of which has seen a 21% increase in turnover since last year. The reason I wanted to employ someone from outside is that I didn't, and don't, want to lose any of you. I was worried that by appointing someone from inside, and there are a few of you I could quite easily have chosen, I just didn't think it would work. I would be faced with some of you saying why not me, haven't I done a good enough job, or don't I deserve the recognition and I didn't want that to happen. Before I announce the person I have chosen, I just want to say that if you all look under your table placemats you will find an envelope with your name on it, but please do not open it now, keep it for later. They all contain the same amount and I have already made the tax payment for you. There is, of course, one person who doesn't have an amount in their envelope and that is because she has only recently joined us. However, in her envelope, she will find a new contract, so I can tell you all now that the new executive post which I have created will be filled by Joanne Webster. Her appointment as our executive has no reflection on the ability of any of you; you are all doing an excellent job, and that is reflected in your bonuses. However, taking everything into account, Joanne has the credentials to take us even further as a company, delivering even better and more accountable services to our customers. I hope you will all wish her well in the post; it is something which she deserves. Thank you all so much."

With that, Warren Fredericks made his way around the room to Joanne to congratulate her.

Although the initial announcement had been greeted with silence, it was soon replaced with shouts of congratulations and everyone moved to towards Joanne to express their best wishes. Joanne was shocked; she just could not believe it and if she had been worried about moving from London to Eastbourne, she now knew that it was the right decision. Not only because of the work and her immediate promotion, but also because of meeting Tom and her developing friendship with him.

Tom stood by Joanne's side while she was congratulated by her work colleagues. He hadn't even congratulated her himself; there wasn't any time before she was surrounded. He could see how much it meant to her, the fact that she was becoming accepted in her new job and position. It was quite amazing how they had all taken to her so quickly, but Tom was in no doubt that there was an air about her that most people found easy to get on with. The last person to stand in line to congratulate her was her boss. Warren gently took her told of her arm and led her to one side, and standing close to her he whispered something in her ear, in a very private manner. Not wanting to appear rude or to give the impression he was trying to overhear what was being said, Tom moved away, closer to the dining hall entrance. While he waited, he took note of all that was happening, and it occurred to him that one of Joanne's colleagues hadn't offered his congratulations – Jefferey. Tom found it quite strange, especially after their conversation from earlier in the evening.

Tom was quite taken aback by the number of Joanne's colleagues who had stopped to talk to him on their way out. Some had mostly engaged in idle chatter, but some were looking forward to him taking their boss up on his offer earlier in the evening regarding some decorating contracts. They were all of one voice, and, like Joanne, were hoping that it was to redecorate their office space, some hinting it was more like working in a funeral parlour than a solicitor's office. It wasn't long before he felt someone clutch his arm. It was Warren.

"Tom, you have one amazing young lady in Joanne. Take care of her, they are very hard to come by," he said.

Tom knew he had to respond, but those quite simple but thoughtful words left a lump in his throat and gave him an immediate flashback to his wife and how she had died. Almost choking and struggling to utter a few words of any meaning, he just replied, "Thank you, I'll do my best."

Taking hold of Tom's hand to say goodbye, he placed his other hand on Tom's shoulder.

"Don't forget to come and see me as soon as you have finished the house. I desperately need to tap into your decorating skills."

"Thank you. I won't let you down," replied Tom.

Joanne and Tom made the short drive back to the house in the taxi in virtual silence. It was late; it had been an exhausting evening, and both had quite a lot to reflect on. It wasn't until they were nearly back at her house that Joanne, touching Tom's hand, spoke.

"I just cannot believe what Warren did. So strange," she said.

"Why strange? He's a businessman, he has kept a close eye on you since you started, and as he said, he had wanted to employ an executive from outside the company and you were pretty close to that," replied Tom.

Joanne gave a giggle and squeezed Tom's hand.

"No not me! I'm talking about you! He was full of praise towards you, that's what was strange," she said.

"I suppose," replied Tom, "but you must have told him about me decorating your house."

"Well, yes, I did, but that was only in general conversation, during work. I did add though that you work fast and have an amazing knowledge of colours," replied Joanne.

"I suppose you failed to mention that I don't live with you in the house but that I live in the barn? He appeared to me to be under the impression that we shared the house."

"Too much information; people will always believe what they want to believe, no matter what you tell them," she replied.

Tom couldn't argue with that, so he didn't respond. In any case, they were home now.

"Would you like a drink?" enquired Joanne.

"I would love a tea although I can make that myself in the barn. However, I still have my clothes in your house, and I would like to change out of this suit if that's okay with you?" he asked.

"No problem," replied Joanne. "I'll make you tea while you change. If you leave your suit upstairs, I will take it into the cleaners with my dress on Monday."

"Thank you," replied Tom. "I was going to ask if I could leave it in your wardrobe as I don't have anywhere suitable to hang it in the barn."

"Sure, not a problem," was the reply.

Tom freshened up his face and washed his hands in the bathroom, and then went into the bedroom to change his clothes. He put his suit back on its hanger and placed it on the handle of Joanne's wardrobe.

As he crossed the hallway towards the stairs, he noticed the bathroom door was open. He had closed it. Instinctively he glanced in; he was shocked to see Joanne just sliding her dress off. Either she caught a glimpse of Tom walking past in the mirror or she heard him.

"I've left your tea in the kitchen, Tom; I'll be down in a minute."

"Thank you," he replied.

He had almost finished his tea when Joanne joined him in the kitchen; he looked up as she walked in. She was wearing a sheer dressing gown. She sat opposite him and picked up her cup.

"That'll be cold by now," he commented.

"No! It's fine for me, really. Did you enjoy the evening?" she asked.

"Very much so," he replied. "Especially your news. I looked around the table when Warren announced it, and although everyone else like you was shocked, there was a look of absolute outrage on the face of one person."

"And whom might that have been?" asked Joanne.

"Jefferey," replied Tom.

Joanne rose from her chair, walked towards the sink and tipped the remainder of her coffee away. As she turned around, Tom noticed that her dressing gown had slid down over her shoulder. She walked back to her chair and sat down, leaving the dressing gown where it was, exposing her shoulder and part of her chest.

They sat there for a couple of minutes, neither of them speaking, but occasionally glancing at each other.

Tom lifted his cup towards his mouth, finishing the last dregs of his tea. He then rose from the chair and walked over to the sink where he rinsed his cup and placed it in the sink next to Joanne's. As he turned around to face her, he noticed that she was leaning over the table with a tired but satisfied look on her face.

"So, you enjoyed it, Tom?" she asked him.

"Yes, I did, it was a very good evening, thank you," he replied.

"And what about me? Did you enjoy my company?" she asked, rising from her chair and walking towards him.

"Yes, of course. You looked really beautiful tonight," he replied.

"That's good," she replied as she placed her hand on his chest and kissed him.

Tom held back, and gently breaking away, he said to her, "It's late, you're tired, and I should be going. Let's not spoil a good evening." As he reached the doorway, he turned and looked at her.

"Get some sleep. I'll see you in the morning,"

Then he turned and left, leaving Joanne leaning against the kitchen sink.

CHAPTER SEVEN

Tom Opens his Heart

Tom woke early; he still had a lot to do. It was only 5:30 am but it was already quite warm. He hadn't slept well, probably not helped by the high humidity, but mostly because of the exploits of the previous evening, which were playing on his mind. He knew it would have been all too easy for him to have accepted Joanne's advances and if he were honest with himself, it was something that under normal circumstances he would not have refused. However, he had trouble coming to terms with what should be 'normal circumstances'. He was still stuck in what seemed to be a perpetual time warp, which, when the situation arose, would lead him straight into a flashback. Had he accepted Joanne's advances, he would have been making love to his wife, something that he found extremely upsetting. He knew that he had to move on, to let go, but he couldn't; it had been five years since that dreadful night, but the memories were as fresh as though it were yesterday. Maybe it was time he sought help, therapy of some kind, but he didn't know where to start.

Tom walked up to the house and taking a key from his pocket, he opened the front door; he was being as quiet as possible as he guessed Joanne would still be asleep. He had some work to finish off in the dining room and the conservatory, so he decided to make himself busy there, but first, the obligatory cup of tea. Clutching his cup, he entered the dining room, but he still wasn't sure that the paper Joanne had chosen was right for that room. He felt it needed a more subtle paper or maybe even just paint, so he finished painting the skirting boards and the door frame and then moved into the conservatory. He had already finished the paint job there, so it was just a matter of laying the tiles. He was over halfway through, but he needed the toilet; he still hadn't repaired the one downstairs, so he had to go to the one upstairs. As he came out, he looked towards Joanne's bedroom – the door was wide open and he wondered if she would be awake.

He walked along the landing to her room, stood in the doorway and peered in. The dressing gown Joanne had been wearing last evening was strewn on the floor; she was lying on her side, her back towards him, her body only half covered by the duvet. He thought about covering her up but decided against it as he didn't want to wake her. As he turned to leave, he got a shock.

Joanne could see Tom's reflection in the small mirror near her bed.

"Where are you going, Tom?" she asked.

"Sorry," replied Tom. "I didn't mean to disturb you. I just wanted to check to see if you were awake."

"I heard you coming up the stairs," replied Joanne. "Did you enjoy looking at my naked body, Tom?" she asked.

"I'm sorry, I didn't mean to look at you like that, but you left the door wide open and I was just trying to see if you were awake," he replied.

Joanne clutched the duvet as she turned over to face him, but it was still only covering the bottom half of her body from her waist down, her arm partially covering her breasts as she lay there. He was still standing in the doorway.

"What makes you think I could sleep, Tom? I've been awake most of the night, thinking about last evening, thinking about you. I heard you open the front door this morning; what time was it now? Five-forty-five?" she asked.

Tom felt a little flustered by the fact that Joanne had caught him looking at her.

"Maybe. I'm not sure of the exact time I came over. I just wanted to make an early start, sorry," he replied.

"Tom, we need to talk."

"Yes, I know."

"What do you know, Tom, please tell me!"

"It's not you, it's me! I'm sorry, very sorry," said Tom and he turned to walk away.

"Tom, please don't just walk away like that!" exclaimed Joanne in a raised voice. "That is not talking this through, that is you just saying sorry and leaving me in limbo, and that hurts."

"Yes, but what more can I say? I'm sorry, but I am just not ready," he replied.

"Tom, would you please come and sit here and talk about it," said Joanne, patting a space next to her on her bed.

Tom took a few steps towards her. She was still lying in her bed, half-covered by the duvet and her arm protecting the rest of her modesty. Tom stopped a few steps away. He was sweating, his heart was pounding, he looked at her lying there and wanted to accept her offer, but at that moment all he could visualize was his wife lying in the bed. He was traumatized and there was nothing he could do.

"Joanne, I'm sorry," he said as he turned away, walking towards the bedroom door.

Joanne jumped out of bed and, picking up the dressing gown off her bedroom floor, she rushed after him.

"Tom, please wait! Where are you going?" she asked.

He half-turned towards her.

"Let's talk in the kitchen or lounge – anywhere but not in your bedroom," he replied.

Joanne followed him into the kitchen. He flicked the switch on the kettle.

"Tea, coffee?" he asked.

"Coffee, please, Tom."

He placed the two cups on the breakfast bar and sat opposite her on the stool. He was trying to focus on her eyes, her face, but it was difficult. Joanne was sitting there, she had not tied her dressing gown and it was just hanging loose. He glanced across at her, trying not to focus too much on her open gown. He quickly refocused on her face while his hands played with his cup.

She sat there, expressionless, waiting for Tom to say something, but whatever the problem was he was finding it extremely difficult, almost impossible, to talk about it.

"Tom, please talk to me. You know this isn't easy for me, either. I like you very much and I feel so comfortable with you and with you being around me. I am not going to hide that from you, I am not going to hide from you, I want you to see me and if I thought it would do any good, I would take my gown off right now and jump on you naked, but I get the feeling you would not be impressed."

That seemed to break the ice slightly as Tom raised a smile which spread across his face.

"There is *nothing* wrong with you, Joanne. As I said yesterday, you are quite beautiful, an amazing woman, but I just can't. I just don't want to let you down," he replied.

"Tom, what are you saying? You would not let me down, I know it. We can work through this together. You are the man I want, no one else, just you," said Joanne as she reached across the breakfast bar and cupped her hands around his. "Please trust me, Tom. Whatever it is, we can work through it," she added.

Tom looked up and straight into her eyes.

"Joanne, believe me, this has nothing to do with you. You are a lovely woman and that is part of the problem. From the very first day that I met you when you came to the barn, I have been struggling with my feelings. Of course I want to be near you, who wouldn't, that is why I have been helping you, but it just isn't working, not for me, and I don't want to deceive you," he said with his eyes fixed firmly on hers.

Joanne had sat quietly listening to Tom's explanation, but he wasn't explaining anything at all. She just couldn't understand his meaning.

"But Tom, why not? I want to be with you, I want you to share this house with me, but you are making it very hard. Please trust me!"

"Joanne, I am trying to be honest with you, but there are things that

I cannot erase from my mind, as hard as I try, and that is the problem."

He sat there, staring at her, seeing the puzzled look on her fac. He knew that he had to be open with her and explain in depth the problem he had. He placed his hands around hers on the table and took a deep breath while trying to compose himself.

"It was five years ago; my wife and I had been out for dinner with our young son to celebrate our anniversary. I was driving, my wife was in the front passenger seat, our son was in the car seat behind her, he was asleep. A speeding car jumped a set of lights; it came out of nowhere. The police report suggested that by the force of the impact its speed must have been at least seventy miles an hour. It all happened so quickly; in those few seconds, my life changed forever. My wife didn't stand a chance, both her and our son died there, in the car, as did the couple in the other car. I was the only one who survived and every day since then, I wish I had died in that car, every day I re-live that nightmare repeatedly, as fresh as if it were yesterday."

Tom paused briefly as he wiped the tears from his eyes, then he took a deep breath and continued.

"People have been telling me for five years that those memories will fade, but when? When will they fade? That is what I want to know. Fade in time means nothing to me because they do not fade, not for me, so when will they fade? That is what I desperately want to know because they haven't faded yet. That is how I ended up here in the barn when I left the hospital after the accident. I had nothing, just an empty house full of memories. I couldn't live there, it was too painful. The house stayed empty, I walked the streets from day to day, sleeping anywhere and everywhere, derelict buildings, on the beach or under the pier, it didn't matter to me, my life had ended that night, just as if I had died too. Every day I questioned why me, why didn't I die too, and every day I wanted to be dead too." He paused to take a drink of water.

Joanne had been sitting there, listening to his explanation. She was shocked. She too had to wipe tears from her eyes. She found Tom's description so upsetting and couldn't imagine how he had coped.

"Tom, I am so sorry, I really wish you had confided in me before now. I feel dreadful for you. But how did you end up living in the barn?" asked Joanne.

"I was living a kind of half-life, moving from place to place, not eating, not drinking. I had no reason to exist; in truth, I just wanted to die, but I was a coward, I couldn't do it myself. Then one day when I was walking in town, an elderly lady fell as she came out of a shop. I picked her up and gathered all her shopping together. She had hurt her arm in the fall and it turned out that it was broken. I went with her in the ambulance to the hospital, and while they fixed her arm, I picked up her car from the town centre. It was the first time I had driven since the accident. That lady was Mrs Wheeler and from that day to this, the barn has been my home." He stopped again, took another drink of water and then took hold of Joanne's hands, holding them tightly and, looking directly into her eyes, he continued.

"I am sorry, Joanne, but that is the way things are. The problem I have now is that whenever I am close to you, or when you try to escalate our friendship, thoughts of my wife come flooding back. In many ways you are so like her, at least that is how it appears to me. The way you walk, the way you talk, even sometimes the way you look. If I didn't know any better, I'd say it's almost as if you are an angel sent to replace her. Last night, before we left the house to go to dinner, when I saw you walking down the stairs in your gown, it was as though you were her. That is why I shy away from you; it is not because I don't like you, I like you very much Joanne, but you must understand the way I feel. If I am to love you, if we are to become lovers, I need to know it is because of who you are, and not because you are so like my wife. That would not be fair to you, and I couldn't live with myself if that were what I did to you, or to belittle the memory of my wife. It is hard, I know, but I am asking you to give me time. I need to get to know you better, to love you for the person you are."

Tom released his hold on Joanne's hand and took a piece of kitchen towel from the roll to wipe his eyes. He looked at her and saw the tears running down her cheeks. He took another piece of kitchen towel and, reaching across the breakfast bar, he gently dabbed her eyes dry. She was stunned; she just did not know what to say. All she could think of now was the times when she had tried to force herself on him. She now understood completely his actions and knew she had to take her time with him if indeed she did want their relationship to blossom.

"Tom, I am so sorry, that must have been so awful for you. I cannot begin to imagine what you have been going through all these years, or how you must have felt! What can I say? I am just so sorry."

Tom rose from his stool and walked round to Joanne. Taking hold of her arms, he pulled her up close to him, kissing her gently on the cheek and then releasing her. He took hold of her dressing gown belt and pulled it together, concealing her body and then tied it.

"Joanne, it is not your fault, you weren't to know," he said as he stood back from her but still looking directly at her. "You are right, I should have told you all this before, but to be honest I just did not know how to; I find it exceedingly difficult to talk about, even now."

"No, it's me who should have listened. I was told when I was thinking of buying the house that your wife had been killed in an accident. I just didn't understand the full impact of what I was told," replied Joanne.

Tom looked at Joanne, still not believing how he had opened his heart to her. She was the only person he had spoken so openly to about the accident, and about losing his wife and son.

"I'm sorry, Joanne, sorry to burden you with my problems, but I had to tell you, to explain to you the way I feel and how it has affected me. I have never confided in anyone before. I am so sorry that you had to be the one to share my pain, but what could I do? I couldn't let you think that you were the problem. I am so sorry, Joanne, please forgive me; anyway, now that is done, I have work to do, so if you'll excuse me, I'll get started." With that, Tom disappeared into the conservatory and continued laying the tiled flooring.

Joanne felt at a loss; she didn't know what to do. She was still stunned by Tom's revelations. She sat there for a while, going over in her mind all the facts that Tom had told her. It was a very traumatic experience for him, and she felt sorry for how it had affected him. She just hoped that he would allow her to try to ease his pain. She wanted to be the one to help him find his life, but she knew it was not going to be easy.

Later, she went into the conservatory to see how Tom was getting on with the tiling.

"Tom, this is marvellous! You have almost finished. It looks very nice," she remarked.

Tom stood up and looked at her.

"Thank you, glad you like it; I have finished the paintwork in the dining room, but I am not sure the paper you bought will look good in there," he said as he knelt back down to finish laying the last few tiles.

"Don't worry about that for now, Tom," remarked Joanne. "You should rest a while. You were up early. I will make you a tea, and I'll leave it in the kitchen for you. I am going to take a shower. Tom, please make sure you come and let me know before you go."

Joanne went up to her bedroom and sat there for a while, still trying to collect her thoughts, and wondering how she could best help Tom, but she knew it would not be easy. Her mind kept returning to the vivid details Tom had given her of the accident. She was sickened by it and was now beginning to understand his actions. She laid out some clothes on the bed and then went to shower. She took her time there, trying to relax her body and her mind.

Tom stayed to finish off the floor tiles in the conservatory, then he cleared everything away and made sure everywhere was clean. He made his way back into the kitchen and sat down to drink his tea. He opened a drawer and took out a writing pad and pen. He stared at the paper; he felt he had to leave Joanne a note before he left.

'Dear Joanne,

I am sorry, but it is only right that I should have explained to you how I lost my wife and son and how it has affected me. I hope you can now understand some of my actions. I have finished the conservatory, hope you like it. I will be back tomorrow to do some more decorating. Please could you let me know which room you would like decorated next, but if you have no preference I will just work through what is left.

Thank you, Tom'

With that, he walked slowly to the front door, closed it quietly behind him and walked down to the barn: his home.

CHAPTER EIGHT

Difficult Times

Tom couldn't sleep. For the last few nights, he had slept on the sofa in the front lounge of the house, not because he had wanted to but because Joanne didn't want to sleep in the big house on her own. He also knew that Joanne had wanted to get all the locks changed on the doors and there hadn't been time to get an alarm system installed. However, he needed to take a break, so he was back in the barn but now he had second thoughts. It wasn't that he regretted his decision, it was more that he too realised that his feelings for Joanne were strengthening and he was struggling with that feeling and how to control it.

It was the events of the previous evening that had fed his decision, and it was those same events that were now playing on his mind. Unable to sleep, he got up, picked up his bucket and walked down to the hand pump. As strange as it may seem, he loved the feel of cold water on his skin, especially first thing in the morning; it woke him up. Having had his wash and got dressed, he sat just outside the barn eating toast and drinking tea. He looked towards the house, thinking once again of Joanne and hoping that she was okay. Although he knew he should go to see her and speak with her before she left for work, he decided not to. He was under the impression that it would be better to wait and give them both some much-needed space.

Tom finished his breakfast and then loaded the wheelbarrow with fencing and made his way down to the perimeter fence at the back of the property. He felt he would be out of the way there, and it was killing two birds with one stone, to coin a phrase. It kept him away from the house and allowed him to fix another section of the fence.

Joanne stirred in her bed. Turning over and opening her eyes, she saw the dim light sneaking through the blinds. She glanced at the clock on the bedside table – it was seven-thirty. She was surprised to see she was on top of her bed; she remembered lying down after her shower, but she must have fallen asleep and lay there on top all night. She sat upright on the edge of the bed and bent down to pick up her dressing gown from the floor. Her thoughts turned to Tom; not so much thinking of all he had told her but more wondering if he had looked in on her before he left. Her heart started pounding; the thought that he might have seen her lying there naked on her bed seemed to excite her, but at the same time she was slightly shocked by the thought of that possibility.

She walked over to the window, pulling her gown on as she did so, and opened the blinds. Peering out from her bedroom she caught a glimpse of Tom walking along, pushing his wheelbarrow. She guessed that he must be going to fix the fence as she remembered him telling her that most of it needed replacing. She stood there for a while, trying to collect her thoughts. Now she knew about the accident that killed his wife and child, she felt she needed to try to find out more. It wasn't because she didn't believe him, but more that she felt if she knew more about exactly what happened, she may be able to help him and understand him more.

Joanne took out her clothes from the wardrobe, quickly got dressed, then made her way down to the kitchen. As she made herself a drink, she noticed the note that Tom had left for her. She sat at the breakfast bar reading it and drinking her coffee. She placed the note back on the table, picked up the pen that was lying there and scribbled a quick note underneath Tom's.

'Good morning, Tom,

I will leave it up to you which room you choose to decorate next. I have no real preference as to which order you continue the decorating, so long as it is all completed eventually. There is no need to rush, though, you can take your time. I am just wondering though, why the note? Wouldn't it be better to talk? I thought you were going to come and see me before you left last night. I was waiting for you …

Joanne xx'

Finishing her note, she placed it in the centre of the table with the flower vase holding it in place. It was eight-thirty – she needed to rush, so she placed her empty cup in the sink, picked up her car keys from the hook and closed the front door behind her. She had wanted to speak to Tom before she left but it would have to wait until she got back later.

Joanne drove into the car park at her office where she could see that Jefferey's car was already there, but there was no sign of Warren's car. She was hoping he would be there as she was expecting a frosty reception from some of the staff after the revelations at the dinner on Saturday. Jefferey was one of those she expected some flak from, and she wasn't wrong. However, it wasn't only regarding her new position as an executive that he had a gripe about as she was about to find out.

"Good morning, Jefferey," she said as she walked through the office to her desk.

"Hi Joanne. Oh, I suppose it is still okay to call you Joanne? Or should it be Miss Webster now?"

"I think Joanne will be fine, Jefferey," she replied as she sat down.

Jefferey had followed Joanne to her desk.

"I'm not sure you should be sitting at this desk now. I would have thought you should be in one of the private offices next to Warren," he said as he sat down in the chair in front of her desk.

"Maybe, but this is okay for me. I am still the same person; a fancy title doesn't change me, not like I feel it might have changed others," she said pointedly.

"Oh, what's wrong? Did you have a difficult weekend with your partner?" asked Jefferey with a snigger.

Joanne looked at him sternly.

"What on earth made you come up with that type of remark? I do not have a partner, and even if I did, it would be none of your business," she replied as she got up to get a coffee.

Jefferey stayed sitting at her desk and waited for her to return.

"You know your partner, Tom, isn't it? Well, he is a really strange guy? Whatever do you see in him?" he asked.

"Look, Jefferey, firstly as I have already pointed out, Tom is not my partner and even if he were that would be my business and my choice. Secondly, he is a very nice man: polite, considerate and extremely useful unlike someone else I am thinking of at this very moment," she replied.

"Oh, very harsh, *Miss Webster*. So I was right about it being a difficult weekend between you two then. I hope the someone else you referring to was not directed at me?" he asked.

Joanne looked straight at him.

"Well, all I can say is if the cap fits, wear it."

Jefferey took the hint and got up to walk away but stopping, he turned round.

"You know, if you are finding your partner difficult, you could always accept my offer," he said to Joanne.

She looked up at him enquiringly.

"And what offer would that be, Jefferey? I certainly do not remember receiving any offer from you," she replied.

"That's because I haven't extended it to you yet, but if you fancy a break from boredom, you could always have dinner with me tonight."

"Thank you, Jefferey. I'll think about your kind offer, and should I change my mind I will let you know," replied Joanne.

"I knew I could break your icy exterior," he muttered under his breath.

Joanne heard the remark and replied with one of her own.

"Never count your chickens, Jefferey."

Jefferey walked back to his desk, feeling quite pleased with himself.

He felt as if he had made some progress and was hoping to have a second bite of the cherry if Joanne accepted his offer.

It was then that Warren walked into the office.

"Morning everyone," he said, his usual phrase each morning, never more, never less. As he reached Joanne's desk, he leant over the partition.

"Good morning, Joanne. My office, please. Bring coffee with you," he said.

Joanne immediately rose from her chair and went to the kitchen where she made coffee, one for herself and the other one for Warren; she entered his office and placed both cups on his desk.

Warren looked up at her.

"Thank you, Joanne. Would you close the door please," he said.

"Certainly," replied Joanne as she turned to close the office door.

Warren moved both cups onto the coffee table as he sat on the sofa.

"Come and sit down here, Joanne. Let's chat. I still know extraordinarily little about your private life, although business-wise I know everything I need to know. I hope it wasn't too much of a shock to you that I made you an executive," he asked.

"It was a huge shock, completely unexpected. I thought you may have promoted Jefferey," she replied.

Warren gave a little laugh.

"You still have a lot to learn, Joanne. Jefferey is a good worker, a good solicitor and very thorough in his work, but he is not an executive." Picking his cup up from the table he continued. "Now, with you, I see you as someone who can control their work whilst keeping a very firm eye on those around them and that is what I need. Anyway, what I wanted to chat about today is you, and what makes you tick. I drove past your property at the weekend. You have a genuinely nice house and a fair amount of land, too. What do you intend doing with it?"

"I haven't even given it a thought yet. When I moved down here and saw it was for sale, I wanted it so much and just had to have it," she replied.

"Sounds reasonable," said Warren. "And what about your partner – Tom? Where does he come into all this?" he asked.

Joanne picked up the cup from the table and took a sip of coffee.

"Well, sorry to disappoint you, but he doesn't really fit in anywhere at the moment, apart from being a very helpful lodger. It's a long story. He actually lives in the barn in the grounds of the property. He was living there when I bought the house," she replied.

"Oh, is that so?" replied Warren, sounding shocked. "Maybe I promoted the wrong solicitor. I thought you would have known better than to buy somewhere with a sitting tenant."

"Well, I was aware of the potential problems of buying the property with a sitting tenant, although he was only living in the barn. However, when I weighed everything up and what with him being a fantastic decorator, I now know I made the right decision. There are so many things that need doing, not only to the house but to the grounds as well. There is no way I would be able to do all that. It would have cost me a fortune to employ someone to do it. I decided to draw up a contract for Tom to sign, allowing him to stay in the barn while I would pay him for the work that he carried out for me," explained Joanne.

"Well, that sounds a perfect scenario, Joanne. Everyone gets what they want. Although it saddens me to hear you explain away Tom in that manner. I mean, the two of you looked so comfortable with each other at the dinner, I just assumed you were a couple and I think you will find everyone else thinks that too," said Warren.

"Yes, I know, and don't get me wrong, he is lovely and a man whom I can trust. It would be wrong of me to explain to you exactly why he is not my partner but for now, all I can tell you is that he is a very honest man with a sad past from which he is struggling to move on," she confided in Warren.

"Sorry to hear that. But my offer to him still stands. Maybe you would convey that message to him for me?" added Warren.

"I will certainly do that and I can assure you he will do an exceptionally good job."

"Excellent and I hope he can sort out whatever it is that is troubling him because you two do look so natural together."

"Thank you, but for now it is just a friendship and I have been reliably informed that that is all it can be," replied Joanne.

"Never say never, Joanne. Time can be a great healer."

"Yes," replied Joanne. "Tom did mention words to that effect when we were chatting, but he said for him that just is not true," she added.

"I am intrigued now. Did he go through a painful divorce?" asked Warren.

"No – much worse than that: his wife was killed in a car accident five years ago. I'm sorry but I can't tell you more than that," she replied.

"That's not good. Five years ago you say? And he is still being affected by it? That's terrible."

"Yes. It was very traumatic for him," replied Joanne.

"Okay Joanne, thank you. I now know a little bit more about you. I must get the papers finalised to make you an executive. That will be all for now. Would you see how Jefferey is progressing on the Saunders case, and would you also ask Edwina to come and see me please?" asked Warren as Joanne turned to leave his office.

"Yes, will do. Thank you, Warren," she replied.

Joanne stopped to speak to Edwina on the way back to her desk, asking her to go to see Warren. As she sat down, she thought she would text Jefferey as she had noticed that he was no longer in the office. She started typing her message, concise and to the point, but polite.

Jefferey, as soon as you have a few minutes could we discuss your report on the Saunders case? Warren wants to review it later today.

Jefferey must have come back into the office without her knowing it, for as soon as she sent the message a reply came back.

'Anything for you, Joanne, on my way.'

Jefferey pulled up a chair and sat down at the desk opposite Joanne, placing the report on her desk as he did so.

"There, all done, *Miss Webster*," he commented.

"Thank you, Jefferey," she replied. "Do you have spare time now so that we can go through it together?"

Jefferey looked at her with a scowl on his face.

"Well, yes, I do have some spare time, but I have already checked it. No point in going through it again."

Joanne looked at him and guessed that most of her battles in the office were going to be with Jefferey. It was clear that he wasn't happy with her being made an executive, reporting only to Warren Fredericks.

Before she could reply, Jefferey was already planning his next forage into her life.

"You know, Joanne, why waste time discussing this report when we can be sitting here chatting about us? I mean, we are going to be spending so much time together so we might just as well make the most of it, you know? Get to know each other better and become more socially active."

Joanne collected her thoughts and knew she had to respond wisely to his remarks.

"Well thank you for that, Jefferey, but unfortunately Warren does not pay us to sit here talking about our private lives. He would prefer very much if we kept them private and concentrated on the job in hand," replied Joanne.

Jefferey sat open-mouthed; it was Joanne's turn to express her thoughts and for the moment Jefferey was speechless.

"I realise you have worked hard on this report Jefferey, and I am sure it's perfect, but what if it's not? Would you rather Warren spots any mistakes, or would it be better for us to check it together before he sees it? That way we both know the report is sound and as it is *your* report, a perfect one would surely add a string to your bow? So, if you will excuse me while I read through it. You can wait here if you like and then maybe you can explain to me how you think we could become more socially active," replied Joanne.

"I'll get the coffee," said Jefferey as he rose from the chair and walked towards the kitchen area.

"Black for me please, Jefferey," she replied.

He placed the cups on her desk and sat quietly waiting for her to finish reading his report. He had almost finished his coffee by the time she closed it and placed it on her desk.

"Well, what do you think?" he asked.

"It might just about get you a C grade at eleven plus but that's about all," she replied.

"What!" he replied with a raised voice.

Joanne looked at him and started to giggle.

"Relax, Jefferey! Haven't you heard of satire? It's good. I think you have covered everything so you can give it to Warren now."

"Thank you, Joanne. I was hoping you would approve it without any changes." Jefferey picked up the report from her desk. "Fancy dinner tonight then?" he added.

Joanne glanced up at him.

"I suppose so, but I am still waiting for you to tell me what your definition of us being socially active actually means," she said.

"I'm still putting my reply together," he replied.

"I would not spend too much longer thinking about it then, Jefferey. 'No' is a short response."

Jefferey turned and walked slowly back to his desk, throwing the report down as he slumped into his chair. He extended his arm to the keyboard and fired up his PC. He was a little perturbed by Joanne's response; he had hoped for a less obstructive reply. Jefferey sat there, his eyes transfixed on the image on the screen.

Joanne too sat looking at her screen, but for a quite different reason. She had decided to spend her time wisely and was searching through past issues of local papers to see if she could match any details of Tom's accident to reports that were in them. Her searches became more frustrating and she was now spending every spare moment she had looking at reports, trying to find the background story she was looking for. She was still searching when she was interrupted by Warren Fredericks.

"I'm off now, Joanne. Did you look at Jefferey's report?" he asked.

"Yes, I did," she replied. "I read through it while he was here with me. He appears to have covered everything. I did ask him to submit it to you for your approval – did he not do that?"

"I haven't seen it yet. I think he has things on his mind now. Maybe you could lean on him a little? I do not like rushing people as that's when mistakes are made, but I did give him a two-week deadline, and it will be three weeks this Wednesday. Would you ask him to forward the link to me? I will read it at home tonight."

"Yes, I'll do that right now, and I'll try to find out what is bothering him too as I am having dinner with him tonight," replied Joanne.

"Dinner?" questioned Warren.

"Yes."

"Was that your idea or his?" asked Warren.

Joanne looked up from her computer screen.

"It was Jefferey's idea, but I thought it might be good for me to get to know him better, just as I intend to do with all our staff," she replied.

"I very much like your idea behind that, Joanne," said Warren as he moved towards her desk and sat in the chair opposite her, "but do be careful. You may not have realised it, but I think most of the staff know what Jefferey is having a problem with," whispered Warren as he leant across the desk towards her.

She looked at him with a questioning expression on her face.

"Are you going to let me into the secret then, Warren?"

"His problem is you, Joanne," he replied.

"Me!" exclaimed Joanne. "Why me?"

"Well, he hasn't stopped talking or asking questions about you since he met you," answered Warren.

"Oh, I see," replied Joanne. "Do you think I should cancel our dinner then?"

Warren rose from the chair and shrugging his shoulders he replied, "That's your decision, Joanne. It's your own free time, but just remember what I have told you, and be cautious, very cautious," he said as he turned to walk away.

"Yes, thank you, I will," she replied.

Joanne sat there for a while wondering what to do. She opened her text messages, clicked on Jefferey's name and started typing.

'Hi Jefferey, would you please email your Saunders report to Warren immediately. I did ask you to submit it to him earlier, however, he has just informed me that you did not do it. He must have it tonight and he has already left the office. I am almost finished here, so if we are still going to meet for dinner, just let me know what time and where. I would prefer to go early if that is okay with you as I'll go straight from work. Thanks, Joanne.'

Her finger hovered over the send button as she recalled all that Warren had told her, however, she was sure that she would be able to handle the situation. She lowered her finger slowly and allowed it to fully depress the 'send' button.

Joanne continued working late into the evening, going through the contracts, checking on her colleagues' previous cases and the ones they were currently working on while waiting to hear from Jefferey, but his reply never came. Joanne decided she could wait no longer; she was not only hungry, but she was tired too and, what's more, she wanted to get home to see Tom and what he had been doing at home.

CHAPTER NINE

Continued Improvements

Tom had spent most of the morning working on several sections of the perimeter fence which was in a bad state of repair. He had tried as best he could over the last four years to keep the fence in a reasonable condition but, in truth, he had been fighting a losing battle. Some sections of it were now falling apart, while others were completely missing. When Mrs Wheeler was alive, he was restricted to just trying to keep the house in the best state of repair that he could, so the fence was placed firmly on the back boiler as it were.

He needed a break and so walked back up to the house. Opening the front door, he removed his shoes and left them outside. He walked through into the kitchen and made a cup of tea. Sitting down at the breakfast bar, he noticed Joanne's reply to his note.

Good morning, Tom, I will leave it up to your which room you choose to decorate next, I have no real preference as to which order you continue the decorating, so long as it is all completed eventually. There is no need to rush though, you can take your time. I am just wondering though why the note, wouldn't it be better to talk. I thought you were going to come and see me before you left last night, I was waiting for you??? Joanne xx.

Tom picked up the pen that was on the breakfast bar, wondering what to write while drinking his tea. He wanted to make some comment, to leave Joanne a message of some kind, but he just did not know what to say. He decided to leave it; maybe he would leave her a note later. He finished his tea and then made his way back down to the new section of fence that he had been working on. He placed the old sections of the fence in his wheelbarrow and took them back up to the barn. Some of the pieces of wood he could use, so he stored those in the barn, and the rest he stacked neatly outside ready to be collected; he changed out of his dirty clothes and then went back up to the house.

With little input from Joanne, Tom decided that he would try to work his magic in the lounge. He knew that the carpets were due to be laid soon so he needed to make sure the decorating was finished before the carpets arrived. He wasn't sure that the paper Joanne had chosen for the dining room was suitable for there, but he thought it would look good in the lounge on the one main wall. He painted the walls first as they didn't take long to dry. He wasn't sure what time Joanne would be home, but he thought he would be able to get most of the papering done too.

Tom set about hanging the paper, having measured the room. He knew the pattern that he wanted to create: one run of paper, two paint, two runs of paper, two paint and then one paper. When he was finished, he stepped back. He couldn't believe it – it looked simply great. All that was required now was for Joanne to like it. For the side walls, there was nothing to do – just paint would be best. The decorating finished, he decided to hang the TV on the wall; he knew exactly where Joanne wanted it.

There was still no sign of Joanne, and it was already seven o'clock. Tom wasn't feeling tired, though, so he decided to carry on for a while. He didn't want to do any painting during the evening, just in case the smell of paint affected Joanne's sleep. He looked at the paper Joanne had bought for the main reception room, and he thought that would look great, so he measured the walls and started to hang the paper. He had only hung a couple of lengths when he noticed the reflection of car headlights coming up the drive. Moments later he heard keys in the front door and then the door closing.

"Tom, are you there?" he heard Joanne call.

"I'm here, in the reception room, hanging wallpaper, but I've only just started," he replied.

"Why are you working this late? You don't have to do it now. Didn't you see my note? I told you there is no rush, you can just take your time," she replied.

Tom turned around to see Joanne standing in the doorway.

"I know you said there was no rush, but I need to finish the messy work before your carpets are delivered, and on top of that I want to speed up so that I can see what Warren wants me to do," he replied.

"What you've done so far looks very good. Tom, I want to talk, but I need to take a shower first. Will you wait for me please?" she asked.

He stepped down from the ladder and looked at her.

"I want to try to get as much of this room done as I can. Maybe I can even finish hanging the paper tonight, so yes, I'll still be here."

"Is that a promise? Are you sure you won't disappear like you did last night?" she asked.

"Have your shower, I won't disappear," he replied, with a grin on his face.

"Okay, I won't be too long but please make sure you are still here because if not, I will have to come looking for you," she replied.

Joanne left the room. Tom completed hanging paper on the longest wall at the back of the room and then continued onto the side wall up to the window. He decided to stop there as he knew that Joanne wanted to chat, and he thought that she must have finished in the shower by now. He tidied all his mess away, neatly stacking it in one corner, then he climbed the stairs to see if the bathroom was empty so he clean up a little. The door was open, so he walked in, only to be confronted with the sight of Joanne in the shower cubicle. He quickly made his apologies, turned around and went back downstairs.

Tom made himself a cup of tea and sat drinking it at the breakfast bar while waiting for Joanne to come down. He didn't have to wait long but he was shocked when she entered the kitchen – yes, she was wearing a dressing gown again and yes, it was secured at the front, but it was thinner than the one she had worn previously so did not leave much to the imagination. He swallowed hard.

"Is it okay if I use the bathroom?"

Joanne looked at him.

"Yes, Tom, of course you can. Sorry about before, I'm so used to leaving the door open, being on my own," she said.

Tom looked at her.

"You're forgiven on this occasion. I didn't see anything anyway," he replied, as he left the kitchen to go to the bathroom.

Tom was feeling a little uneasy about going back down to the kitchen and sitting chatting to Joanne with the way she was dressed, but he had to accept the fact it was her house and apart from walking out, there wasn't a lot else he could do. He knew there were things needed to be said and he thought it was best to clear the air rather than bottle things up. He certainly felt easier being around Joanne since he had explained to her the constant problem he was faced with. He walked slowly back down to the kitchen and sat on the stool at the breakfast bar, directly opposite her.

"Have you been in the lounge yet?" he asked.

"No, I haven't – why? Have you been working in there too?"

"Take a look and you'll find out," he replied.

Joanne leapt from her stool and rushed to the lounge. Turning the light on, she was in total shock. She just could not believe what she was seeing.

"Tom!" she shrieked. "You're a diamond! Come here, now!"

He got off his stool and walked slowly towards the lounge. As he got to the doorway, he could see Joanne in the middle of the dimly lit room, spinning round and round on the spot with her arms outstretched. She just did not stop, round and round she continued. He wasn't sure how long for; it seemed as though she had endless energy until she collapsed on the floor in a heap.

Tom rushed towards her and gently lifted her into sitting position.

"Sit there for a while. You've made yourself dizzy. What was all that about?" he asked.

Joanne tried to reply but she was still out of breath.

"Just sit there and don't move. I'll get you some water," he said and went to the kitchen. He filled a glass with water from the fridge and picked up her phone from the breakfast bar; going back to the lounge he knelt beside her and offered her the glass.

"Here, drink this slowly," he said as he brushed her hair away from the side of her face.

Joanne took a couple of small sips of water from the glass and then a couple of longer sips. Tom could see that her face was slowly returning to its usual colour.

"Do you feel better now?" he asked her.

"Yes, thank you, Tom, I feel much better. What would I do without you?" she remarked, looking straight at him.

"Maybe you'd be lucky and find someone who will love you," he replied.

Joanne placed the glass on the floor and cupped her hands around his.

"No, Tom! I could never find anyone to love me like you could and don't tell me you don't love me because I know you do, maybe not in a sexual way, but I know in your own way you do. I can see it in your eyes, in your actions and … just look at this room, Tom! There is no way on earth you could have decorated this room the way you have if you did not love me. It is so special, it is so beautiful, and I love it. I love *you*, Tom."

With that, Joanne leant forward and kissed him on the lips. He didn't respond but he didn't pull away either, not immediately, anyhow. He then placed his hands around her waist and slowly pushed her away until she broke off her kiss.

"I am so pleased that you like it, Joanne. I hoped you would," he said.

"Tom, I meant it! It is so beautiful. I love it and I love you, Tom," she replied.

"I know, I know, but what can I do?"

Joanne pulled him towards her again and kissed him slowly, then releasing him she said, "Let me help you, Tom, let me help you."

He looked straight at her.

"Joanne, you look so beautiful, you are beautiful, and just sitting here in the middle of the room you look perfect, you *are* perfect. Please may I take a photo of you, just as you are now?" he asked.

"Tom, of course you can! You can do anything you want to, you don't have to ask, you know that," she replied.

"But I'll need to use the camera on your phone. I have a camera in the barn, but I don't want to miss the moment – is that okay?" he asked.

"Yes, of course you can use it," she replied. "It's here. Where do you want me then?"

"Just where you are; don't move at all, just straighten your body a little, a little more, that's it, hold it there, that's perfect," said Tom as he checked the photo.

"Can I move now?" asked Joanne.

"No! Not yet, just a couple more. Okay, can you just undo the top three buttons?" asked Tom.

"Hey, are you sure?" she asked.

"Yes, it will be fine, trust me."

"But I thought that is just what you asked me *not* to do! I can take it off completely if you like," she said.

"No! Don't do that. Just undo the next button too, please," asked Tom.

Joanne fumbled with the fourth button down, and then after pulling her dressing gown away from her body she leant slightly forward, just as Tom had asked her to do.

"How's this," she asked.

"That's fine," remarked Tom.

"Is that all now?" asked Joanne.

"Just one more. Can you let your dressing gown drop off your right shoulder and almost down to your elbow?"

"Now you can see my breast," added Joanne.

"Don't panic; now just let your left hand cup your exposed breast. Okay, that's perfect," said Tom. "You can rest now."

Joanne got up from the floor. It seemed as though she had been there for ages. She walked over to where Tom was standing and planted a kiss firmly on his cheek while hugging him around the waist.

"Thank you, Tom. This room is gorgeous! Wherever did you get the idea to align the paper like that? I would never have thought of doing that," she said as she cuddled up close to him.

Tom looked at her.

"I was just trying to create something that looked modern for you. I'm so pleased that you like it, thank you," he replied.

"Can I look at the photos you took please Tom?" she asked.

"Of course you can. I hope you like them," said Tom as he passed her the phone with the last photo he had taken showing on the screen.

"Oh Tom, this is so touching. You make me look beautiful, and such a sexy pose," she said as she laid her head on Tom's shoulder. "Show me the others please," she added as she passed the phone back to him.

Tom flicked through the photos one by one, pausing at each one for Joanne.

"They are great photos, Tom, thank you, but what are you going to do with them?" she asked.

"I have a plan," replied Tom. "You'll just have to trust me."

Joanne raised her head from his shoulder and kissed him.

"I trust you implicitly, but how can you take such lovely photos with a phone? They are so sensual," she replied.

"My wife, Anne, was a photographer and a good one at that. I learnt a lot from her. The idea is not to give too much away in photos like these, but to let the viewer use their imagination."

"I want you to take more photos of me, Tom. However, wherever and whenever you like," she added.

"I have my wife's camera in the barn. I'll get it out and see if it still works," replied Tom.

"Thank you, Tom, I'd like that," she replied.

"So, what did you want to chat to me about?" asked Tom.

"Sorry, Tom, you distracted me with the beautiful room. I feel as though I owe you an apology," said Joanne.

"Apology? What for?"

"I put you on the spot because of my advances to you and I was wrong. I'm sorry, I shouldn't have let myself get carried away. You have been the perfect gentleman all along, even though I have put you under unbearable pressure. So much so that I forced you to open up to me about the accident involving your wife and son, and I can appreciate how difficult that must have been for you. Apart from that, I have been expecting you to accept my advances even when I have been hiding my past from you. I hope you find a way to forgive me?" she asked.

"Joanne, stop, you don't have to do this, you don't have to explain yourself to me," he said as he saw tears start to form in her eyes.

"No, Tom, please let me finish, I want to explain because if we are going to try to make this work then we have to trust each other and believe in each other. My marriage wasn't great. I got married too young, I realise that now. My parents tried to warn me, talk me out of it, but I was headstrong, still am really as you have found out, but I'm older now. Anyway, I was still studying for my law degree, my husband was an office manager, we hardly ever saw each other and when we did, we were both tired. Then the worst possible thing happened: my parents were killed in an accident while on holiday. Well, that was the end of my world. My husband started coming home later and later from the office, then he wouldn't come home at all, sometimes for two or three days. I guessed he was having an affair, but I let it ride until he came home after being away for three days and asked for a divorce." Joanne leant down and, picking up the glass of water, she took a few sips before continuing.

"At that point, I knew my marriage was over, but I had no one to talk to. My parents were dead, my aunt lived too far away, and my friends were his friends too. That is why I had to get out and move down here. At first, I wasn't sure I was doing the right thing, but now I know I was right. I know that I have made the right decision, not because of the house, or that I am near my aunt or even that I have somehow got myself a really good job. Tom, the reason I know I was right is because I have found you. I know I can make rash decisions, but you are not a rash decision, please believe me, please trust me. I love you, Tom."

Tom sat there, not knowing what to say or how to respond. How could he follow that? He was speechless.

"Please say something, Tom," said Joanne as she held him tight.

"You are so beautiful, Joanne, and I have very strong feelings for you, but I am not sure if the timing is right," he replied.

Joanne was upset. She had been hoping that Tom was making some progress to release himself from his past, but it appeared she was wrong.

"Tom, please don't torment yourself like this," replied Joanne.

"It's late and you need to sleep, and I need to get some fresh air," said Tom as he pulled himself away from her grasp. He walked slowly towards the hallway, pausing to look at Joanne before continuing to the front door of the house. As he reached for the door handle, he turned to see her standing in the doorway of the lounge, a look of anguish on her face, tears running down her cheeks. He turned away, stepped out into the cold evening air and closed the door behind him.

Tom walked slowly down to the barn, not knowing what to do. His head was spinning and his throat was dry. He closed the barn door behind him and sat in the chair. He was feeling tired, but he remembered what he had said to Joanne about his wife's camera. He got up and went over to the storage boxes and took it out. It felt heavy, heavier than he remembered it, maybe because he was tired. He sat back in the chair, the camera on his lap, struggling to keep his eyes open … It was a clear evening, stars were shining brightly, the road ahead was clear …. Then nothing. Where was he? He was upside down. How did he get here? His head began to clear. He looked to his left where he could just make out the lifeless body of his wife. He tried to turn round but it was too painful. He couldn't see his son, he couldn't move. Then he felt someone shaking his shoulder and he heard a faint voice: 'I think this one is still alive.'

Then he heard a louder voice.

"Tom! Tom!" he opened his eyes; it was Joanne and she was kneeling there in front of him in the barn, holding his wife's camera.

"Tom, you dropped this. It was on the floor by your chair. Are you alright?" she asked as she gave him the camera.

"Sorry, Joanne, I must have fallen asleep. I was dreaming," he said as he got up. "I need you, Joanne," he added as he held out his arms to her. "I just want to hold you. Is that okay?"

"That is perfectly okay with me," she replied. "Come to bed now, Tom, you can hold me all you want," she remarked and she took his hand as they walked together back to the house.

CHAPTER TEN

The Morning After

Tom opened his eyes; he was staring at the ceiling. He'd forgotten the last time he had slept in a bed; it felt strange. His arm was partly trapped under Joanne's body, her head and shoulder still resting on his chest with her arm still wrapped around his waist. With his free arm, he reached out and picked up her phone, which was on the bedside cabinet where he had put it after they had been looking at the photos he had taken of her. It was five-thirty in the morning.

He was trying to piece together the events of last evening but was that necessary? He wasn't sure. All he knew now was that he felt at ease with himself, and he felt comfortable in the presence of Joanne. He had a lot to thank her for. She had faith in him, and she was helping him to come to terms with his loss, helping him to close one chapter of his life and move on to the next. He realised now that life was indeed just like a book: you can't be stuck on the same page, reading it repeatedly because, in the end, you cannot change what is written there. Life is the same, you cannot change what has happened, you remember it, yes, maybe never forget it, but you cannot change it. He was now coming to terms with that, and it was Joanne who was helping him.

He tried again to free his trapped arm, but he didn't want to wake her. He wasn't sure what time they went to sleep but he knew it was late and she was tired. After a few tries, he managed to slide his arm slowly from under Joanne's body and ease himself out of the bed. He placed a pillow beneath her head and shoulders where his body had been and kissed her softly on her forehead before going to the bathroom.

Tom looked in the cupboard and pulled out a clean towel. After taking a quick shower, he wrapped the towel around himself and walked back into the bedroom. Joanne was still asleep; she hadn't moved from the position he'd left her in. He dried himself off but as he didn't have any clean clothes, he wrapped the towel around himself again and casually walked down to the barn to get some. While there, he looked in the box where his wife's camera had been for the charger. He placed his clothes and charger and a few toiletries into a bag and walked back up to the house.

Back in the bedroom, he found that Joanne was still asleep, although it was still only 6:30 am. Walking quietly across the room, he picked up the camera and plugged it in to charge the battery. Tom threw the towel on the floor and got dressed; when he had finished, she was still asleep. He decided that she was not an early morning person. On the floor by the side of the bed he found her dressing gown, so he picked it up and gently laid it over her.

He went down to the kitchen. He decided he would make her coffee and take it up to her in bed. He looked around the kitchen, checking the cupboards and fridge to see what he could get her to eat. Then he remembered that she was carrying a bag when she arrived home the previous evening. He found it and digging around inside it, produced some brioche rolls. *Perfect, they will do*, he thought. He placed everything on a tray and took it up to the bedroom.

He put the tray down on Joanne's dressing table and then picked up her coffee and rolls and placed then on the cabinet by the side of her bed. He then walked back to the dressing table and sat on the stool drinking his tea, he looked at his watch it was almost seven-thirty. He didn't know what time she had to be in the office, but he guessed it would be around nine, which meant he would have to wake her soon, although he didn't want to do that as she looked so peaceful.

He picked up the camera and looking at the screen he noticed that it was twenty-three per cent charged. He was thinking of taking a photo of Joanne as she lay there on the bed, but he decided that was not the proper thing to do; he should at least wait until she was awake and gain her consent. As he looked back towards her, he was hoping that he wouldn't have to wait too long; then she stirred and moved her position on the bed, followed almost immediately by more movement. She lifted her hand and patted the bed a few times; she had clearly expected Tom to still be there, but the bed appeared to be empty, apart from herself; she opened her eyes, confirming that she was indeed alone.

"Tom, Tom?" she called. "Where are you?"

"I'm here, Joanne," he replied.

She looked in the direction the voice came from and saw Tom sitting on the chair by the dressing table.

"What are you doing there?" she asked.

"I am just waiting for you to wake up. I didn't want to disturb you," he replied.

Tom picked up the camera from his lap and pointing it towards her he asked, "May I?"

"But of course," she replied with a smile on her face.

Tom fired off a few photos, with Joanne occasionally changing position slightly, then she sat up more in the bed, allowing the gown that Tom had placed over her to fall away, exposing her naked breasts; he kept firing all the time, catching every movement with a still shot.

"Why did you get up so early?" she asked.

He placed the camera on his lap and looked up at her, sitting there on the bed.

"You know what they say, the early bird catches the worm," he answered.

"And did you catch your worm, Tom?" she asked.

"I'd like to think so, I'd like to think so."

Joanne swung her legs over the edge of the bed and placed her feet firmly on the floor. Then getting up, she slowly walked over to where Tom was sitting; picking up the camera from his lap, she placed it on the dressing table. Placing one leg either side of his knees, she placed her arms around his neck and pulled herself onto his lap.

"And will this worm always be enough for you to feast on?" she asked as she looked inquiringly into his eyes.

"Always, Joanne, always," he answered in a soft but firm voice, then kissed her gently on her shoulder.

Joanne moved his head to the centre of her chest and held his head tightly there. She could feel his moist lips against her skin.

"Then you can feast on me anytime you want to," she said as she lifted his head away from her chest and kissed him firmly on the lips. She broke off her kiss and took his hands from her waist, guided them to her shoulders and then slid them slowly down her chest to her breasts, where she left them. She then placed her hands around the back of his neck and looked him in the eyes.

"My body is yours, Tom, whenever you want it, wherever you want it. As soon as you're ready, I will be waiting."

Tom looked at Joanne. He found it hard to believe how relaxed he was around her; everything seemed so natural, just how love should be. He knew now that he could love her and commit to her, it was just a matter of taking one step at a time and he felt lucky that she was prepared to wait until he was ready.

"Thank you, Joanne, thank you so much."

Joanne held him close to her.

"Tom, are you mad? Why do you want to thank me? It is I who should be thanking you because I know that you are genuine, and not just some guy looking for a quick fix."

"Last night, Joanne, when you came to the barn, I had every intention of coming back up to you, but I searched for my wife's camera and I sat down in the chair, just reminiscing. I was feeling drained, tired, and just fell asleep. Then I felt a hand on my shoulder shaking me. Up to that point, I was in the car, hanging upside down, with my wife dead next to me. When the hand grabbed my shoulder, I heard a voice: *This one is still alive*, but this time when I opened my eyes, it was *you* standing there. It was a sign, it was as though you had been sent to rescue me, thank you, thank you so much. If I cannot love you, I will never love anyone else ever again," remarked Tom.

Tom could see the tears forming in Joanne's eyes. He took a tissue from the box on the dressing table and gently wiped her eyes dry.

"Don't cry, please don't cry," he whispered.

"I'm sorry, but your words are without doubt the loveliest anyone has ever said to me. I love you so much," she replied.

"I know, I know you do, thank you. However, as much as I would like to stay here all day like this, do you realise it is now nine o'clock?"

"What!" shrieked Joanne. "I need to shower and get to work, but I must ring Warren first, to let him know I will be late."

Warren's phone only rang twice before he answered.

"Joanne, how are you? How can I help you?" he asked.

"Warren, I am so sorry. I have been unavoidably detained this morning, but I will be in by ten o'clock. I do apologise," she said.

"Joanne, no need for apologies. Your time is your own. How did everything go with Jefferey last night?" he asked.

"I didn't meet him. I was working in the office until nine o'clock last night, but he didn't reply to my message about where we were meeting for dinner," she replied.

Warren paused for a few seconds before responding.

"And you're worried about being a few minutes late this morning when you were here until nine o'clock last night? You need to relax. I just thought maybe you and Jefferey had a late evening as he is not in yet either."

"Okay, thank you, Warren," she said. "I'll be in soon."

"Hold tight," said Tom as he stood up, still holding Joanne.

"Tom, where are you taking me?" she asked.

"I thought you wanted a shower which is where I am taking you."

Tom guided her into the shower and turned the water on.

"It's cold!" she shrieked.

"That's okay, it will cool you down. I thought you were getting a little too hot to handle in there," remarked Tom.

He left Joanne in the shower while he made the bed and then took the breakfast things downstairs. He was just finishing cleaning up in the kitchen when there was a knock at the door.

'Strange,' he thought, as no one ever knocked.

When Tom opened the door, he was shocked to see Jefferey standing in front of him but probably not as surprised as Jefferey was to see Tom opening the door.

"Oh, Tom!" exclaimed Jefferey, somewhat surprised. "What are you doing opening the door? Aren't you supposed to be living in the barn? I'm Jefferey by the way, Joanne's friend. Does she know you are in her house? What are you doing here, anyway?" asked Jefferey in a troubled voice.

Tom stood there, not quite believing the onslaught that he was receiving from Jefferey.

"I know exactly who you are, and what I am doing here in the house is none of your damn business," replied Tom.

"I need to speak with Joanne, and it's urgent. Can you call her please?" asked Jefferey in a kind of rattled voice.

"Well, I am sorry to disappoint you, but I cannot call her," answered Tom.

Jefferey was even more rattled now.

"What do you mean? Why can't you call her? What have you done with her?" he asked.

"Firstly, I haven't done anything with her, and secondly, as I said previously, it's none of your damn business anyway. If you must speak with Joanne, I am sure you will have plenty of time to do that during your working hours. Thank you for calling, Jefferey, goodbye," replied Tom.

Tom went to close the door, but Jefferey put his foot in the way.

"You know what, Jefferey, the last person that did that ended up in hospital after having a pitchfork mysteriously go through his foot," said Tom.

"Are you threatening me then?" asked Jefferey.

Tom sniggered as he replied. "Threatening you? Certainly not. If I had been, you would already be on your way to the hospital. I was just quoting a fact."

"Think yourself clever, don't you? Well, I want to know where Joanne is and I am not leaving here until I've seen her," he replied.

"Some people just never give up. You're certainly not going to see her as she's unable to come to the door now and by the way, I never once said I was clever. You are the one who appears to think I am cleverer than you. But I *was* just wondering how fast you can run," replied Tom.

"What? Why do you need to know that?" asked Jefferey.

"Just curious, that's all. I'm wondering if I set the dogs on you, would you be able to make it back to your car before they get you," replied Tom.

"You're mad, totally mad. I'll wait in my car."

"A very wise choice I think," replied Tom.

Tom closed the door and went back upstairs to see how Joanne was doing. She was just getting out of the shower when he entered the bathroom.

"Late again, Tom. I was waiting for you to wash my back, but you took too long," she said.

"All thanks to your friend, Jefferey," answered Tom.

"Jefferey? What's *he* got to do with it?"

"He's sitting outside in his car. Said he wants to see you urgently. He tried to come in, but I wouldn't let him. I told him I'd set the dogs on him," replied Tom.

"Dogs? What dogs? We don't have any dogs!"

"We know that, Joanne, but he doesn't," replied Tom.

Tom waited for Joanne to dress and then they both went

downstairs. He opened the door and called to Jefferey, who got out of his car, looking frantically around to make sure there were no dogs about. He didn't trust Tom for one minute and he didn't like him either.

Joanne stepped out of the door and called to her colleague.

"Jefferey, what are you doing here? This is my private house. You have no reason to be here. What do you want?" she asked.

"Sorry," replied Jefferey. "I just wanted to make sure you were fine last night after getting home so late. You know, just making sure your partner wasn't annoyed with you that I kept you out."

Joanne was confused. She looked at Tom who was standing behind the door and whispered to him, "The man is deranged. He didn't even turn up to take me to dinner. I was sitting in my office all evening waiting for him. I think he needs help."

"Jefferey, what are you going on about? You are not making any sense! We can talk at work," she replied.

"No! We can't because we can't talk in private there, just the two of us," he exclaimed. "Please, let's talk in the car. I need to make sure you are alright."

Joanne turned to Tom.

"I'll try to get rid of him. Let me see what he wants," she said.

"Okay, I'll wait here, just shout if you need me, and don't forget the dogs – Salt and Pepper," he said jokingly.

Joanne walked down to the car where Jefferey was still waiting.

"What is it you want, Jefferey? You're not making any sense," said Joanne.

"Can you just get in the car, please?" requested Jefferey.

"No, I will not get in the car with you. Whatever it is that you want to say to me, you can say it out here," she replied.

"I just don't want that partner of yours to hear our private conversation, Joanne," he replied,

"Jefferey, are you crazy? We are 50 metres away from the house. I know Tom has excellent hearing, but even he would not be able to hear what we are saying from where he is standing. Just say what you've got to say and leave," replied Joanne.

"I am sorry for last night, Joanne. I hope I didn't hurt you, but we agreed to become socially active, and I hoped that partner of yours wasn't annoyed because I kept you out late," said Jefferey.

"I think you should leave, Jefferey," said Joanne, becoming increasingly annoyed by his lying.

"No, wait, Joanne. Do you agree that you wanted us to become socially active?"

"No, Jefferey, get your facts right. You were the one who first mentioned that you wanted us to become socially active, whatever that might mean, and as I said, it would be nice to get to know you better. I have no problem with that."

"It's good to hear you say that. I thought you were giving me the push, so can we still do it then, you know, the socially active bit?" he asked.

Joanne looked at him. "Yes Jefferey, we can still do it if that is what you want," she replied.

"Thank you, Joanne. You are fantastic, great and so fit," replied Jefferey.

"Anytime you like, Jefferey, just let me know," she said.

"How about tonight, can we do it tonight?" he asked.

"Yes," she replied, "if you want to."

"Yes, please, Joanne. Sorry about last night, I just wasn't ready, too tired I think."

"Okay then, but don't let me down, Jefferey. Don't pull out at the last minute. See you later," she said as she turned and walked back up to the house.

Jefferey wound down the window and shouted, "Looking forward to it," then he drove off down the drive.

Joanne entered the house and closed the door behind her where Tom was still waiting.

"What the hell was all that about then?" he asked.

Joanne shrugged her shoulders. "I haven't a clue! I think the man seriously needs help."

"Help?" enquired Tom. "I think he needs more than just help. I think he desperately needs to see a shrink," he added.

"Maybe you are right, Tom, but Warren asked me to get to know all the staff, so I told him I would meet with them all individually to find out more about them and see what makes them tick. Jefferey was meant to be first in line, and I was meant to meet with him last night, but he didn't reply to my text. I waited and waited but he didn't reply so I came home. It's so annoying because I could have been here all evening with you," explained Joanne.

Tom placed his hands on her shoulders and pulled her towards him, planting a kiss on her forehead.

"Don't worry, we've always got tonight," he said.

"That's the problem – he wants to meet me tonight now. He said he was tired last night and wasn't ready," replied Joanne.

"No problem, we have lots of time; your work has to come first, you have a huge responsibility," he said.

"Thank you, Tom, you're so understanding."

"Come on, you have to go now, or you'll never get to work. Can you drop me in town on your way?"

"Yes, of course, but can you drive, Tom? I need to rest, it has been such a rush this morning. It's not far at all. If I direct you there, you'll know where to come when you have to see Warren about the decorating."

"Sounds a good idea to me," he replied.

"Just head towards the rail station and I'll show you from there," said Joanne.

The traffic was light, which pleased Tom as he had hardly driven at all since the accident and although he hadn't forgotten what to do, things change with time and so does the road layout. In five years, it was amazing how many roads had seen changes, some now 'no entry' and 'one way', and some with a reduced speed limit. Although driving didn't frighten him, it was just like learning all over again and what really surprised him was the increase in the number of bad driving decisions, which led him to wonder how there were not more accidents.

Joanne opened her eyes, surprised to see that they were almost at her office.

"That was quick, Tom. It's not far from here. Do you want to get out somewhere or do you want to take me directly to the office?" she asked.

"If your office isn't far from here, I may as well take you all the way there," he replied.

"Okay, take the next turning on the right and then the second on the left," replied Joanne, "as you take the left the entrance to the small car park is immediately on the right," she explained.

As Tom pulled in through the gates of the car park, Joanne pointed out her designated space right next to Warren's.

"Another safe journey accomplished," remarked Tom.

Joanne looked at him.

"Oh Tom, I am so sorry. I can see it is still painful for you. I shouldn't have asked you to drive, I wasn't thinking," she said as she held Tom's arm firmly and kissed him on his cheek.

Tom looked at her as they were getting out of the car.

"Come on, enough of this. I'm okay. You have to get in the office and sort that Jefferey out."

"Thank you, I will. I love you so much! See you tonight."

Tom gave Joanne a kiss and a hug as they said their goodbyes. He stood and watched her as she walked to the entrance door, where she turned and blew him a kiss. Tom waved goodbye, then turned and walked off into town.

CHAPTER ELEVEN

Chance Meeting

Tom didn't have to get a lot in town, but he expected to be out most of the morning. He had decided it was time to re-connect with the outside world, so first stop was going to be a phone shop, something that took him much longer than expected. He really had shut himself away and even in five years things had changed so much. He found it all too much; he visited a couple of different outlets where the sales staff all ensured him that their contract was the best, but he had no odea if that was true or just sales talk. Having thought about it, he returned to the first shop he had visited, where the staff there were less pushy and their phones were just as good as anywhere else.

With the phone in hand, he managed to reset his old email and couldn't believe it when he found that the photos of Joanne he had taken were there, ready to be downloaded. He had sent them to himself from her phone but didn't know until that moment that the transfer had worked. He sat there on a bench in the shopping centre to check the photos, thankfully they had all transferred correctly.

He made his way to Lismore Road. He wanted to get the photos enlarged and he knew there was a shop along there that could do exactly what he wanted. He was hoping the photos would be good enough for them to enlarge, a surprise for Joanne.

"Good morning, Sir, how can we help you today?" said the assistant behind the counter.

"I'd like to get three photos enlarged and placed onto canvas; would you be able to do that for me?" he asked.

"We will certainly see what we can do for you, Sir, but a lot will depend on the images and their quality. As much as you may want them transferred, we pride ourselves on only transferring and enlarging images if they are suitable," replied the assistant.

"I have the photos here on my phone," replied Tom as he took his phone out of his pocket.

"May I see them, please?" asked the assistant.

Tom opened the photos in the phone's gallery and showed them to the assistant.

"These are the three that I want to be transferred to canvas. The face on one I would like as one hundred and twenty-two by eighty-one centimetres and the two side-view ones as sixty-one by forty-one," explained Tom.

"Do you have these images stored anywhere else, Sir?" asked the assistant.

"No, these are the only one that I have," replied Tom.

"May I download these, Sir? Then we can check them and see if they are suitable for the size of prints that you require?" asked the assistant.

"Sure, no problem. Will you be able to let me know today if they're suitable?" asked Tom.

"I can do that for you as soon as I have downloaded the images, Sir; if you would like to wait, it shouldn't take too long," replied the assistant.

Tom waited for a few minutes to find out if the images were suitable for canvas when the assistant returned; it was good news.

"They seem, fine, Sir. The large one will be one hundred and forty pounds and the two smaller ones will be fifty pounds each. In total, that will be two hundred and forty pounds, please. The enlargements will be ready for you in three to six days, and we will contact you as soon as they are ready."

Tom asked if it would be possible for the prints to be delivered once they were ready, and was told it would be fine but that there would be an extra charge. He paid for the prints and the delivery and then made his way back towards the town centre.

He had one more stop to make and that was just to get a card, then he was going to go straight to the taxi rank to get a taxi home. On the way, he spotted a Coffee Republic and decided to pop in there to get a snack and a coffee as he was feeling hungry. He found a cosy corner and had just sat down when he spotted Warren Fredericks walk in, and he managed to make eye contact while Warren was waiting to be served. Warren collected his coffee and baguette and walked straight over to the table where Tom was sitting.

"Good morning, Tom. How are you today? May I join you?" asked Warren.

"Yes of course. I'm fine, thank you, just having a light refreshment before heading back home," he replied.

"And playing with a new phone by the looks of things," commented Warren.

"Haven't used one of these things in almost five years," replied Tom. "I have an old one, but they have changed so much in that time, so I decided to treat myself to a new one."

"Are you going straight home from here then?" asked Warren.

"Yes, I still have decorating to finish at Joanne's house, so I need to press on with that," he replied.

Tom took a sip of coffee from his cup while Warren was eating his baguette.

Placing the cup back on the table, Tom looked across to Warren and asked.

"Why did you enquire if I was going straight back home?"

"I was just wondering if you had some time to spare, that was all," replied Warren.

"Well, I have almost completed the main rooms that Joanne uses, so there is no great panic to get the rest done," said Tom.

Warren looked at Tom with a broad smile on his face.

"I was hoping you'd say that, Tom. When we have finished here, would you like to come back to the office with me to see what decoration needs doing there and discuss any plans you might have?" he asked.

"That sounds an excellent idea, Warren. I know from what Joanne has told me that you are anxious for me to get started; what were you thinking for the re-decoration?"

"I have no plans at all, apart from the fact that I want the office brought up to date, and yes, I would like you to get started as soon as possible. However, can I ask you a favour?" said Warren.

"Of course, fire away," remarked Tom.

"I realise it will probably be awkward for you, being in such proximity to Joanne while you are carrying out the re-decoration, but could you please disassociate yourself from her while you are in the office?"

"That goes without saying," replied Tom.

"Brilliant. Let's get on our way then if you are ready. It's only a short distance back to the office."

"Yes, I came down in the car this morning with Joanne so I know where your office is now," replied Tom.

They had crossed the car park and were just about to enter the office when Warren took Tom by the arm.

"Tom, just before we go up into the office, I did see Joanne briefly this morning and she explained the reason why she was late; she told me that you had a visit from Jefferey Philips. What can you tell me about that?" he asked.

"It was rather strange. I was downstairs in the house, Joanne was getting ready upstairs, there was a knock at the door and when I opened it, Jefferey was standing there, asking to see Joanne as a matter of urgency. I told him that he couldn't see her because she was getting ready, and he could speak to her at work. Then, because I wouldn't let him see her, he asked me what I had done to her. He was just not making any sense. I tried to close the door, but he stuck his foot in the way. I think that was when I told him I would set the dogs on him, the problem being we don't have any dogs. However, he took the hint and said he would wait in his car but that he wasn't leaving until he had seen Joanne," explained Tom.

"What happened then? Did he leave?" asked Warren.

"No, he waited for Joanne to come to the door, then insisted he speak to her in his car, but she refused to get in and just stood by the door while Jefferey stayed in the car."

"Okay, thank you for that. I think I need to have a word with young Mr Philips," remarked Warren as he opened the entrance door for Tom and beckoned him to enter.

They climbed the stairs and walked straight through the office to the far end where Warren's office was situated.

"Take a seat on the sofa for a moment please, Tom. I will see if Joanne is free to join us," said Warren.

"Thank you," replied Tom as he took his place on the sofa.

While he was alone, Tom had time to have a look around and study the décor in Warren's office; it was obvious from what he saw that some tender loving care was missing.

He also noticed a few things that needed changing or refurbishing, and some items that were so out of date that they needed replacing. Then there was also the colour scheme – it was disastrous. Having already taken a quick glance earlier as they'd walked through the office, Tom was now of the opinion that there would be at least a month's work required, maybe even more, but that would be controlled by how much Warren was prepared to spend on the alterations. Tom was still making mental notes when Warren returned with Joanne.

"Okay, Tom, Joanne has a few minutes to spare so while the three of us are here, we need to decide what we are to do about Jefferey. What he did this morning and for whatever reason he did it, it was wrong, so we need to make sure there is no re-occurrence. I have listened to what both of you had to say about the incident and Jefferey has a problem. So how are we going to deal with this, without it causing too many problems within the office framework? It seems obvious to me that I will have to speak to him to see what is going on. Do either of you have anything to add to that?" said Warren.

A moment of silence followed before Joanne gave her thoughts on the matter.

"I think this is a problem that I have to iron out with Jefferey. It may stem from the fact that I was promoted to an executive position, something that he thought he deserved."

"I take your point," replied Warren, "but then that also involves me and the business since I was the one who chose to promote you, so it seems to me that if he has a problem with that then maybe he shouldn't be here."

Joanne was stunned. She had read through notes from past cases Jefferey had led, and he was a good solicitor.

"But Sir, wouldn't it be better to try to find out the background to the problems Jefferey is having, before having what could be a knee jerk reaction?"

"Joanne, you can be quite forthright at times and not afraid to put your opinions forward, and I like that. As much as I think you could be wrong, I can certainly see where you are coming from with your thoughts, so I think on this occasion it may be best for all concerned to try your line first," commented Warren.

Tom had sat quietly through the discussions so far, but he had his own ideas about what might be causing Jefferey's problem, and he thought this should also be considered.

"Can I add a thought to all this?" asked Tom.

"Yes, of course, Tom," replied Warren.

"I am not sure that Jefferey's problem is with Joanne gaining promotion when she had only just started here. I get the impression that it is more to do with me," said Tom.

Warren was interested in Tom's idea.

"Ah, okay, can you explain in more depth why you feel that?" asked Warren.

"Yes," replied Tom. "I know I only get to see one side of the story. However, it probably contains the most important factor. Jefferey does not like me, he made that abundantly clear at your office dinner. He has convinced himself that I am Joanne's partner and he feels that a low-life odd-job man like me has no business invading the life of such a well-acclaimed and financially stable solicitor. It's as though he saw himself as getting a slice of Joanne's cake, but he was beaten to it," explained Tom.

Both Warren and Joanne sat in stunned silence; they both knew that if Tom were right, then they had a fundamental problem, one which could only get worse.

"I do value your opinion, Tom," remarked Warren, "but I must add that Jefferey has worked here for almost five years now, and not once has he been, or caused, a problem. That in no way condones what happened this morning but I am just stating facts," added Warren.

"So, what is the answer then?" asked Tom. "Surely it cannot be right for him to continue in his current vain? And how can it be right for him to come to Joanne's house, uninvited, as he did this morning?"

Joanne was also concerned by the fact that Jefferey had turned up on her doorstep as he did, and she wanted answers. She knew that there was little Warren could do as it was out of working hours but nevertheless, something had gone wrong, and she wanted to find out how.

"Warren, I would like to know how Jefferey managed to get my address because I certainly didn't give it to him," she remarked.

Warren was also concerned, but he did not have the answer that Joanne was looking for.

"I am extremely sorry, Joanne, all I can is offer my apologies and try to make sure that something like this never happens again," he replied.

"I appreciate your concern, Warren, but that does not change the fact that Jefferey should not know where I live and, if Tom is right about what he has said, there may well be other visits. Am I expected to get an injunction against him from entering the grounds of my property and if so, what will that do for the atmosphere in the office towards both me and other staff members?"

"Joanne, everything you have said is right, but I am just worried that anything I may say to Jefferey might make things a whole lot worse. It is an exceedingly tricky situation, one which affects us all and will continue to do so until we find the underlying cause," replied Warren.

Joanne was beginning to realise that she was the only one who could sort this whole sorry business out.

"Look," she said. "I have a meeting with Jefferey tonight. Let me see what I can do before we take any other action. I will try to impress on him that he should not be turning up on my doorstep, demanding to know where I am and what I'm doing. It is, as Tom rightly said, none of his damn business. I think I need to find out exactly what his problem is because now we are only guessing. I do realise this may not work but all I am asking it that you both let me try tonight and then take it from there. If we need to, we can arrange another meeting so that I can explain what happened," said Joanne.

After a few tense moments, Warren agreed that Joanne's suggestion was probably the best way forward for now. Tom, however, was not entirely convinced. His reservations regarded Joanne's safety and he made this known before reluctantly agreeing to their plan of action.

"Having spoken to Jefferey this morning, he worries me in as much as he doesn't appear to be in control of what is happening. I know you may think this strange, but some of the things he was saying just do not make any sense. I am still sure he is trying to get at me, but I worry that he may, in the end, do that through you, Joanne," remarked Tom.

"Tom, I will be okay," replied Joanne. "I will have to go now as I have a client meeting in fifteen minutes and I need to get a drink first." She got up and walked towards the door before turning to them and saying, "Let's look on the positive side, and hope that I can sort this out tonight."

Joanne went straight to the reception desk.

"Hi Linda, I have an appointment with Mr Sullivan in fifteen minutes. Could you apologise for me and let him know I am running a few minutes late?" she said.

"Okay, not a problem," Linda replied. "I'll let him know."

Warren and Tom reverted to the subject of re-decoration and after seeing what he had so far, Tom was anxious to look around the rest of the office.

"Is it okay if you show me around the office now Warren? I can already see here that there's quite a bit needs doing."

"I'm not sure if that is still a good idea, Tom. Maybe Jefferey will be suspicious seeing that he had a confrontation with you this morning. What do you think?" asked Warren.

Tom thought for a moment and then he replied.

"I think it would appear more suspicious if I just left and he saw me. He would automatically wonder why I had been here. If I continue to look at the office, you just introduce me and tell him I am looking around before starting on the re-decorations."

With that, Warren began the tour around the office, with Tom making notes of any structural alterations he thought were required. He also made use of his new phone, taking photos of areas within the office to help him plan his intended work. The last area in the office they visited was Jefferey's desk.

"Jefferey, this is Tom – I think you met at the dinner? He is just looking around to see what extent of re-decoration is needed in the office," said Warren.

"Hi Jefferey," said Tom.

Jefferey looked up and grunted something completely inaudible, to which Tom responded.

"Thank you, Jefferey, sorry to have disturbed you. Hopefully, I can make the offices brighter and a more pleasant place to work." He then turned to Warren. "Thank you, Warren, I think I have seen enough. I will let you have my report and suggestions within a couple of days."

"Thank you, Tom, that's great. If I agree to everything, when would you be able to start?"

"Well, I can start the painting almost immediately, once you have decided on colours and exactly what you require. As for any structural work, and I will be suggesting some in my report, then that would depend on your budget and the ordering of any materials that I might require."

"Thank you, Tom. Could you wait one minute, and I'll show you out?"

Warren then turned to Jefferey. "Please would you put the Saunders report on my desk now? I must read it today."

Jefferey looked up.

"Sorry, Warren, I'll do that right now," said Jefferey as he picked up a file from his desk.

"Okay. Tom, I will show you out now, thank you for coming in and I will look forward to seeing your quote."

Warren walked down with Tom to the main entrance and taking his hand he said, "Tom, I noticed Jefferey's reaction to you in the office and I can now understand your concerns about Joanne. Don't worry, I will take good care of her."

"Thank you, I'll send my quote in with Joanne, in a sealed envelope, of course," replied Tom.

Tom left the office and slowly walked back to the station where he took a taxi to the house. He had enjoyed his morning; it was something different to what he was used to, and, in some ways, it was his first step in re-engaging with the real world. He knew that was something for which he had a lot to thank Joanne for and he was looking forward to her coming home that evening.

CHAPTER TWELVE

Frosty Exchanges

Joanne was reading through the transcript of the trial she was working on when she was interrupted by Warren.

"I'll be leaving soon, Joanne. Is your meeting with Jefferey still on for tonight?" he asked.

"I think so. He hasn't told me otherwise, but then he didn't last night, either. He said earlier that he would let me know where we would go for dinner, but I'm still waiting for him to confirm that with me. I'm not prepared to sit here waiting half the night again, so if I don't hear from him soon, I'll be going home myself," she replied.

"I don't blame you, Joanne. If Jefferey is being awkward, there's not a lot you can do. Oh, I nearly forgot – I was asked to give you this," he said as he passed a piece of paper to her with a number on it.

"Whose number is this? It's not one I recognise."

"Tom asked me to give it to you earlier. He bought himself a new phone."

"Thank you. That's a good sign," remarked Joanne.

"I'll see you in the morning. Good luck for tonight. I hope you can sort it all out."

"Yes, me too," replied Joanne.

She sat there for a moment, still not having heard from Jefferey. It was feeling a little like a *déjà vu* moment. She looked at the piece of paper that Warren had given her and added the phone number to her address book, then she typed in a message.

'Do you have any plans on where you might sleep tonight? It's cold and lonely in that barn.'

Joanne sat staring at her screen, but there was no reply to her message. Maybe Tom was busy and hadn't seen it. She waited and then a message flashed up on her PC: it was from Jefferey.

'I was thinking you probably don't want to get socially active with me, but then I thought maybe you are busy. We can go whenever you are ready. I'm here waiting for you now. Jefferey'

What type of message is that? she thought to herself. *Where the hell are you?* What was Jefferey playing at?

'Okay, Jefferey, you say you are ready and I'm ready and waiting too, but do you mind telling me where you are so we can both be in the same place? Joanne'

She was waiting for his reply when Tom text, which was of much more interest to her.

'Sleep? I can do that on my own, but it might be nice to try something different.'

Joanne replied straight away.

'What might the nice bit include?'

Then she got a message from Jefferey.

'I'm waiting for you at Bill's. See you soon.'

Joanne instantly sent Tom a message before leaving the office.

'Just got a message from Jefferey. I'm meeting him at Bill's now. See you later and looking forward to it.'

Tom was still very worried about where this might be leading.

'Okay, be careful, I just do not trust him.'

Joanne collected her things, left the office and drove to Lismore Road where she parked and walked the short distance to Bill's. Jefferey was already seated at a table and patiently waiting for her to arrive. She walked over and sat down.

"Good to see you are here and not keeping me waiting all night like last night," remarked Joanne.

"Still bitter, I see," replied Jefferey.

"I don't suppose you would feel bitter after waiting all night to be contacted and then that person didn't contact you or didn't reply to messages and then dares to turn up on your doorstep first thing in the morning while you were still in the shower! What do *you* think? Yes, I am still bitter."

"Oh! So now the super-cool calm executive loses it, all because of an insignificant disagreement?"

"Jefferey, what are you going on about? What disagreement? You are just not making any sense," said Joanne.

"Oh, come on! Is your memory that short? That's not good for an executive! You should know everything and remember everything."

"Look, if you are going to go on all evening talking rubbish, then I'm off. I hear enough rubbish from clients all day long but I don't expect to hear it from another solicitor as well. Whatever it is you want, you can stuff it; I don't care and if you ever turn up at my property again, uninvited, I will set Salt and Pepper loose on you!"

"Salt and Pepper?"

"The dogs. Believe me, you wouldn't want to meet them."

Jefferey sat there for a while looking at her; he sensed that he could not get the better of her, well, not yet anyway, so he decided he needed to reset the situation.

"Look, I'm sorry, I didn't start this very well, did I? I didn't intend to annoy you."

Joanne was mystified by his sudden change of attitude, but she decided to accept his apparent apology as she wanted to find out what game he was playing.

"Well, I guess that is a veiled attempt at an apology, Jefferey, and one which, for now, I will accept, so are we going to eat now or what?"

That seemed to break the ice, for a while anyway, but Joanne was still finding it hard to fathom out where Jefferey was going and what he was on about. He seemed confused at the best of times, almost as though he was living in a different world.

"So, tell me, Jefferey, why did you come to my house this morning? What was the reason behind that? I mean, what was so important that you needed to invade my privacy, when you could easily have confronted me at work?" asked Joanne.

"Sorry, it was a mistake," he replied.

"Oh, come on, Jefferey, cut the crap! You don't just turn up at someone's house and then palm it off as a mistake. What were you after? What were you looking for? I guess the mistake was not that you drove there, the mistake was that you didn't find what you wanted – isn't that the truth?"

"What are *you* going on about, Joanne? You're not making any sense. I told you it was a mistake and that is all it was," replied Jefferey.

"Yes, I accept that it was a mistake because you hadn't planned on Tom opening the door. You were fully expecting me to answer the door, so what was it that you wanted to ask me that was so important it couldn't wait until we were in the office?"

She sat waiting for Jefferey to reply but he sat in silence, not moving. He just kept staring at the table.

"I'm waiting! Jefferey, what did you want to ask me? Surely you can't have forgotten in the space of twelve hours, and if you *have* forgotten, it couldn't have been that important in the first place, could it?"

"Can't you just leave it? I made a mistake and that is all that matters now, but I guess you will never let me forget that so I will just have to live with it," replied Jefferey.

"I am sorry Jefferey, but it is not as simple as that. I want to know why you turned up on my doorstep uninvited and now you don't even have the decency to tell me why. If you expect that to be the end of the matter, then you are deluded."

"Okay, okay, enough. I wanted to speak to you to tell you that I think you are making a big mistake. However, instead of you opening your door, it was that Tom guy. I was shocked, I hadn't expected that, and I just did not know what to say," he finally replied.

"Jefferey, you are not making any sense. And how is it any business of yours who is in my house anyway? I will choose to see and speak to whomever I want to, and nothing you or anyone else can say will make me change my mind, so you had better get used to it," replied Joanne.

"But why the odd-job man? You are a beautiful lady and intelligent with it. You could do much better than him."

"Well, it is obvious to me that this is just not sinking in, Jefferey. I just told you it is none of your business whom I want to choose as a friend," said Joanne.

"So, tell me then, Joanne, what was the real reason for your partner being in the office this morning?"

"Look, Jefferey, if by my partner you mean Tom, then he is not my partner, and he was in the office on business he had with Warren, so I am the wrong person to be asking that question. However, it appears that Warren wants Tom to re-decorate the office and make some changes to the office spacing. I am sure you can appreciate how much the office requires some tender loving care," replied Joanne.

"Oh, without doubt, Joanne, it has required that for some time," replied Jefferey.

"Seeing that we have worked our way around to work Jefferey, have you submitted the Saunders file to Warren yet? He keeps asking me to remind you that it is overdue."

"Yes, I did that before I left," he replied.

"On a personal note, Jefferey, if you don't mind me asking a personal question, that is?"

Jefferey looked at her. "No, I don't mind. Ask me whatever you like."

"You're not married are you, Jefferey?" asked Joanne.

"No! Never have been. Does that surprise you?" he replied.

"In a way, yes, but then I guess it's just a matter of finding the right person."

"I think that plays a big part," remarked Jefferey. "And you, Joanne? I take it you aren't married?"

"No. I am single at the moment, but divorced," replied Joanne.

"That can be nasty," commented Jefferey, "as is well known in our chosen profession."

"Yes, that's true, and best not to make the same mistake twice," she remarked.

Jefferey looked up at Joanne. "But sounds like you'll be getting married again soon, I expect."

Joanne looked towards Jefferey with a frown on her face. "Why would you expect that?" she asked.

"Well, you're living in your house with your boyfriend or partner, whatever you want to call him," replied Jefferey.

"Jefferey, is there some problem with your hearing? I have told you several times now Tom is neither of those things, so maybe you should let that sink in. You should never judge a book by its cover," she added.

Jefferey sat there in silence and it appeared for once that he did not have a prepared answer to throw back at her.

Joanne felt she wasn't getting anywhere and decided that she needed to accelerate the conversation.

"What about you then, Jefferey. Do you have a special lady in your life at the moment, but just haven't got around to asking her to marry you?"

Jefferey sat there in silence for a few moments, playing with the glass on the table, before replying.

"No, there is no one close at the moment, but there is someone I really like, but she already has someone else."

"Oh no, that's sad," remarked Joanne.

"Tell me about it. It's painful too," commented Jefferey.

Joanne looked at her phone, she hadn't realised it was so late. She had one message and one missed call, both from Tom.

"You'll have to excuse me for a minute, Jefferey. I need to go to the ladies."

"Okay, no problem," he replied.

Joanne checked the message from Tom.

'Hope everything is going well and that you won't be too late.'

Joanne replied to his message.

'Are you missing me then? Should be leaving here soon.'

Joanne returned to the table and sat down.

"Jefferey, is there anything else you would like to discuss while we are here? Anything to do with the business or anything else?" she asked.

"No, not really," he replied, "although maybe we could commit to this socially active theme and do it more often? What do you think, Joanne, could we do it more often?" he asked.

"I don't see why not, Jefferey, as long as we both want it and it works for us," she replied.

"I was hoping you would say that," said Jefferey. "I will leave the ball in your court then, and whenever you want to get together, just let me know. If you can't get away during an evening, we could always pop out during a lunch break," he replied.

"I like the lunchtime idea, Jefferey. It might also relieve the stress. Sorry, but I have to go now, it's getting late."

"Thank you, Joanne. I hope you found it has been a worthwhile evening?"

"Yes, after a false start, it was good and very worthwhile," replied Joanne.

"Okay, I will try not to get overawed by the moment next time and try to perform better," he replied with a smile on his face.

As they both got up to leave, Jefferey picked up Joanne's handbag from the table.

"Don't forget your bag," he said and passed it to her.

"Thank you, Jefferey. I will see you in the morning. Good night."

Joanne walked back to her car which was only parked about fifty metres away. She instantly sent a message to Tom before driving off.

'On my way home now. Hope you aren't too tired! See you in ten minutes.'

Joanne placed her phone in the holder on the dashboard and started the short journey home. She was so looking forward to having a coffee and a shower. She parked her car at the top of the drive, walked to the front door and took the key from her bag. She looked around for Tom but there was no sign of him downstairs. She tried calling out.

"Tom, I'm home," but still there was no response. She made herself a coffee and took it upstairs to her bedroom. She sipped a couple of mouthfuls, removed her clothes and threw them on the bedroom floor. Taking another mouthful of coffee, she picked up a bath towel and headed into the bathroom. Now she knew where Tom was – she found him in the shower! She placed her towel on the radiator and joined him.

"Hey, don't you believe in knocking?" he asked.

Joanne laughed. "No need for that, it's my house, so my rules apply!"

She picked up the bottle of shower gel and proceeded to quirt it all over his back, then she took the sponge from its holder and squirted shower gel on that, too, before thoroughly washing his back. When she had finished, she calmly put more gel on the sponge.

"Turn around, please."

"What?" he exclaimed.

"Oh, come on, Tom, surely you are not that shy?" she asked.

"Well, no, but …" he tried to reply but Joanne cut him short midsentence.

"But what?" she asked.

"Well, you haven't seen me naked before."

"Is that so? Well, it may surprise you to know but I'm not standing here in the shower with all my clothes on, either. Come on, don't be a baby, turn around."

Tom very slowly and gingerly turned around.

"There, that wasn't too bad, was it? Oh, I can see now why you were shy! Where did I put that magnifying glass?" she laughed as she continued to wash his body.

"Hey, cheeky," replied Tom. "It's my turn now," he added as he picked up Joanne's sponge and began washing her body.

"Tell me, why exactly do you wear a bra?" he asked.

"Hey, they're not *that* small!"

"It's okay, small is beautiful," he replied.

"You've got a cheek," she said as she playfully kneed him.

"Joanne, you are perfect. I was just getting my own back."

Joanne turned the shower off and walked into the bedroom before starting to dry herself.

"How did your meeting go with Jefferey, then?" asked Tom.

"Oh, you should have been there. It started badly. I ended up threatening him with Salt and Pepper."

"Really?" asked Tom. "Did he fall for it?"

"You bet he did," replied Joanne. "It quietened him right down. I threatened to walk out as well but he apologised, and we reset and started over again."

"Did he talk sense or was he still living in a dream world?" asked Tom.

"Sometimes he is still really strange: one minute he's talking normally and then he is going on about me and him being socially active," replied Joanne.

"Socially active?" queried Tom. "What the hell does that mean?"

"I haven't got a clue, but he just keeps going on about it as though it's the only phrase he knows."

"Did you get the impression that I had something to do with the way he is acting?" asked Tom.

"Oh yes, he definitely gave me that impression, but I also think he has a gripe against me being made an executive," added Joanne.

"Strange man," remarked Tom.

"Oh, he also asked what you were doing in the office today. He didn't say so, but I got the feeling he thought you were there to complain about him turning up on our doorstep," said Joanne.

"You confirmed that I was there just chatting about the redecoration that Warren wants, didn't you?"

"Yes, and he seemed quite happy with my explanation," added Joanne.

Tom sat on the edge of the bed watching Joanne as she finished drying herself and then when she sat in front of the mirror, drying her hair and running the brush through it. He knew the time was close when he would be able to love Joanne for the person she was. The flashbacks of his wife were diminishing, which in no way meant that he was forgetting her but more that he was beginning to accept the reality of life as it was and that he had to move on. His thoughts were becoming less muddled and for the first time, as he sat watching her, he knew what he wanted.

"Anyway, that's enough about Jefferey. What about us, Tom?" asked Joanne.

"Well, maybe I've been a little bit too presumptuous as I didn't ask you but am I correct in thinking that I can sleep here with you again tonight?" asked Tom.

"Tom, it is the only place you are *allowed* to sleep! I don't want to sleep alone when I have you here. I just love your cuddles and having your body next to mine," replied Joanne.

"Thank you. I hope I will be able to give you everything you want, but the gently does it approach is working for now," commented Tom.

When Joanne had finished drying her hair, she sat on the edge of the bed, her back to Tom. He stretched out an arm and let his fingers slowly trace the contours of her backbone from her neck down to the cheeks of her bottom. She lay down beside him.

"Time is a great healer, Tom, and we can have lots of fun together during your healing process. What do you think?" she asked.

Tom turned onto his side, leaning over Joanne. He kissed her neck, then her chest, moving slowly down her body over her breasts, to her stomach, while the fingertips of his right hand moved slowly down the length of her arm from her shoulder down to her fingers, then effortlessly moving across her thigh. He could feel the nervousness and tension building in his body and in Joanne's too. He lifted his head and looked into her eyes.

"I think we should just let it flow."

"Oh yes!" whispered Joanne as she relaxed and responded to his touches; she could feel the excitement running through her whole body as Tom explored every part of her.

CHAPTER THIRTEEN

On Reflection

Joanne turned over in bed, expecting to feel Tom's body next to her, but he was not there. The bed was empty and the space left was cold, not even the warmth of his body was left. She got up and went to the bathroom, full of disappointment. Maybe he would reappear after her shower buy when she had finished, the bed was still empty.

She went downstairs, expecting to see Tom sitting in the kitchen, his favourite place, but there was no sign of him. He was missing. She looked in every room but there was no sign of him anywhere. She went back to the bedroom, put some clothes on, then went back downstairs. She picked up a torch from the kitchen and walked down to the barn.

The barn doors were closed and the place was in darkness. Joanne pulled open the door.
"Tom? Are you in there, Tom?" she called, but there was no answer. She switched on the torch just to make sure he wasn't sitting there, but the place was empty. She walked along the perimeter fence and around the property, but there was no sign of him anywhere.

She walked back up to the house and called him again, just in case he had come back while she was looking for him.
"Tom, Tom? Where are you, Tom? Please don't do this. Are you here?" but there was no answer. She picked up her phone and tried to call his number, but he wasn't answering it. She sent him a message.

'Tom, where are you? Are you Okay? I'm worried about you. Where are you, Tom. Please contact me. I love you, Tom.'

Joanne removed her shorts and put on a pair of jeans. She took some socks out of the drawer and put them on, then, going to the wardrobe, she took out a jumper and placed it over the T-shirt that she was already wearing. She went back downstairs and picked up the car keys from the wall safe where she kept them.

It was still early but Joanne needed to find Tom, so she drove down to the town and looked around the places he had talked about from his dark days but there was no sign of him. She drove to the sea front, parked the car, got out and walked along the front but she could not see him anywhere. She tried ringing him again, but he was still not answering, so she sent him another message.

'Tom, please tell me where you are and I will come and get you. Please, Tom, please I am so worried about you. I love you, Tom, please come back home.'

Joanne walked back to her car and sat inside, locking the doors as it was still dark – four o'clock in the morning. She didn't even know what time Tom had got up, so he could be anywhere. She rang his number again, but this time she left a message.

'Tom, where are you? Please don't do this, I need you, Tom, I love you, it's not your fault – we can sort it out, please come back home, we need to chat, Love Joanne.'

Then she sent him another text message:

'Please, Tom, don't do this, none of this is your fault, Tom, I love you, we can beat this together, all my love Joanne.'

She heard a tapping sound at the window. She must have fallen asleep. It was a police officer. She opened the window to speak to him.

"Are you okay, Miss?" he asked.

"Yes, officer, I'm fine. I've been looking for a friend. I must have fallen asleep, sorry," she replied.

"Have you been drinking, Miss?" he asked.

"No, certainly not, officer," she replied.

"You said you were looking for your friend. What is your friend's name?" asked the officer.

"His name is Tom, Tom Maddox, officer."

"Were you meant to be meeting him here then, Miss?" asked the officer.

"No, I was looking for him. He was missing when I woke up," she explained.

"And have you reported him as missing?" asked the officer.

"No! Not yet I haven't, but I will if he doesn't turn up within a couple of days," she replied.

"Okay, Miss, nothing has shown up on our name check, so it doesn't appear that he has been hurt in an accident or anything like that. You take care, Miss. Good night."

"Goodnight, officer, thank you," said Joanne.

Joanne sent Tom another message.

'Tom, please contact me. I love you, Tom. I am parked near the lifeboat museum; I will wait here another thirty minutes then I will go home'

And then yet another:

'Tom, none of this is your fault. I am sorry Tom, I have been putting too much pressure on you, I know that now and I accept the fact that this is my fault. I thought I was helping you whereas I have probably made things worse. Please forgive me, Tom, you can sleep where you want. If you want to go back into the barn, that is fine by me. Or you can have a bedroom to yourself. I am sorry, Tom; please just contact me. I am worried.'

She waited patiently, hoping that Tom would send her a message or ring her, but she was unlucky in that respect. The thirty minutes had passed, so she decided that she would have to go home.

Joanne started her car and drove slowly, looking on each side of the road as she drove, but Tom was nowhere to be seen. She had to accept the fact that he had disappeared and that she had probably played a large part in the reason for his disappearance. She drove through the gate and up the driveway, parking close to the front door.

Joanne opened the front door and instinctively called out.

"Tom, Tom? Are you there?"

She was both shocked and relieved when she heard his voice.

"I'm here, Joanne, in the kitchen," came a somewhat slurred reply.

Joanne rushed to the kitchen and saw Tom sitting there, quite obviously the worse for wear. She flung her arms around him and kissed him several times.

"Tom, where have you been? I have been looking everywhere for you! I have been so worried, but you are here now," she said.

Joanne looked at him and saw the gash on his forehead and a graze on his cheek.

"What happened to you? Where did you go?" asked Joanne.

Tom looked at her.

"Sorry, Joanne, I couldn't sleep. I needed to clear my head so I thought I would take a walk down by the stream. It had been raining, the path was slippery, I fell and hit my head on an old tree stump. I think I must have knocked myself out. I don't know how long I was there, but when I opened my eyes, everything was blurred, I couldn't focus. I lay back down and felt for my phone, but it wasn't there. It must have fallen out of my pocket when I slipped down the bank, there was nothing I could do, I had to lie there until I could focus, and the dizziness cleared. I sat up and even then I didn't feel right, but I knew I must get back here. I guessed that if you woke up you would be looking for me, so I had to try walking, but standing up just made me feel worse. I knew I had to do it, then I started vomiting, twice I think, maybe three times. My head was pounding, my hip was hurting more, I was okay while I was lay down, but the further I walked, the more painful it became. I think I knocked it when I fell."

Tom continued to explain what happened and how he had struggled to get back home.

"I felt I was going to vomit again, so I sat and rested. I saw a fallen branch a little further down the slope, closer to the stream. I managed to get to it and broke off some of the thinner branch spurs and was then able to use it as a walking stick to support me. I got back up the slope and with the help of the branch, I was able to make it back here. I came in and called you but there was no sign of you. I couldn't understand why you weren't here. I couldn't think straight, I couldn't understand the chronology of events. I looked outside and it was then I noticed your car was not there. That made things worse! I didn't even know if you had come home last night … the shower, the bed, maybe I had dreamt all that, and the more I thought about it, the more confused I became. I went back upstairs to the bedroom and sat on the bed, trying to remember what had happened, to see if it were real or if it had been a dream. I was looking for clues, but I couldn't find any. I came back down and just sat here in the kitchen waiting for you. I was dozing off then I heard you call and when I looked up and saw you, that was when things started to fall into place."

Joanne sat listening to Tom's recount of what had happened. She needed to get him to the hospital as she felt sure that he may still be concussed.

"Tom, you don't need to worry about that now. I need to get you to the hospital to get you checked out," she said.

"No, wait, I haven't finished. I'm sorry Joanne, I messed up again last night, I don't know what is wrong with me. It all felt so good being with you, the shower, lying on the bed watching you standing there naked while you're drying your hair and brushing it. Then feeling you lying next to me, it all felt so natural, kissing you, kissing your breasts, your body, it all felt so natural, my hands exploring your body for the first time, I could feel the excitement running through my body and I could sense your excitement too, and then bang, it was as though my wife was standing there watching us. What could I do?"

Joanne took hold of his hands.

"Tom, leave it, you don't have to do this, you don't need to explain that to me."

"Joanne, please, I have to tell you. I know my wife loved me dearly and I loved her very much too. At times, I feel as though she is still here watching over me, it's as though she is telling me we are still married, and I shouldn't be with you. Last night, I felt her walk into the bedroom. I could feel her eyes looking at me, watching me, watching us, then she spoke to me, she asked me what I was doing and why I didn't love her anymore. I'm sorry Joanne, I just can't do this."

Joanne took a tissue from the box sitting on the breakfast bar and wiped away the tears rolling down Tom's cheeks.

"Tom, come on, we have to get you to hospital. We can talk about this later, come on,"

Joanne helped Tom to the car and made sure his seat belt was fitted, then she rushed around the car and jumped in. Thankfully the hospital wasn't far away, maybe only ten minutes at the most.

She kept looking at him; he wasn't doing a particularly good job of holding his head up straight. It was leaning to one side.

"How are you feeling, Tom?" she asked, but there was no answer.

"Tom, Tom? Can you hear me, Tom?"

Joanne held the steering wheel with one hand and grabbed Tom's wrist with the other. His pulse seemed very weak. She felt she needed to hurry but there was a line of traffic in front of her. Tom gave a murmur or something like a grunt, but then she clearly heard him say *sick*.

"Don't worry, Tom, if you need to vomit, just do it, I can clean it up later," said Joanne.

Tom still wasn't very coherent, and he was drifting in and out of sleep, but still, Joanne was trying to keep talking to him.

"Tom, if you can hear me, we are almost there. We are just passing East Sussex College. Two more minutes and we will be there. Just hang on, Tom."

Joanne pulled up outside the Accident and Emergency department and rushed inside, asking for a porter with a wheelchair. A porter came straight out with a trolly, followed by a nurse and a doctor; they got Tom out of the car and laid him on the trolly.

"I have to park my car; his name is Tom Maddox but that is all I know. I will come in as soon as I have parked," explained Joanne.

The nurse turned to Joanne, saying, "Sorry, but you need to stay with the patient. We can get one of the porters to park your car for you."

With that, Joanne followed them back into the hospital and the porter who brought Tom in took Joanne's keys and went to park her car.

Tom was wheeled straight into a side cubicle and transferred onto one of the beds.

"I will be back in a couple of minutes to get some details from you," said the nurse.

In no time at all, a doctor was there with another nurse, both asking questions.

"Can you tell me his name age and date of birth, please?" asked the nurse.

"I know his name, that is all, it's Tom Maddox. The only thing I can tell you that might be of help is that he may have been brought in here five years ago with his wife and son, when they were all involved in a car accident. He was the only one to survive," replied Joanne.

"He has a nasty bump and gash on his head. Do you know how he got them?" asked the doctor.

"He told me he slipped down a slope while taking a walk on my property and hit his head on a tree stump. He also said that he thinks he passed out for a time, and he has been vomiting," replied Joanne.

"How many times did he vomit?" asked the doctor.

"He told me about three or four times, but also once on the way here in the car."

"Were you with him when he fell?" asked the doctor.

"No, I don't even know what time it happened. I woke up at about three o'clock and he wasn't in bed, he was nowhere to be seen in the house. I looked everywhere but I couldn't see him. I tried ringing his mobile and messaging him, but he never answered. I think he lost his phone when he fell," replied Joanne.

"So, if you weren't with him when it happened, how do you know all this?" he asked.

"When I couldn't find him, I went back to the house, by which time he had recovered enough to get home. He was sitting at the breakfast bar in the kitchen; he was awake, but his speech was slow and a little slurred. He told me that when he woke, he felt okay apart from his head pounding, but when he tried walking his hip hurt. He found an old fallen branch on the floor, so he used that to lean on to help him get home. When I looked in the sink, he had vomited there and as I said, then again in the car on the way here, but he said he also vomited two or three times before he got home. I'm sorry, that is all I can tell you."

"Do you have any idea what time this happened?" asked the doctor.

"No, I can only guess. As I said, I woke about three o'clock and I think I first rang him at about three-thirty, let me check, yes, three thirty-five, and he didn't answer then, so maybe he had already had the accident before then," replied Joanne.

The nurse came back into the cubicle.

"Are you sure your friend was brought in here after the car accident because we can't find any trace of someone with that name."

"No, I am not one hundred per cent sure as I didn't know him then, but I can probably find his details for you. I know where most of his things are stored," said Joanne.

"If you could, that would be a help," replied the nurse.

"Before you go, is there anything about the accident you might have forgotten to tell us?" asked the doctor.

"No, I am sure I told you everything that Tom told me. I will look for his details and get back as quickly as I can," said Joanne.

She was just about to leave when she turned and said, "He had a problem seeing when he first woke after his fall. He said his eyes couldn't focus properly and he felt dizzy. He added that he lay back down, and he thought he may have fallen asleep again and then when he woke the second time, he felt better, his eyes were better, although still blurred, but he could see more," said Joanne.

"Okay people," said the doctor, "we need to organise an MRI scan and do blood tests, and we need a scan on his hips, too. And we need them yesterday … we may not have much time."

Joanne rushed back to the house and straight down to the barn; she didn't know where to start looking, everything was stored in separate boxes. She just had to open each one to see what was inside. It was strange: Tom seemed so organised but none of the boxes were labelled, so he must have an amazing memory to know exactly what was in each one.

She opened box number nine.

"Well, at last, this looks promising," she said to herself. It contained all sorts of different paperwork, all neatly stored in separate envelopes:

Anne Greenfield – my one true love
Tommy Maddox – our beautiful son
Me

She opened the envelope marked 'Me' and hit the jackpot: so 'Tom Maddox' was 'Raymond James Maddox'. It was all there in front of her. Joanne was stunned. It was so sad, he was clearly using 'Tom' in memory of his son. The pain he must have been going through was unimaginable; there was just so much to look through, but she didn't have the time. She quickly sifted through the papers, took his passport, and the hospital discharge document from after the accident.

Joanne rushed back to the hospital emergency department where she showed them his passport to verify his identity and his hospital and NHS numbers which were both on the discharge document. While she had been home, he had been transferred to the Acute Medical Unit, to which she was now redirected.

She pressed the buzzer on the wall next to the entrance door and waited for someone to come and speak to her.

"Can I help you?" asked the nurse.

"Yes, I am here to see Raymond Maddox. You may still have him registered as Tom Maddox."

"Ah yes, some confusion there, but his relative just gave A&E the corrected information. May I ask who you are?" she asked.

"I am that person and I have all his information here, but I am not his relative, I am his partner, and he has nobody else. My name is Joanne Webster. It was me who brought him to A&E so my name and details should appear on his admittance paper," replied Joanne.

"Thank you. Would you like to follow me? Tom isn't here now, he's still having tests and scans, but you can wait in his room. This is it, please take a seat, I'm not sure how long his tests will go on for, but you are welcome to stay as long as you like. I will tell the ward sister you are here and she give you an update on Tom's condition as soon as she can. Can I get you a drink – tea or coffee?" asked the nurse.

"Oh, thank you, a coffee would be great. White no sugar, please," replied Joanne.

"If you would like something to eat, I can give you toast or cereal?" she asked.

"Thank you, some toast would be great," replied Joanne.

Joanne was eating her toast when the ward sister entered the room.

"Hello, I'm Josephine Calleja, the duty sister. Thank you for coming and for the updated information on Mr Maddox. For the moment we will continue to refer to him as Tom as I believe that is his preferred name now."

"Yes, that's right," replied Joanne.

"Unfortunately, things do not look favourable now, but you gave Tom the best possible opportunity of complete recovery by getting him here as soon as possible after you found him. There may be some internal bleeding which would account for the fact that he was conscious when you found him but then lost consciousness on the way here. A bleed in a confined space like the brain would cause loss of consciousness. I am in no way trying to frighten you, but I am just being frank."

"Thank you, I do appreciate your honesty. Do you know how long it will be before Tom is brought back here?" asked Joanne.

"I am sorry, but I do not know the answer to your question. If they do find evidence of a bleed while undergoing tests and the scan, it is more than likely he would be taken straight into surgery, but of course, we will keep you informed of what is happening. You are of course welcome to stay here as long as you like."

"Thank you, thank you very much," replied Joanne.

CHAPTER FOURTEEN

Worrying Times

Joanne took her phone out of her coat pocket and sat down in the chair, waiting for Tom to be wheeled back into his room. She decided to make use of the free time she had to text both Susan Caton and Warren Fredericks.

'Hi, Susan, I won't be in today. I can see by your schedule that you are booked for training today and tomorrow. As you are ahead in your expected level, your training will be to take over my cases for the next two days. All the information you need is on the desktop on my desk. I can keep an eye out for problems on my laptop, but I will not have that until later today. The code for my desktop is twenty-five twenty-seven. If you have any problems or find something you do not understand, don't hesitate to call me. Thank you. Joanne'

'Good morning, Warren. I won't be in for the next two days. I have transferred my work to Susan as I believe she is the only one capable of not messing things up. I am in Eastbourne District General Hospital with Tom. I brought him here earlier; he had an accident in the early hours. Joanne'

She had just finished sending the work messages when the doctor in charge of Tom came to see her.

"Joanne, good morning. It is not great news but it could be a lot worse so I will not beat about the bush. Your partner has been incredibly lucky. Had you have not got him here when you did, he would almost certainly have been dead by now. He has had a major bleed which caused him to lose consciousness despite apparently recovering for a bit. We have managed to stop the bleed and relieve the pressure, however, we noticed there are a couple of lesions on his brain. I'm not sure how long they have been there, but he may require further surgery. We will keep him here for a few days under observation, which was the good news, the sad news is that we cannot yet tell whether this incident will affect his memory; only time will tell, so you must be prepared for the fact that he may have forgotten some things. However, only time will tell. We will keep him in surgical recovery for a couple of hours, so if you need to get anything, it might be an idea to do that now, then you will be here when he wakes up. You are welcome to come and go as you please."

Joanne was stunned: the full facts of Tom's injuries were not easy to swallow. She did not know what to say or do; it felt to her as though the entire world was caving in around her. True, she had found a man with a past but one whom she knew she could not only love without question, but also a man that she would do anything for. Now, he was on the brink of being snatched from her. Joanne didn't know what to think anymore, or how to cope. The tears were running down her cheeks and she could taste those same salty tears on her lips which only seemed to increase their flow. A feeling of total loss flooded over her as she collapsed onto the chair behind her. Thoughts were replaying in her mind: how did they get to this stage? Was Tom's accident her fault? She was in turmoil – the man she loved was in danger and she blamed herself.

The doctor was still waiting for Joanne to say something.

"Joanne, are you okay? Should I call a nurse for you?" he asked.

She fought back the tears and cleared the lump in her throat. "Please can I have some water, doctor?" she asked.

The doctor opened the door and called for a nurse to fetch some water; Joanne almost emptied the whole glass. The nurse stayed in the room with the doctor until Joanne had sufficiently recovered her composure.

"Are you feeling better now?" he asked.

"Thank you, doctor, I will be okay. It has just all come as a terrible shock to me. I am struggling to take it all in, but thank you for being honest," she replied.

"There is no point in giving you false hopes because should the worst materialize, it would be that much harder to accept," added the doctor.

"Thank you, yes, you are right. I need to go to the house and pick up some clothes. I will leave my phone number with the ward staff, but I should be back in just over the hour," replied Joanne.

With that, they both left the room, the doctor continuing his chat with the nursing staff. Joanne rushed back to her car. She had so much to do: she wanted to pick up some clothes for herself and she wanted to go back to the barn, to box number nine, and see if she could find out anything else about Tom. If she had time, she also wanted to look for his phone.

Joanne pulled up outside her house and started on the trail of Tom's missing phone; from his description of events earlier that morning, Joanne felt she knew where to start looking, but she didn't have much time. She started walking down the slope towards the stream; yes, Tom was right – it was quite slippery and she nearly fell herself. Then she saw what looked like slide marks: that must have been where he fell and slipped down the bank. Looking further down towards the stream, she saw what was probably the tree stump that Tom hit. She was struggling to keep her footing and she could see why he fell, bearing in mind it was pitch black when he was here. He must have hit it quite hard as there was a patch of what appeared to be dried blood there. She couldn't see his phone, but then she thought she would try ringing it. She could hear it but couldn't see it. She walked carefully further down the bank towards the stream and there it was. She picked it up – it was dry but dirty.

Now all she had to do was negotiate the climb back up to level ground, which she managed without too many problems. From there, she went straight to the barn and to box number nine. She decided to take the box with her to save time. Once back at the house, she placed the envelopes from the box and some of the other paperwork into her laptop carry case, all ready to take with her back to the hospital.

She took some clothes from her drawers and put them in a backpack and then went into the shower. Standing there, her thoughts returned to the previous evening when she had arrived home to find Tom in there; she recalled opening the shower door and getting in with him. It was that decision which ultimately started off the chain of events that led to Tom's accident. As she washed her body, she remembered how she felt when Tom was washing her and how her body had been tingling all over, but now, she didn't even know whether she would ever experience that same feeling ever again. If only she could reset the clock to the previous evening! Knowing what she knew now, she would never have opened that shower door.

She dried herself off, threw the towel into the tub and walked into the bedroom to get dressed. It was quite warm in the hospital, and she decided that if Tom were connected to machinery, it would make the room even hotter.

She put her knickers on and then picked up a pair of shorts. Should she wear a T-shirt or a loose top? She decided on a loose white top. She ran the brush through her hair – she didn't have time to dry it – but she would put the blowers on in the car which would help.

She picked up the laptop case and the backpack with a change of clothes in it and made her way back downstairs. She stopped off in the kitchen and took a couple of drinks from the fridge. Okay, she now had everything she needed … oh no, except for the chargers for the phones! She quickly rushed back upstairs and picked them up. Then it was straight back downstairs and into the car.

The traffic was starting to build up as it was late afternoon now. It was still twenty-seven degrees, so she opened the windows and turned the blowers on full power, hoping that her hair would be dry by the time she arrived back at the hospital.

She parked her car and went straight to the ward where she pressed the buzzer and waited for someone to let her in.

"Hi Joanne, we were about to ring you. We just heard from the recovery suite that they should be bringing Tom back within the next thirty minutes," said the nurse.

"Oh, that's great news," replied Joanne. "Do you know if he is awake yet?"

"I'm sorry, I don't know that because I didn't answer the call, but the ward sister will be in shortly to make sure the room has been prepared correctly, so maybe you could check with her," replied the nurse.

"Thank you very much, I'll do that."

Joanne was sitting quietly looking through messages on her phone. There were quite a few from work colleagues who must have heard from Warren that Tom had been involved in an accident. The one from Warren was quite touching:

'Joanne, so sorry to hear about Tom's accident. I do hope that he will be Okay and it is not too serious. Don't worry about us here. You must give Tom all the support he needs, this is something he could well do without after what he went through previously and just as he was finding a new lease of life with you. Our love and best wishes are with you both at this time. Take care and give my best regards to Tom. And keep me updated. If you need anything, no matter what, just contact me. Warren, and Judith.'

The one from Jefferey was not so touching but she guessed that was to be expected:

'So, Tom has been in an accident and is in hospital? Such a shame. Guess you'll have more time to become socially active with me, then.

I'll be waiting for your call. Just want to see so much more of you, if you get my meaning😊🙈🙈'

Then the door opened and they were wheeling Tom back into his room.

"Sorry, Joanne, but could you just wait outside for a couple of minutes while we get Tom settled and make sure everything is connected?" said the ward sister.

While she was waiting outside Tom's room, his doctor came out and sat next to her.

"Joanne, your partner has been through a very traumatic day. He appears to have coped okay, but it is still too early to tell. I hope you can stay because from the information we get from you, we will be able to tell exactly how well he is recovering. You will be pleased to know that he regained consciousness, but he is tired and he will sleep a lot. When he wakes, we need you to talk to him, speak about the recent occurrences and things in the past and see how he responds."

"Thank you, doctor, I have no intention of going anywhere as long as you are happy for me to stay, then stay I shall," she replied.

The doctor continued. "We have controlled the bleed and relieved the pressure on his brain, and hopefully he will return to normal in a couple of weeks. If you have to go to work, it would be better to get someone to stay with him. He shouldn't be left on his own for any length of time. Try to make sure he doesn't get too excited; he mustn't partake in any strenuous exercise and where possible he should take a shower, not a bath. We have prescribed medication for him, and it is of the utmost importance that he follows the chart with regards timings and dosage. I think that is all, Joanne. I hope you are not too easily bored as I expect the ward sister will repeat word for word what I have just told you."

"That's quite okay," replied Joanne. "I know you have to make sure that your instructions are completely understood."

The sister opened the door to Tom's room.

"Okay, Joanne, you may come in now, everything is ready for you. Your partner is sleeping now, but he will wake up from time to time, and when he does, try to talk to him as much as possible. We need to ascertain if he has suffered any memory loss."

"Thank you, Sister. Is he in danger if he sleeps for too long?" asked Joanne.

"Yes, he could be, so we will continually monitor him over the next twenty-four to forty-eight hours. He will probably be like this for most of that period, drifting in and out of sleep but after that he should show a marked improvement as he returns to what will hopefully be some normality."

"Thank you," said Joanne.

"Okay, I will leave you to it, but don't forget to try to get him talking when he wakes up and make a note of anything strange. If you need anything or if you are worried about anything at all, just use the buzzer. I will get one of the staff to bring you a drink, a hot drink if you like? Which would you prefer – tea, coffee or hot chocolate?" she asked.

"That's very kind of you. I'd like a coffee, please; white with two sugars," she replied.

Joanne sat in the chair next to the bed and took out some of the papers she had found in the box where Tom had stored them. She did feel a little strange that maybe she was invading his privacy, but the boxes were not sealed, and they were, after all, on her property. She also convinced herself that it was for the best that she found out as much as possible about Tom and his life with Anne, his wife; all she knew was that she was a photographer.

She was also looking for any photos of Anne and his son. It was now obvious to Joanne that 'Tom' senior had been undergoing some mental torture since the accident. What she had found was: full names, birth dates, birth certificates, wedding certificate, death certificate; it was all there.

There was a knock on the door. It was a nurse with Joanne's coffee.

"I'll put it down here for you," she said.

"Thank you," replied Joanne. "If I need to go to the toilet, is that okay? Or should I call you so that Tom is not on his own?"

"No, he must not be left on his own, so you must use the buzzer and one of us will come and watch him," replied the nurse.

"In that case, is it okay if I go now?" she asked.

"That's fine," replied the nurse. "I'll wait here for you to come back."

While she was out of the room, Joanne sent a message to Warren, thanking him for the kind message he had sent earlier and letting him know that she was staying at the hospital all night with Tom. She also responded to the message that Jefferey sent.

'Jefferey, you are a rat.'

As Joanne opened the door to Tom's room, the nurse called to her.

"I think you're just in time, Joanne, as it looks like Tom is waking up."

Joanne stood by the side of the bed and held his hand in hers.

"Tom, can you hear me," she called gently. "Tom, listen to me, if you can hear me, squeeze my hand once. Tom, can you hear me?"

There was no reply, but he was making occasional movements, and all his vital signs were stable. The nurse was sure it was only a matter of time before he woke up. Joanne sat back down and waited patiently for that one moment when she could hear Tom's voice. She didn't have to wait long.

"Water, please," he muttered.

Joanne jumped up and took his hand and squeezed it tight.

"Tom, you made me jump, here just sip it slowly," she said as she held the glass of water to his lips and placed the tip of the straw in his mouth.

Joanne pressed the buzzer so she could let the nursing staff know that Tom had woken up. Within seconds, the nurses were there, wanting to check him to make sure all was okay.

When the nurses had left, Joanne leant over and kissed Tom on his lips while squeezing his hand gently.

"I have been so worried about you! How are you feeling? I love you very much, Tom," she said.

"I'm not sure; weak, tired, confused. How did all this happen, Joanne?" he asked.

"Do you remember any of it, Tom? How this started?"

"More water first, please."

"Okay but slowly – just sip it, Tom," said Joanne.

"I remember everything or almost everything: the shower, watching you brush your hair, in bed and then–" Tom stopped.

"And then what, Tom? Why did you stop?" asked Joanne.

"My wife – she was there, standing right beside us, watching us. I went to the bathroom and when I came back, she had gone; you were asleep and I didn't want to disturb you. I went downstairs to get a drink and sat there thinking …" He stopped again, and took a few sips of water. "I was thinking about us, about everything. It seemed perfect to me: you saying how much you loved me, and me falling for you, and you accepted me into your home. I mean, what more could I ask for? But it just wasn't that simple, there would have been three of us in the relationship and our love could never be consummated. That was when I went for a walk. I was trying to think about how I could tell you, and then I fell and hit my head, I remember it all now."

Joanne interrupted him. "Tom, that is really good news because they were worried that the pressure from the bleed on your brain may have caused some loss of memory, but it appears as though you are okay."

They sat talking for a while, Joanne asking questions and Tom providing the answers; it certainly appeared that he hadn't suffered any loss of memory which had been the doctor's main concern. Although it was early days and Tom still had a long way to go before he had fully recovered, Joanne was so pleased; her fears and worries for the moment at least were allayed. As she leant forward and kissed him, Tom moved his hands up her back over the thin top she was wearing. He stopped suddenly, then moving his hands to her shoulders, he pushed her slightly away and glanced down.

"Is that for me," he asked, "because of my comments?"

"What do you think?" Joanne asked.

It was at that point the nurses knocked on the door and told them it was time for Tom's medication and that he needed to sleep. They turned the lights down low, and Joanne settled down on a small fold up bed. She didn't sleep well; she was still worried about him in case he should experience a relapse. Whenever she did manage to doze off, she was woken by the nurses coming into the room, constantly checking on Tom. Of course, she still had to tell him that she had searched through his belongings to find his details, something she was not looking forward to. There was also something which he had mentioned during their chat when he woke up after his operation. He'd said he didn't know how he was going to tell her! But tell her what? That is what Joanne wanted to find out.

While he was still sleeping, she called one of the nurses so that she could go and take a shower and change her clothes. Then she went to the ward kitchen to get a cup of coffee before going back to his room. He was sitting up in his bed, the nurse holding his glass of water while he drank from the straw.

"I thought you had gone," he said as she walked into the room.

"Why?" exclaimed Joanne. "Why would you think I had gone? I have been here all night, making sure you were okay. I just went to the washroom to freshen up and change my clothes."

"Okay, sorry, I didn't know," he replied.

"It's okay, Tom. Now, how do you feel this morning?"

"I feel alright, I just have a splitting headache."

Joanne knew it was now or never; she had to tell him she had searched through his private papers.

"Tom, there is something I have to tell you. While you were unconscious, I went back to the barn and searched through your private papers – the hospital needed to know your personal details. I'm sorry," she said.

Tom turned to her but she didn't like the look on his face.

"It doesn't matter anymore, don't worry about it," he replied.

Joanne didn't understand his attitude; it had changed since last night, and she was wondering if this was something to do with his operation and the bleed on his brain.

"Tom, can I ask you a question?"

"Yes, sure, what is it you want to know?"

"It was something you mentioned last night. You said you went for a walk because you didn't know how you could tell me something – but tell me *what*, Tom?"

He sat stone-faced and silent.

"Tom, please, what didn't you know how to tell me?" she asked again.

He looked at her. "Come here please," he asked.

She got up from the chair and moved closer to the bed. He reached out and clasped his hands firmly on her arms, pulling her towards him, then he kissed her on each cheek, before releasing his hold on her arms, allowing her to stand up straight.

"I can't do this, Joanne, it's too complicated," he said.

"But what is complicated? You are making it complicated yourself!"

"Joanne, please try to understand. How can I love you when I love my wife? I just can't do it," he replied.

"Look, I told you I would wait. Yes, I made a mistake, more than once, but my mistake was not falling in love with you, my mistake was not giving you space. I am prepared to do that, Tom; I am prepared to wait for as long as it takes."

"But I can't stop loving my wife," he replied.

"Tom, Anne is not here, she is not your wife, you don't have a wife, you are no longer married, you are a widower. You must wake up to the fact that no matter how much you loved her and how much you still love her, you can never bring her back. It is the same with your son too, isn't it? Isn't that why you call yourself Tom, which is not your actual name? So, what is it going to be for the rest of your life? Is it Tom, or

Raymond, or plain Ray?"

Tom sat there, but didn't say a word. Joanne was wiping the tears from her eyes when there was a knock on the door and the ward sister walked in. She took one look at Tom and saw Joanne wiping away her tears, then she turned again to the door.

"Sorry, I forgot something. I will come back in a few minutes," she said as she left the room.

"Tom, your accident last night isn't going to change anything, only you can change that. Maybe you just don't want to change or have no intention of changing, in which case, I will be waiting for nothing. I need to know your intentions," she said as the tears started to flow again.

"Sorry, Joanne, I can't make that commitment," replied Tom.

Joanne picked up her things and walked towards the door. Turning to Tom, she said, "Goodbye, Raymond."

Before leaving, Joanne went to the nurses' desk.

"Is it possible to speak with the ward sister, please?"

"Of course, come with me, please."

The nurse walked her down to the office.

"Come in, Joanne, and take a seat please. Are you sure you are okay?"

"I can't stay with Tom any longer. He doesn't need me, he only wants his wife, but please, can I ask a favour?"

"Which is?" asked the sister.

"When he is fit to be discharged, please don't let him go home by taxi. Contact me and I will come and get him," she asked.

"Don't worry, it's done. I will put that request in his records."

"Thank you," said Joanne as she got up to leave.

"One question, though, how do we contact his wife?" asked the matron.

Joanne turned to her with tears rolling down her cheeks.

"You can't; she died five years ago."

Joanne felt bad as she made her way towards the door leading out of the ward, walking slowly along the corridor, tears still streaming down her face. She didn't know if she had made the right decision or not. Maybe she was being too hard on Tom, she didn't know; all she could remember were his words: that he couldn't love her because he still loved his wife. It appeared to her that he had put a brick wall between then and there was no way she was ever going to be able to dismantle it.

As she got in her car and her emotions became too much for her, she was so distraught, she could not stop herself from sobbing. Then she was screaming, trying to let out her frustration and banging her fists on the steering wheel.

CHAPTER FIFTEEN

Painful Decisions

Joanne pulled up outside her house and rushed upstairs to her bedroom where she took off her clothes and threw them on the floor, before going for a shower. She spent rather a long time there, maybe trying to wash her thoughts away, but it didn't work; she had never felt so confused as she did at that very moment. She felt as though she was in limbo and she couldn't stop thinking about Tom, but she now knew her thoughts on that subject were useless. If the business of the last forty-eight hours had proved one thing to her, it was that she was head over heels in love with him.

Having finished in the shower, she grabbed a towel and walked into the bedroom while drying herself; she sorted out her clothes for the day and lay them on the bed. Picking up her phone, she rang Warren and placed the call on speaker as she continued to dress.

'Thank you for contacting me. However, I am unable to accept your call now, but please leave a message after the tone and I will return your call later.'

"Warren, it's Joanne. There has been a sudden change of plans and I will be in the office today after all, but I urgently need to talk with you, please, if you are available. Thank you."

When she'd finished dressing, Joanne went straight down to the kitchen and made herself a coffee, took out a bowl from the cupboard and poured in some cereal followed by milk. While she was eating, she checked her messages; there was one new text so she clicked on the button: it was from Tom. All she could do was stare at it.

'*Sorry*' was all it said.

She was shattered; she felt even more upset now, even more confused. *What type of message is that?* she thought to herself. She soon found herself typing a reply.

'*I don't want your apologies, Raymond. What I need is you and your love*' then she hit the 'send' button.

Finishing her breakfast, she placed everything in the dishwasher and then went to the lounge to collect Tom's documents so she could return them to the barn. It was dry outside, there had been no rain for a few days now, but for speed, she jumped in the car and drove the short distance down there. She grabbed the papers and placed them neatly back in their box where she had found them.

She stood for a moment and looked around as she recalled the first time she met Tom and how she hadn't got off to a good start with him, not dissimilar to the situation she was in with him now. She hadn't wanted it to end this way and once again she felt the tears rolling down her cheeks to her lips. She slowly raised her hand and wiped away the tears; it was then that she realised that when she split from her husband there were no tears, no sadness, only relief and joy and now she knew exactly why that was.

As she turned to walk away, Joanne noticed a jotter pad on the desk. She picked up a pen as she wanted to leave Tom a message, but her feelings were getting the better of her.

'*Dear Tom (Raymond)*

I wish you well and a full recovery. How did we get to this situation? I guess we both equally played our parts but now you have decided that you no longer want to be involved with me. Please remember that it is your choice and yours alone.

Love you always Joanne xx'

Joanne closed the barn door and got in her car to drive the short trip to work. Pulling in through the gates, she saw that the car park was almost empty. *That's good*, she thought to herself. And now she needed to place Tom on the back burner and catch up on what had been happening at work.

She walked into the office and went straight to her desk where she switched on her PC and then connected her laptop to transfer some work she had managed to complete at home. As there was no one on reception, she opened the surveillance camera on her PC so she could monitor who was coming into the building. She looked at reports from the cases they had been working on, and one stood out amongst the rest: the Saunders case, which was the one assigned to Jefferey.

She found it hard to believe that Jason Saunders, the defendant, had received a custodial sentence of not less than five years, which was crazy and an injustice. She looked at the office files and could not understand why an immediate appeal hadn't been lodged; that should have been automatic after the handing down of a sentence of that nature. It was a clear case of the punishment not fitting the crime. Yes, she knew that Saunders was guilty but there were highly mitigating circumstances. She looked for the download of the court transcripts but once again they weren't there and no request had been lodged for them, something else that should have been automatic.

Joanne felt bad; she had not been covering her duties as an executive and the fact that she had taken her finger off the pulse could have dire effects, not only for the business but more importantly for their clients. She knew she had failed in her given task and there was only one reason for that: she had placed herself above all else. So it was time to make some changes and some painful decisions.

She continued looking at finished cases to make sure there weren't any other glaring mistakes that she had missed and then started typing a letter. She checked her phone to make sure she hadn't missed any messages but there were no new ones. She then went to the kitchen to get a coffee and, before taking it back to her desk and waiting patiently for Warren to come in, she had a few spare moments, so she picked up her phone, pressed a saved contact and waited for them to answer.

"Good morning. Acute Medical."

"Good morning. This is Joanne Webster. Could you tell me if the medical team have assessed Raymond Maddox yet and, if so, what was their conclusion?"

"Ah, Miss Webster, would you please hold? The ward sister would like to speak to you. I'll just transfer you."

"Okay, thank you," replied Joanne.

"Joanne, hello, it's the ward sister here. The doctors have seen Tom – or Raymond – this morning and they are quite happy with his recovery. They do not think there will be any lasting brain damage. He was incredibly lucky to have you to make the decision to bring him in, though. He will have another couple of scans today but if they are clear, then he will be released from the hospital on Friday afternoon."

"Thank you very much. That sounds like very good news," replied Joanne.

"Joanne, could I ask a special favour? This is a request from me and no one else," said the sister.

"What is it?"

"Is there any way that you could ask someone else to come and sit with him, or at least visit him? I have seen a change in him ever since he's known you won't be here to help him," she said.

"I am at work today, and there have been mistakes made during my absence, so I have to be here. What time do visiting hours finish?" asked Joanne.

"Well, as he is still officially critical and he needs to be kept alert, then if you were to visit him there are no restrictions. I know what you told me and I can understand that you both have your own thing to sort out, however, my concern at this time is for his well-being."

Joanne thought about what the sister had asked, and she could understand the logic of her request, but she was not sure she could manage the mental strain of pretending everything was okay when it certainly wasn't.

"Joanne, are you still there?" asked the sister.

"Yes, I am here, sorry, I was just thinking about your request. You know, this has all been very upsetting for me, too. I don't want to belittle Tom's accident or what he is likely to be going through at this time; I very much want him to recover as quickly as possible, but I am not sure I can do it. I will try, but for now, I cannot promise."

"I understand, Joanne. I will be here late tonight to catch up on paperwork so maybe we can chat then. Goodbye and thank you," said the sister as she put the phone down.

"Damn this! Why does life have to be so hard?" said Joanne out loud as she put her phone down on her desk.

"Surely you never expected it to be easy, Joanne?" commented Warren who was passing just as Joanne made her outburst.

"Sorry, Warren, I didn't see you come in," replied Joanne.

"No problem at all," said Warren. "I like someone who shows a bit of spirit and punch. As for your problem, I am free most of the morning, so whenever you are ready."

"Thank you, I'll be with you in a few minutes," she replied.

Joanne checked in with the reception desk, letting them know that she would be in with Warren, then she went to the kitchen to make two cups of coffee. On the way to Warren's office, she stopped off at her desk to pick up the letter she had typed and placed it in the envelope that she had prepared. She knocked on Warren's office door and entered, placing the coffee on his desk as she sat in the chair opposite him.

"Well, what's the problem?" he asked.

"Well, I'm sorry, but I feel I have no alternative but to tender my resignation," she said as she slid the envelope across the desk towards him.

"Refused," said Warren as he ripped the envelope in half and threw it in the bin.

"But you didn't even read it, so you don't know my reasons!" protested Joanne.

"I don't need to and I am certainly not letting you go without a fight, something you need to encompass in your private life. When I walked past your desk, you asked why life had to be so hard – well, it is only hard if you let it be. You know, I learnt many years ago from an engineer friend of mine when we were looking at some plans together. I commented on what then appeared to be a major problem with them. Would you like to guess his reply?" asked Warren.

"Sorry, I wouldn't know."

"He said there are never problems, only obstacles, and when you think about it, it is true because once you remove the obstacle, the problem disappears. Anyway, what do you intend doing about the obstacle or, in your case, obstacles?" he asked.

"I am not sure yet."

"So, you thought that rather than deal with the obstacle you would just leave? Well, it doesn't work like that. You are here to do a job, a job which I know you can do, so just get on and do it. I will back you 100 per cent because I trust you," said Warren.

"But what about the Saunders case. I took my eye off the ball for a minute and look what's happened! You are aware of the major problem we have there, aren't you?"

"Well, yes, one of our clients has been incarcerated for a term of not less than five years, but why? We both read the reports and there was nothing in them that warranted such a heavy sentence, so you need to sort it out. As for your private matter, that doesn't warrant you resigning, everyone during their life has family problems, they are no different to business problems, so identify the obstacle and remove it."

"Yes, well, about that – I am afraid you will have to put the redecoration of the offices on the back burner for now. Tom's accident caused him to have a bleed on the brain. He has had an operation to stop the bleed and relieve the pressure, but he is still in hospital and will need a recovery time of maybe two to three months," said Joanne.

"Okay, the redecoration is on hold – not a problem. And if Tom is still in hospital after such a serious accident, then what the hell are you doing here?" he asked.

"Well, I have urgent work to do here!" she replied.

"Excuses! You have the best laptop money can buy. You can do everything from home that you can do here," he quite pointedly remarked. "So what is the *real* reason you are here?"

"He doesn't want me, Warren. He can't love me because he is still in love with his wife."

"But hang on a minute, didn't you say his wife died in an accident?"

"Yes, five years ago, along with his son. The other thing is, his name is not Tom, Tom's his son's name. He's been using his son's name which just adds complications to everything," explained Joanne.

Warren looked troubled. "So what's his real name then? Did you find out."

"Yes, I had to look through some boxes he has stored in the barn; his real name is Raymond James Maddox," replied Joanne.

Joanne sat there, waiting for Warren to say something but he was quiet, just staring at her, no expression on his face nothing, just a blank look.

"Are you okay, Warren? You don't look well."

"I'm fine," came the answer. "I will be okay in a few minutes."

When Warren finally broke the silence, his concerns were solely for Tom and how it was Joanne's responsibility to help him recover and to overcome the debilitating memory of his wife.

"Joanne, look I understand Jason Saunders is behind bars when he shouldn't be, and he is still our responsibility, and yes, I do expect you to find out what went wrong. However, as unfortunate as it is, there is now a process which we must follow and the appeals process cannot be rushed. Even if we were to produce extenuating circumstances, I doubt it would change things immediately, but I am sure you know that. What you must do though is to help your partner recover. I know you are telling me he can't love you, but I am sure that is just because he is not allowing his wife's death to be finalised and he needs help to do that. That person has got to be you, Joanne, because you know that you love him, and it is only someone that loves him unconditionally who can help him."

"Yes, I know you're right. Thank you, Warren," replied Joanne. "Look, I know you have to go out, but going back to the Saunders case, there was nothing wrong with the report that Jefferey compiled; we both read it, I would have expected eighteen months at worst but was hoping for nine months, less time served in custody which would mean he would be free almost immediately. I could not find any process of appeal which should have been requested by Jefferey or a full transcript of the case and as for the judge's summing up of the report, I find that quite absurd. I have now requested all of those and will start my investigation into what went wrong as soon as I have them."

Warren thought for a while, then said, "Do you not feel you should ask Jefferey first before looking into the trial transcripts?"

"No. I know for sure there is something strange about this, so I want all the information in front of me before I tackle him," replied Joanne.

"Sounds good to me. You know exactly what you have to do and, as I said earlier, I will back you up one hundred per cent."

"Thank you. I will start my investigation as soon as I have all the information I need from the court. Just so that you know, when you walked past my desk this morning and heard me make that comment out loud, it was not directed at work. I had just spoken to the sister on the ward where Tom is being treated, and she asked me the same thing that you asked me: she asked me to help Tom. Thank you for your very positive advice," said Joanne as she opened the door of Warren's office and went back to her desk.

She sat down and picked up her phone, pressing the fast dial button; she didn't have to wait long before the phone was answered.

"Acute Medical, how may I help you?" asked the voice at the other end.

"Hello, sorry to trouble you, it's Joanne Webster again. Would it be possible for me to speak with the ward sister please."

"Hold the line please, I'll transfer you."

"Joanne, how can I help you?" said the ward sister.

"I was just wondering if there is anything I need to bring in for Tom when I come?"

"You're coming? That is incredibly good news! I won't tell him, I'll let it be a surprise. A change of clothes would be good and maybe some shaving things. What made you change your mind?" she asked.

"My boss agreed with you that I should help Tom as much as I can, so I couldn't argue. I will be in later, maybe about mid-afternoon so that I can stay for a while."

"Don't forget what I said, Joanne. You can stay all night, so please think seriously about it."

"Okay, thank you, I'll see you later."

Joanne walked through the office to the lobby area to speak to one of the receptions.

"Hi, Therese, how are you today?" asked Joanne.

"Thankfully it has been fairly quiet so far Joanne, not many people in the office today; how is your partner – Tom, isn't it?" she asked.

"He will be okay, thank you, the injury wasn't as bad as they first thought, and if his tests show clear tomorrow, he should be out on Friday," replied Joanne.

"Oh, that will be good, just in time to be together for the weekend."

"That's what I came to see you about. I spoke to Warren this morning and we agreed that I could do most of my work from home or the hospital, so I won't be about as much. If anyone wants me, I will either be reached via email or on my mobile. I will be leaving soon to go to the hospital, but you shouldn't be too lonely this afternoon as those people who were on a course this morning should be back around lunchtime. We haven't got any clients due in apart from Mrs Saunders," added Joanne.

"She's cancelled; she rang earlier and said there has been a last-minute change of plans," said Therese.

"Oh okay, so you shouldn't be bothered by anything this afternoon, then. Have you heard from Jefferey today? I thought he was meant to be processing all the files from the Saunders case?"

"Yes, I have, he phoned to say he has a stomach upset and probably won't be in today. Did you want to talk to him?" she asked.

"Oh no, I was just going to ask him if I could look at the files, that's all, but there's no rush. I'm not sure when I will be in again, but Warren knows where I am," said Joanne as she left and headed home.

CHAPTER SIXTEEN

Help is Needed

Joanne got in her car; the hospital was only minutes away, but she needed to go back to her house first. She wanted to change out of her work clothes and put on something a little more suitable, something that she hoped would catch Tom's eye.

While on her way home, she remembered that the sister had asked her to bring a change of clothes for Tom, along with his shaving gear. He had very few clothes in the house, so she would have to go to the barn to find something for him to change into. She decided to check there first and so she drove down and pulled up outside the barn doors.

Joanne looked around but she didn't find a lot. She started to open some of the boxes. Although most were full of documents and photos, there were a few boxes, containing women's clothes, some of which were quite suggestive. Joanne didn't know if his wife had worn them, or if they were used by the models when creating her photo shoots. But if they *had* been Anne's … is that what Tom would like *her* to wear, she wondered. If it would help him to get over the loss of his wife, then she was prepared to try it.

She picked out a few of Tom's clothes, mainly T-shirts and shorts, and having placed them in a bag she took them with her to the car and then drove up to the house. She went straight to her bedroom, undressed and grabbed a towel from the wardrobe before going to the bathroom to take a quick shower. Once out, she dried herself off and walked back into her bedroom to sort out some clothes to wear. Having decided on a sheer, loose-fitting bodice with ties down the front and a free-flowing skirt, she placed them neatly on the bed before choosing something to change into for the next day, just in case she was asked to stay with Tom overnight again. She placed her change of clothes in a small bag before getting dressed and then checking in the full-length mirror to make sure that her choice of clothes was not too risqué for the hospital, she went back into the bathroom, threw her wet towel in the wash basket, and picked up some toiletries. She then placed everything in a backpack and made her way downstairs.

She got in her car and drove straight to the hospital, parked, and made her way through to the Acute Medical Ward, pressed the entrance bell and waited for the door to be opened for her. Instead of going straight to Tom's room, she first went to the ward sister's office to see if she was still there.

"Joanne, I'm so pleased that you managed to make it back here, thank you."

"How is Tom?" asked Joanne.

"Well, he was responding well, as you know, but then later this morning he showed signs of a relapse: he stopped talking, he is drinking but refusing food. We need to try to get him back on the road to recovery as soon as possible, Joanne, the pressure is building up and it's not good; it could cause another bleed."

"Is that my fault Matron?" asked Joanne again.

"No, Joanne, we're not here to play a blame game, our only concern is to get Tom better as soon as possible and to do all we can to aid his recovery. You have already done more than enough; without you, he would be dead and that is a fact. But although you have done so much, we are asking you to do more, to go the extra mile, if you like, for Tom. Because without you he is in real danger of going backwards. We know it is hard for you, but what you must realise is that when Tom is telling you that he doesn't want you, that he doesn't love you and that you cannot have a relationship with him, that is not Tom speaking; it's his late wife playing on his mind. Joanne, mental illness is one of the biggest killers in this country and it is often worse for men than it is for women. Most women have someone they can confide in, someone to tell their problems to and gain help. For men, it is different; they are meant to be strong, they are supposed to act like *men*, not whimpering women. They don't have a close person to talk to, so they hide their problems within themselves, forming a buffer, until that barrier brakes, then all hell lets loose. For now, we as a medical team are asking for your help; you are the one link that can help Tom recover. Yes, we can still do everything we would normally do without you, but you are the one who loves him and who can guide him. Joanne, will you help us? Will you help Tom?"

Joanne wiped the tears from her eyes; it hurt her so much now to know that she had walked out on him earlier, but it hadn't fully sunk in what he was going through, but the way the sister explained everything made it much easier for her to understand, which, she guessed, was why she was a sister.

"Yes, of course. I'll do everything I can. Tom will have to push me out before I leave that room," replied Joanne.

"Thank you, thank you so much," added the sister. "Come on, let's go and tell Tom he has a visitor."

Joanne followed her towards Tom's room where she knocked on the door before entering. Joanne stood outside waiting.

"How are you feeling now, Tom?" asked the sister.

"I'll be okay," he replied.

"That is not what I asked you, Tom. I need to know how you are feeling now and if you are in the right frame of mind to have a visitor"

"Who is it?" asked Tom. "I don't need any visitors."

The sister beckoned Joanne to move forward and stand in the doorway.

"What, not even this one?"

Tom looked towards the doorway when he saw who his visitor was.

He moved his hands to his eyes as if to wipe away the tears. Then he flung his arms out wide in front of him as Joanne rushed forward and filled the gap between them.

"Thank you, thank you so much!" he said and then he kissed her full on her lips and didn't stop for at least five minutes.

The sister pulled the blind down on the window for some privacy as she closed the door and left them to it.

Joanne freed herself from Tom's clutches and stood there in front of him.

"Do you like my outfit?" she asked as she twirled around and then turned back to face him.

"Wow," he said. "Yes, absolutely stunning."

She turned so her back was towards him and said, "What about if I take off this little jacket? Does that improve your view?"

She placed the jacket on the chair and then turned around to face him.

"Do you like what you see now?" she asked him.

"Oh yes, I like that very much, thank you. You are perfect. Come here, let me cuddle you again," he said, holding his arms out.

Joanne shook her head and said, "Wait, one more thing."

"What is it?" he asked. "What thing?"

Joanne stood there, her arms outstretched like a ballet dancer, then she began to pirouette, and as she did so, the hem of her skirt ballooned out and lifted to her waist revealing the tiniest of thongs.

"How does that look now, Tom?" she asked.

"Stunning, absolutely stunning! I just don't know what to say, no words I can utter could ever explain your beauty," he said as he held out his arms once again, enticing her to move forward and into his clutches. He slid his hands down her back and then up under her skirt, to the firm cheeks of her bottom, squeezing and caressing the naked flesh. Releasing his grasp on her cheeks, he slid his hands up under her blouse, tracing the contours of her body then sliding his hands to the front as he gently caressed her naked breasts.

Joanne pulled away and took his hands in hers.

"Hey, they told me you are not to get excited for at least two to three months, so you will just have to control yourself for now," she said as she leant forward and kissed him.

"Then why dress as you have?" he asked.

"Because I love you and I wanted to please you," she replied.

"Well, you have certainly done that," he replied. "Thank you, Joanne. I love you so much, but I just don't know how I can prove it to you."

"I know, but don't worry about that now, all you need to concern yourself with is how to get better. That is, of course, the main reason for me dressing in this fashion. I have to give the doctors a report every day on how you are progressing, so I needed to wear something that was sure to catch your attention so that I could gauge your reaction," she said as she sat on the edge of the bed and then lay down beside him to cuddle him. Joanne felt so good to be back next to him; it was where she belonged.

They lay there quietly in each other's arms for a while before Joanne spoke seriously to him.

"Tom, please don't tell me that you don't love me or that you can't love me because of Anne. I know you loved her with all your heart, and I am not asking you to forget her or to love me with the passion and fervour that you loved her; all I am asking is that you are true to yourself and true to me. I am here not only because I love you, but because I want to be here and I want to help you get better."

She lay there expecting him to say something, but the silence was deafening; perhaps the truth had struck home at last.

"Tom," she said as she looked at him. "Oh well, that explains a lot – you're asleep."

She eased herself off the bed, trying not to wake him; she picked up her jacket and put it back on.

On the way back to Tom's room she made herself a coffee and picked up a couple of biscuits. Seeing the sister in her office she knocked on her door; looking up, the sister beckoned to Joanne to enter.

"Tom is sleeping now. I just wanted to say thank you for being so understanding, you have helped me to acknowledge my place in all of this and to realise that it is in Tom's best interest for me to be here. Thank you."

The sister smiled as she replied.

"Well, the gamble paid off because he's asleep! He's has been so irritable all day, but as soon as you arrive, he's sleeping peacefully. Well done!"

"I could stay tonight if you need me to. I have brought a change of clothes for myself as well as for Tom, and apart from nipping home at some stage tomorrow for a shower, I can be here all day then too. I have my laptop with me so I can do some work and keep in touch with what is happening in the office. Anyway, I just wanted to say thank you, and I am sorry for taking up so much of your precious time. I will go back to Tom now, just in case he wakes up and wonders where I am. I don't want him thinking I have gone again."

"Joanne, that is what I am here for, but it needs us all to pull together, yes Tom is out of immediate danger, but we all saw how quickly that changed when you told him you were no longer prepared to stay with him. We are worried as he is showing signs of mental stress that rekindle his thoughts after that terrible crash. When you walked out, he suddenly realised he was on his own again, which was not good seeing what he has just been through. That is why it is important that he knows you are here," explained the ward sister.

Joanne left the sister's office and went back to Tom's room, where thankfully he was still sleeping peacefully so he hadn't missed her. She sat down and took out her laptop; she was urgently waiting for the transcripts of the Saunders case, and she was hoping they had arrived. Looking through her emails, there was one from the court, but it didn't have all the attachments she wanted, though it had the most important one and that was the defence report which had been presented to the court by Jefferey.

Joanne downloaded the document file that the court had sent her and opened it on her laptop. She read it through twice, but from what she could remember the file she had in front of her now was not the one that Jefferey had shown her, and it definitely wasn't the one that Warren agreed to. She made sure she was connected to her desktop and then searched for the copy she had taken of Jefferey's report, but it wasn't there. She knew exactly where she had saved it, but it had disappeared. This was weird … she couldn't understand it.

She opened messenger. *That's good, Therese is still on-line.*
'Hi Therese, not many bodies in the office today. I can't see Susan online – has she been in today?'
'Hi Joanne, no she was finishing off her training module at home, and she has already submitted it.'
'Okay, not a problem. Is Warren still there?'
'No, he left about an hour ago.'
'Therese, I am going to try to get into the office tomorrow for a couple of hours as I need to speak with Warren and Susan. I can contact Warren myself to see when he will be in, but could you contact Susan and ask her to let me know what time she will be available for me to meet with her tomorrow? Thanks'

Joanne was trying to come to terms with the fact that it appeared very much as though Jefferey had either sent the wrong report to the court by mistake, which she thought was very unlikely, or he had deliberately sent the wrong information which, if correct, was a serious offence. Both scenarios would require further and immediate action which Joanne would have to instigate. Part of the immediate action required would be to get everyone to change their passwords; she drafted a short email to everyone and sent it out.

'Dear colleagues, it has been drawn to my attention that our password security system may have been hacked, which poses a serious breach and needs to be corrected immediately. You are now all required to change your passwords with immediate effect. Thank you, Joanne Webster.'

Joanne was interrupted by the sound of Tom's voice: he was awake.

"Hey, what are you doing?" he asked.

"Wow, Tom! You had a good sleep. How do you feel now?" she asked.

"Good, thank you, Joanne," came the reply. "Are you going to stay with me all night tonight?" he asked.

"Yes, I'm sorry, but you are going to have to put up with me all night. Is that a problem for you?" asked Joanne.

Tom delayed his answer; Joanne could tell he was thinking of something to say.

"No, of course not, except that I would rather be awake so that I can watch you, since sleeping seems such a waste when you are here," replied Tom.

"I know, and I very much like you watching me too, but there is a time and a place for everything, and this is neither the time nor the place," replied Joanne with a huge smile on her face.

Joanne's reply brought a smile to Tom's face too, something that had been missing for a day or two.

"Is that so?" asked Tom. "Do you honestly like me watching you?"

"Yes, Tom, I do, it makes me feel good. I can almost feel your eyes continually focused on my body and it sends tingles down my spine," she replied.

"Wow, thank you. I love watching you, not only when you are naked though. I love watching you all the time, the way you move, the way you do things; it excites me."

"Okay, mister, time to change the subject. *No excitement* is what the doctor ordered, which is what the patient has to accept," she replied.

"Now you are being a spoilsport," said Tom.

Joanne had closed her laptop to concentrate on Tom. She put it back in her backpack and placed it on the floor by her chair.

"Tom, I need to ask you some questions, is that okay?" she asked,

Tom looked worried by her request. "What questions?"

"Okay, what questions? Just some general questions about the past because the doctors have asked me to, just to see if the accident has caused any loss of memory," she replied.

"Okay, fire away," he replied.

"Do you have any siblings?"

"No! Just little old me."

"Where are your parents?"

"They are both dead now. They married late, they were both in their early fifties when they married and in their late fifties when I arrived and I was their only child."

"What is your very first recollection?"

"Being in a cot, in a small room and seeing my parents come in, all dressed in white and wearing face masks."

"Scary," replied Joanne.

"Tell me about it," replied Tom. "That is why I remember it, and according to my mother I was only six months old. I was born with enlarged tonsils and adenoids and had to have them removed."

"Where did you live as a child?"

"On a farm."

"Well, you seem to have answered those questions without any problems. How did you get here? To the hospital?"

"In your car, I think. I can remember getting in the car, and vomiting I think, then the next thing I remember is being woken after the operation."

"Yes, it was my car, and you are right, you did vomit. The reason you can't remember anything after that is because you were unconscious. You passed out while we were still on the way here in the car."

"Are we nearly finished, Joanne, or can we continue this later? I am feeling very tired again, not sure why," said Tom.

"Yes, sure, we can finish now. You did very well and don't worry too much about the fact you keep feeling tired; sleeping is part of your recovery. The doctor told me that you would probably sleep a lot more than usual. Sleep now and we can do this tomorrow, when you have more energy."

"Thank you, Joanne. Can you promise me that you won't leave while I'm sleeping?" he asked.

She walked over to the bed and sat down on the chair. Leaning forward, she took Tom's hand in hers and said, "I promise you; I will not go anywhere, apart from the bathroom, that is," she replied.

"Thank you, Joanne. I want to get better and to do that I need you to be here to help me," replied Tom.

"And what about after you are better, Tom? Will you still need me then?" asked Joanne.

"I will always need you," he replied.

"Would you like me to cuddle you, Tom?" she asked.

"Yes please, I would like that very much," he replied. Joanne sat on the edge of the bed, swung her legs up onto the bed and lay down by his side. She placed her arm over his chest and cuddled up to him.

She was pleased with the way that he had responded to the questions she had asked him; it appeared to show that he had not suffered any major memory loss owing to his accident. While she lay there next to him, he drifted off and she thought she may as well take the opportunity to catch up on some sleep herself.

CHAPTER SEVENTEEN

Awkward Times

Joanne hadn't slept well; the bed wasn't exactly comfortable, but what disturbed her sleep most was the nurse coming in every so often to check on Tom; even so, she still woke up early. Tom was still sleeping, so she let the nurses know that she would take the opportunity to go to the bathroom to take a quick shower. Ten minutes later, she was back in the room to relieve the nurse who had been watching him while she showered. She quickly got dressed and sat waiting for him to wake up and deal with whatever the day had in store for her.

She picked up the chair and moved it from the side of the bed over to the window, then connected her laptop and logged in. There were no new messages or emails which gave her time to completely read through the documents that she had received from the court. It became clear to her that had Jefferey submitted the correct document, there was no way a sentence of five years could have been handed down.

Joanne knew now she needed to go into the office to speak firstly to Susan, who may be able to throw some light on what was a very worrying incident, and secondly and most importantly to discuss the next proceedings with Warren. First, though, she had to arrange her day around Tom, and he would be awake soon as it was at about this time that the nurses came to do their rounds.

She was just moving the chair back by the side of the bed when she noticed that Tom was stirring and opening his eyes.

"Good morning, Tom. How are you feeling this morning?" she asked.

"I feel quite good, no headache at the moment," he replied.

"That is good news. I think you're allowed to get out of bed today. I brought you in a change of clothes so maybe we can take you for a shower," said Joanne.

"A shower would be nice. Are you sure it will be okay?" asked Tom as he started to get out of bed.

"No, don't get out just yet, you are still connected to a monitor and I need to check with the nurses first to make sure it's okay to get you out of bed," she explained.

She left the room to find a nurse.

"Excuse me, nurse, I think the sister said yesterday that it would be okay for Tom to get up today, but I just want to check if that's still the case?" she asked.

"Yes, that's fine. We're going to come along soon to get him up and sit him in the chair for a while," replied the nurse.

"Will it be okay if he has a shower as I have brought some clean clothes in for him?"

"Yes, that will be fine as long as you are going to be there with him and remember not to allow the force of the shower to be directed onto his head," replied the nurse.

"Okay, thank you, as soon as you are ready to help me get him out of bed, I'll take him to the bathroom," replied Joanne.

Joanne went back to the room with a skip in her step.

"Okay, mister, you are allowed up and you can also have a shower, but we have to wait for the nurses to come and get you out of bed, then I can take you," she told him as he laid back against the pillows on his bed. "So just rest there for now and they'll be in shortly to get you up."

It was only a few minutes later when there was a knock on the door and one of the nurses entered the room.

"Good morning, Tom. It's your lucky day! You're allowed to get out of bed today to have a shower, but we just have to check your readings first to make sure everything is okay and then we will get you up," said the nurse.

"Is he okay?" asked Joanne when she saw that the nurse was writing some notes on his chart.

"Yes, everything would appear to be fine. Well done, Tom, I'll just fetch the ward sister as she wants to be present when we get you out of bed," said the nurse.

Joanne waited until the nurse had left the room before she walked over to the bed and gave Tom a lingering kiss on the lips.

"You are marvellous, Tom. You are making such a good recovery now. Well done," said Joanne as she stood upright and took a couple of steps back from the bed.

Tom held out his arms to her, beckoning her to come towards him. Joanne moved back closer to him and she felt his arms wrap around her waist.

"I love you, Miss Webster," he said as he kissed her.

Joanne pulled away, breaking their kiss.

"Are you sure, Mr. Maddox?" she asked.

"I am now, Miss Webster. I couldn't have done this without you. Thank you for believing in me, thank you for coming back, thank you for wanting to love me, thank you for being you, and …"

"That is quite enough thank yous for now, Mr. Maddox, all I want is your love, not your words," she replied as she stood there, looking at him, tears forming in her eyes once more.

At that moment, the door opened, and the ward sister came in followed by the nurse.

"Come on then, Tom, let's get you out of that bed and see what you're made of," said the sister.

Joanne moved to the far side of the room so she could dry her eyes discreetly, then she turned around and watched as Tom swung his legs around and sat on the edge of the bed. He then put his feet on the ground and stood up.

"Wow, that feels good," he said as he took a few steps with the help of the nurses guiding his movement.

"Do you feel okay?" asked the sister.

"I feel fine, thank you," he replied.

"Okay, now turn around and walk over to where Joanne is standing," said the sister as she released her hold on his arm and left him to walk on his own.

"Are you okay, Tom?" asked Joanne as he appeared to wobble a little.

"Yes, I'm fine," replied Tom. "Where is the shower room?"

"It's straight across the passage, Tom," commented the sister. "I think we can leave him in your hands now, Joanne," she added as she left the room.

"Okay, Mr. Maddox, time to get you in the shower," said Joanne.

"Oh, that sounds promising," replied Tom as they walked towards the door.

"Hey, I told you about that last night, Tom – no excitement."

Tom had his shower and got dressed and was back in his room just as they were serving breakfast. The staff offered Joanne something too, but she said she would get something later. Tom sat on the chair eating his breakfast while Joanne placed both sets of dirty clothes in a bag and then put them in her holdall.

She was all set to go to the office, she just wanted to wait for Tom to finish his breakfast and then she would check with the ward sister that it was okay. She also wanted to tell her about his answers to the prepared questions she had asked him earlier.

Tom had almost finished his breakfast when the nurse came in to let Joanne know that the ward sister was now in her office.

"Okay, I'm just going to see the ward sister to tell her how you got on with the questions I had to ask you last night. I'll only be a few minutes."

Joanne knocked on the sister's door and waited to be called in.

"Joanne, so, how is Tom doing?" she asked.

"He appears to be doing okay. Here are the answers he gave to the distant memory questions. I didn't ask him the other set as he was getting tired and wanted to sleep."

"No problem, thank you for these. He gave some very good responses."

"Yes, I was quite surprised but at the same time very pleased for him," replied Joanne. "I know I said I was going to be here all day, but I have to go into the office for about an hour this morning. I hope that will be okay."

The Matron looked up at her. "But yes of course. What time do you intend going?"

"I was thinking of going now so that I am back for when the doctors do their rounds," replied Joanne.

"That would be good if you can do that; they usually come at about eleven, but I have a message here saying that they expect it to be about eleven-thirty today. Do you think you could be back by then?" she asked.

"Yes, I would very much hope so," replied Joanne.

"Okay then, I'll see you later."

"Yes, thank you, sister," replied Joanne.

Joanne went back to Tom's room to let him know that she just had to pop into the office for an hour or so, but that she would be back before the doctors did their rounds.

"That's okay," said Tom. "Just as long as you do come back."

"Of course I'll be back, mister. I have to get you better and then wait the two or three months until I can excite you," said Joanne as she leant forward and kissed him goodbye. "I'll see you soon, don't worry, bye," she said as she closed the door behind her. She called at the nurses' station to make sure that one of them would be able to stay with Tom while she went to the office.

Joanne rushed down to her car and made the short trip to her office. As she pulled into the car park, she could see Susan's and Warren's cars but no sign of Jefferey's. Not to worry, she thought, as she didn't need to see him today anyway and if she was correct in her thinking, she needed to gather more evidence anyway.

Joanne pushed the buzzer on the main door and walked up into the office.

"Good morning, Therese," she said as she walked past the reception desk.

"Oh, Joanne," she called. "Jefferey rang in this morning and he said he would not be in until Monday as his upset stomach still hadn't cleared up."

"Okay, thank you for that, Therese. No problem, I guess we'll see him when he is ready," she commented as she continued her walk through the office. Next, she stopped at Susan's desk.

"Good morning, Susan. Could I have a word with you when you are ready?" asked Joanne.

"Yes of course, just give me five minutes, please," replied Susan.

"Okay, no problem, bring a drink with you if you want one," remarked Joanne.

Joanne put her laptop down on her desk and then went to see Warren.

"Good morning, Warren. Are you going to be available for the next thirty minutes to an hour?" she asked.

"Joanne, of course. I always have time for you. Have you got something for me?" he asked.

"Yes, I think I have but let me speak to Susan first. Did you take a scan of Jefferey's original report by the way?"

"Yes, as always. I'm very surprised that you didn't, though," remarked Warren.

"Yes, me too! But can we discuss that when I come back please?" asked Joanne.

Joanne went to the kitchen area to get herself a coffee, and by the time she arrived back at her desk Susan was already there waiting for her.

"Susan, I'm so sorry to keep you waiting – I just had to sort something out with Warren. Just give me a couple of minutes to get my desk top up and running. While we are waiting, what I want to ask you has nothing to do with you, but I just need you to think back to a few days ago when I asked you to cover my urgent work. I know you would have had to come here to use my PC. Did you at any time walk away from it and leave my desktop on? It is not a criticism as I know we all do it."

"I'm sorry, Joanne, has something happened?"

"I believe so, Susan. I had a court report on my PC, but now it has gone, and I am not sure how it disappeared or got deleted, it just doesn't make any sense. So, can you think again of what happened when you were using my PC – did anyone distract you?"

"I'm sorry, Joanne, I just can't think," replied Susan. "But you think someone used your PC to delete an important file?" she asked.

"That's about it, Susan, yes, and there is no way it was done accidentally, either," replied Joanne.

"How do you mean? Are you saying it's an inside job, someone in this office?" she asked.

"Yes, Susan, that's exactly what I am saying, but for now I know I can trust you not to mention a word of this to anyone else. I need to find out who it is – I do have my suspicions but that is all they are."

Susan sat there, ashen-faced.

"Joanne, I know I used your PC, but you allowed me to do so. I accept that I must be a suspect, but I swear it wasn't me. I would never do anything like that," replied Susan with a worrying look on her face.

Joanne was quick to dispel Susan's worries.

"Susan, believe me, you are not a suspect, so you have no need to worry about it," replied Joanne, trying to put Susan's mind at ease.

"Coffee, I need another coffee," said Susan.

"I was just thinking the same thing," remarked Joanne. "I'll get yours; how do you have it?"

"No! Wait, that's it!" said Susan with a raised voice.

"What– what's wrong?" enquired Joanne.

"How stupid of me!" shouted Susan.

Joanne stopped in her tracks and sat back down in her chair.

"What is it, Susan? Tell me!"

"I remember now! I was sitting at your desk, reading your casework reports, when I heard a voice. It was Jefferey and he said something like *Good morning, Joanne*, and then proceeded to correct himself. I can't remember exactly but something like, *Oh, you're not Joanne*. I asked him what he wanted because I was busy and did not want to make any mistakes. Then he asked why I was sitting at your desk using your PC. I told him you had asked me to cover your work because you were not going to be in. I realised he did not like me covering for you because he said something like he should have been the one to cover for you, not me. Anyway, I could see he was getting even more irate, so I asked him if he wanted coffee. I went to get him one and left him sitting in the chair where I am now. When I came back with the drink, he was standing behind your desk. He said he had been looking out of the window and then remarked how much better the view was from your office than his. I thought nothing of it. I don't know if that has any relevance to what happened to your files, but I must have been away for five or six minutes. I am sorry, Joanne, it was the coffee thing that jogged my memory."

"Thank you, Susan. Yes, that may help, but as I said before, our conversation this morning is in the strictest of confidence. I'll get you a coffee now."

Joanne came back to her desk, sliding Susan's coffee towards her.

"I hear you completed your training course and gained a distinction which doesn't happen often. Well done! My trust in you to cover for me was well-founded," said Joanne.

"Thank you, Joanne. I am hoping all the hard work will be worth it in the long run."

"In your case, Susan, I am sure it will be. Do you realise, though, that gaining a distinction at this point allows you to skip some parts of your final year and do them later which would allow you to earn a higher salary whilst completing the deferred parts of the course?" asked Joanne.

"Yes, so I believe, but I would like to complete the course fully now and then gain extra commendations later if I'm suitable."

"That's a good choice, Susan, and is exactly what I did. Keep your feet firmly on the ground and your head on your shoulders and I am sure you will have an exemplary career in front of you."

"Thank you. I was amazed at how thorough you are in your work and what a stickler for detail. I noticed both aspects while reading through your cases when you asked me to cover for you; I know I can learn a lot from you."

"I have to go and speak with Warren now, Susan. Sorry to have taken up so much of your time this morning, but you have been very helpful. It's amazing sometimes how a cup of coffee can make all the difference, if you get my meaning."

"Yes, Joanne, I get your meaning exactly," replied Susan with a grin.

Joanne picked up her cup and took it to the kitchen, then went to Warren's office. She knocked on the door and he beckoned for her to enter. He was on the phone, so she sat down on the sofa. It was further away from his desk and allowed her to sit comfortably without fully hearing his conversation.

"Sorry, Joanne, that was my wife. That's the tenth time already this morning," he commented.

"She must be missing you, Warren!" remarked Joanne.

"Either that or just trying to annoy me when she knows I'm busy," he replied with a smile on his face. "So, what have you got for me, Joanne?"

"Nothing concrete yet, I'm sorry to say, but it would appear the loose ends may come together fairly soon."

"Okay, and would you care to explain?"

"Having read Jefferey's report on the Saunders case, we both know that a five-year custody term for the crime he Saunders is accused of is nothing short of immoral, so how did it happen? Well, having requested a download of the court transcripts and also managing to get a copy of the judge's summing up, it was plain to see the judge and the jury took their decision based on a report which we had not seen. I looked for the copy of Jefferey's report on my PC but it has disappeared, and could not be put down to deleting the file in error because it has even been deleted from our cloud backup which could only be done from my PC. That is why I asked you this morning if you had a copy of the original report that Jefferey gave us. If you look through it, you will see that the report from the court and the one you have are different. That leaves the question of why Jefferey would not submit the report that we had both agreed to. Furthermore, there is the mystery of the missing report. Last week, I asked Susan to cover for me for the two days I was off. I have spoken with her this morning, and it now appears that on one of the days, Jefferey went to my office on the precept of speaking to me, but finding Susan there annoyed him. To try to placate him, Susan left him sitting in there and went to get the coffees. When she returned, Jefferey was standing behind my desk, close to my PC. He brushed it off as having been looking at the view from out of my office window. In summing up, Jefferey knew we had seen his report and he knew that I copied everything so when I was out of the office and Susan was at my PC, it allowed him time to delete the file and folder, not only from my PC but from the cloud too."

Joanne sat waiting for Warren's comments; after such a long statement, she was expecting him to raise some questions. However, after he had given her description of the events some thought, his only comment was, "That is pretty serious stuff. What do we do now?"

"The problem is, I have no concrete evidence and if I am correct in my beliefs, Jefferey will know that too. This goes deeper than his dislike or jealousy of me; there is something more worrying than that. Why would he intentionally submit a report that he knew was almost certain to end with the defendant receiving a long custodial sentence? I think we have to ask ourselves what benefit that would be to him."

"Joanne, you are very thorough, and I'm not sure what I would do without you. *Jefferey!* My God, in all my time as a solicitor, I have never worked with someone who has behaved in such a corrupt way."

"Please do remember Warren that I have no proof of all of this. I think that is where the difficulty will start: proving everything. I think I need to get a solicitor pass to visit Jason Saunders. Firstly, to apologise and to let him know we have already started the appeal process and to see if he can throw any light on this sorry business. I need to find out how he got on with Jefferey, and whether they had any disagreements."

"Yes, of course, you have to do whatever is necessary."

"There is one other thing. I am aware that things are tight at the moment, but I am hoping that you could see the benefit of appointing an assistant for me."

"Joanne, I can see the logic, but an assistant would cost substantially more than we can afford now. We would be looking at an increment of at least twelve thousand pounds a year."

"Yes, but would you think about it if the increment was more like five thousand two hundred a year?"

"Well, if you can find someone to take on the responsibility of becoming your assistant on those terms, then you are free to appoint them with my blessing."

"Thank you, Warren, thank you so much," remarked Joanne.

"Before you go – I'm feeling rather hungry. Do you have time for food in your busy schedule?" he asked.

"I have about forty minutes before I need to leave to get back to the hospital – is that okay?" she replied.

"The sandwich bar it is, then. I'll see you there."

"Okay, I'll be five minutes."

Joanne left Warren's office and went to see if Susan was still around.

"Ah Susan, could you spare me five minutes please?"

They both walked down together to Joanne's office.

"Take a seat please, Susan, this will only take a few minutes."

"Am I in some sort of trouble?" she asked nervously.

"Why would you be in trouble? Have you done something wrong?"

"Well, that business earlier – it was awkward."

"Susan, you told the truth. Anyway, let's get this over and done with, then we can both share the benefits. I took on board this morning how you said you think you could learn a lot from me."

"Yes, Joanne, I know I could, but it's getting the time."

"That's why you are here now, Susan; I desperately need an assistant and what better way could there be for someone to learn from me than to be my assistant? Do you think that post would interest you?"

"It would interest me very much, but it might mean I would have to give up my part-time job."

"So, what if there was a salary increment of one hundred pounds a week, plus a free parking space downstairs?"

"When do I start?" she asked.

"Right now – will that be okay? I will get the papers drawn up over the weekend and we can see Warren on Monday to get them signed."

With that, Joanne stood up and held out her hand towards Susan.

"Welcome! I know you will be the perfect assistant and I hope that I can be of benefit to your learning curve."

"Thank you so much, Joanne! You have no idea how much this means to me."

"Oh, I think I do Susan, and that is why I am giving you this opportunity. Oh, the other thing is I will get this copied for you," she said as she took a card out of her pocket. "It's a company benefit that allows me to spend twenty pounds a day on food while working but I never spend more than ten pounds, so we can share it. It will save you buying your lunch."

"Thank you so much! I will not let you down."

"I have to go now. I may be in the office for a while tomorrow, but if not, you have my mobile number, and I will have my laptop so you can always contact me. Oh, and best keep this to yourself until Monday when Warren will let everyone know of your new position. If I don't see you tomorrow, have a good weekend. Bye."

Joanne picked up her things and rushed down to the car park. She put everything in the boot of her car and then walked round to the sandwich bar. Warren was already halfway through his baguette when she sat down opposite him at the table.

"Sorry, took me longer than expected."

"No problem. So was, Miss Caton happy?"

"Poor girl was overwhelmed. I could hear it in her voice, but she deserves the recognition."

"Yes, I'll agree with that."

"Hang on, I didn't tell you whom I was going to offer the job to, so how did you know?"

"As you said, she deserved it. I was in the office last week when she covered for you quite admirably, she just got on with it, no problems, no tantrums, a true professional."

"Well, I'm pleased that you agree. I gave her a parking space and allowed her to share my lunchbox vouchers. I hope that's okay with you."

"I think that is the least I would have expected after such a small increment for what is a particularly important position. You have chosen well, but then that is why I chose you as an executive. So, what do you think is happening with Jefferey? I get the feeling that whatever it is, it won't be good?"

"Me too though I am not sure what he is up to. But I will find out and it will be dealt with. I am sorry Warren, but I have to get back to the hospital now to see the doctors and find out when they will release Tom."

"So, you are still calling him Tom, then? How is he doing? I do hope he will make a full recovery; give him my best wishes."

"I will thank you, and yes, it is still Tom … for now. Bye Warren."

Joanne left Warren in the sandwich bar, rushed back to her car and then drove to the hospital.

CHAPTER EIGHTEEN

Some Good News

Joanne parked her car and walked straight through to the Acute Medical Ward; she hoped she was on time as it was twenty minutes past eleven, so the doctors' rounds would soon be finishing.

She pressed the buzzer on the wall by the side of the ward door and waited to be let in. She couldn't see any signs of the doctors but as she walked past the ward sister's office on the way to Tom's room, she heard voices. She thought that it might be the doctors, already discussing their patients.

Joanne opened the door to Tom's room; he was lying on the bed, asleep. She walked quietly over to him and kissed him gently on his forehead. He stirred momentarily, so she kissed him again, but this time nothing. She went over to the sink and washed her hands which were rather sticky after eating the baguette in the sandwich bar.

She walked back over to the bed; she wanted to make sure that Tom was awake when the doctors came round. She leant over and kissed him, but this time on his lips, a long lingering kiss. At the same time, she moved her hand under the bed covers and slid it down to his groin, which did the trick. Now he was returning her kiss and placing his hands around her waist and pulling her towards him.

"I hope you are not trying to excite me," he said.

"Of course not! Whatever gave you that idea? I was just making sure you were still alive," she replied.

"And what did you find?"

"Something that requires further investigation, but unfortunately not right now."

"I was waiting for you to come back, but you were a long time. I must have fallen asleep; is there a problem at work?" asked Tom.

"Nothing for you to concern yourself with. You don't need to worry about my work, it will all get sorted," replied Joanne. "But you probably needed the sleep. I was told that it was likely you would be sleeping a lot more than usual, but I'm here now, and I needed to wake you up before the doctors do their rounds. We need to know what progress you are making and when you will be allowed to come home."

Tom looked at her as he clasped her hand in his.

"I can't wait, Joanne. I know you have tried to be here with me as much as possible, but when you are not here, I miss you so much," he replied.

"Wow, thank you! Are you sure?" asked Joanne.

"Yes, I am sure. If I didn't have you in my life, I'd be sleeping in doorways or under the pier because life would mean nothing to me."

"Hey, come on, cheer up! I'm here with you and that is where I am staying," replied Joanne.

"But your work – it is important to you, too. Let me guess: is it Jefferey causing a problem again?"

Just then, the moment they had been waiting for had arrived: the door opened and in walked the ward sister along with a selection of doctors. It looked like the whole medical team; the room was heaving with barely any air left to breathe.

The ward sister started off the proceedings as she introduced Joanne to the doctors.

"This is Joanne, Mr Maddox's partner. She has been a great help and has managed to stay with Mr Maddox for most of the time."

"Thank you for the introduction, Sister," said one of the doctors who then looked in the direction of Tom and Joanne as he continued speaking.

"I am Dr Will Grey, and this is Dr Jenny Walsh from the neurological team. You have had a miraculous escape, Mr Maddox. The head injury you received was quite nasty, a heavy impact with a solid object and a deep wound. You suffered a substantial bleed on the brain and although re-gaining consciousness after the initial accident, you lost consciousness again soon after, which was caused by the pressure building up from the bleed. After the initial tests were carried out, it was decided to operate immediately to relieve building pressure and you did regain consciousness soon after, which was a good sign. Since then, you have made steady progress every day, another good sign. In cases such as yours, we are looking for continued timely progress with no setbacks and although you did have a brief period of no response, we have been informed by Sister Evans that this was not due to your injury but by outside influences and we have accepted that. You have shown no signs of any short- or long-term memory loss and although you are still at an early stage in your recovery, we are prepared to let you continue to recover in your own home."

The doctor continued.

"There are of course stipulations that must be adhered to; if not, you may well end up back here, but we will give you a list of dos and don'ts before you leave. Do you have any questions?"

"Only one, doctor," replied Tom. "When can I leave?"

"You have to give us time to get everything together for you, but I should think by four o'clock," said Dr Grey.

"Thank you very much," replied Tom.

With that, Dr Grey turned to Joanne.

"Joanne, Sister has told me how you have done everything asked of you to aide Mr Maddox's recovery and that is one reason why we are prepared to release him from our care at this early stage. We feel that he would make more rapid progress in your care and in his own home. However, and this is a major factor, this does come with some quite stringent rules which do have to be adhered to by the letter. Sister will issue you with a full list of what Mr Maddox can and can't do, and I cannot impress on you enough the need to follow everything that will be on that list. It is a tall order, I know, but I am looking for your total commitment regarding the recovery program."

Joanne looked at Tom and then at the doctor and to his team.

"Yes, of course, I certainly understand the need for my full cooperation and I have already made arrangements at work which will allow me to work from home whilst having my newly appointed assistant cover any office-based problems. In a dire emergency, should one arise, and I must leave the house, I have today arranged that my aunt will be at home with Tom. I hope that will give you the confidence to implement your proposed release of Tom to home care," replied Joanne.

"That sounds perfect; you appear to have covered every eventuality. If you have no other questions at this time, then I think we can move on, Sister."

"Excuse me, Dr Grey," said Joanne. "Do you have any idea exactly how long the recovery procedures you mentioned will be in place for?"

"Not too long, but it will depend solely on how well you implement everything that is on the guideline sheet that we will give you. However, as a minimum, four weeks, but it could be longer, depending on the progress made. Anything else you would like to know?"

Joanne looked at Tom, who shook his head.

"No thank you, doctor, I think you have covered everything for now," replied Joanne.

"Great. Well, we wish you all the best Mr Maddox and I'll look forward to seeing you at your outpatients follow up appointment."

Once they had all left the room, Joanne walked over to Tom and gave him a hug.

"Well done, Tom, you have been terrific. We'll soon have you better once we get you home."

"But four weeks, it is too long! I can't wait, I want you now, I want it all," he replied as he kissed her hard on her lips.

Joanne responded in kind but broke off their kisses after a minute or two.

"Hey, remember what the doctor said, no getting excited! You will just have to wait. Then, when the time is right, we will see what happens."

"Thank you, Joanne," commented Tom.

"Thank you? What for? Why are you saying thank you?" she questioned.

"For putting your trust in me, when we are still not sure what will happen," he replied.

"It's simple, Tom. I love you, no matter what happens. We will work it out together."

Tom was about to kiss her when they were interrupted by a knock on the door.

"Lunchtime," said the nurse as she brought in Tom's food on a tray. "What would you like to drink?"

"Tea, please," replied Tom.

Joanne got up and leant over towards Tom and kissed him on his forehead.

"While you are having your lunch, I will pop home and pick up some clothes for you to wear for going home later. I'll be back as soon as I can."

"Okay, see you later," replied Tom.

Joanne went straight down to the car park and got in her car. She was on the way home when her phone rang; it was Susan.

"Hi Susan, I am driving at the moment. How can I help? Is there a problem?"

"Sorry, Joanne, I didn't want to bother you, but something has been playing on my mind all day and I decided that I had to mention it to you."

"Okay, so what's the problem, Susan?"

"I was taking little Billy to my mum's this morning, but the road was blocked, badly parked cars again; so, I had to take a detour. I noticed as I was driving there was a small removal van outside the block where the

Saunders live."

"Okay, maybe just coincidence. How many families live in that block?"

"Oh, I don't think it was coincidence, Joanne," she replied.

"Why? What makes you think that then?" asked Joanne.

"Well, a small sofa was being loaded into the van, and I noticed that Mrs Saunders had someone to help – it was Jefferey!"

"Jefferey! I very much hope you were mistaken, Susan! Maybe just someone who looked like him as you drove past?"

"That's what I thought at first too, but when I turned in to the next road, Jefferey's car was parked just around the corner."

"Have you mentioned this to anyone else, Susan," asked Joanne.

"No, I haven't told a soul, except for you, of course."

"That's good, Susan, we need to keep it that way, for now. Just make a note on your PC that you have told me but make sure you password protect it. There is not much we can do for now, but thank you. This all sounds very suspect."

Joanne pulled up outside the house and took her laptop and dirty clothes from the boot of the car. She left the whole lot in the kitchen, then went upstairs and collected the dirty clothes and towels from the bedroom, rushed back downstairs and placed them all in the washing machine. *That's the problem with being away from home,* she thought to herself, *the things you normally do automatically don't get done.*

She went back upstairs and sorted out some clothes for Tom, then quickly changed her own. She went into the kitchen and took a couple of sausage rolls from the fridge and placed them in the microwave, and made herself a coffee while they were warming up. She picked up her coffee, took the sausage rolls from the microwave, and sat down at the breakfast bar.

Joanne picked up her phone and pressed one of the quick dial buttons, taking a large bite of a sausage roll while waiting for an answer

– bad timing.

"Hello," said the voice on the other end of the phone.

"Aunty, it's me, Joanne, sorry I have a mouthful of a sausage roll. Can you hear me okay?" she asked.

"Just about, dear, where are you?"

"I am at home, Aunty, but I am just going back to the hospital to get Tom. They are discharging him this afternoon."

"Oh, that's quick, dear! Is he okay?" asked Aunt Matilda.

"Yes, Aunty, he has made good progress and they are very pleased with his recovery so far. He still has to be careful what he does, though, but I will be here with him most of the time."

"Yes, dear and if you can't be there, I will make sure he behaves himself."

"Yes, thank you, Aunty. We've been so busy recently – I was thinking maybe you could come and visit over the weekend if you want to."

"That would be lovely, dear, I would like that very much."

"Okay, I'll give you a ring later once I have got Tom home and then we can sort out when you want to come over."

"Thank you, dear. I'll wait for your call later, then."

"Okay, Aunty, I have to go now but I'll speak to you later. Bye," said Joanne and she ended the call.

Joanne was just finishing her sausage rolls and coffee when she heard a phone ringing but it wasn't hers. Then she remembered she still had Tom's phone in her bag.

"Hello."

"Mr Maddox?"

"No! This is his partner, Joanne. Tom's not here now. Can I help? Who's calling, please?"

"This is Pixels to Canvas. Mr Maddox ordered some canvas prints from us. I'm just ringing to let him know that they will be delivered tomorrow. Will that be okay?"

"Oh, well, yes. I suppose so. There will be someone here all day. Do you have any idea what time they will be delivered?" asked Joanne.

"Not at the moment but I could get them to ring Mr Maddox about an hour before they arrive. Will that be okay?"

"Yes, that will be great, thank you. I'll let him know. Sorry, where did you say you were from?"

"Pixels to Canvas. We transfer digital photos to canvas prints."

"Okay, thank you. I'll tell him," she replied.

Joanne made sure that she had everything she needed and then she got back in her car and drove to the hospital, stopping on the way at a local convenience store to buy a couple of boxes of chocolates for the ward staff. She pulled into the car park, picked up the bag with Tom's clothes in and the chocolates, and made her way to the ward.

She was just about to press the buzzer on the entrance door to the ward when she saw the ward sister coming along behind her.

"Hello Sister. I'm just back – I had to go and get some clothes for Tom as he had nothing suitable here to go home in."

"Okay, it's great he has made a good recovery, but now the hard work starts for you, to make sure he abides by the rules."

"Yes, Sister, I know, and I will make sure he carries them out to the letter, you don't need to worry about that."

"I will be in with you soon as I think we have almost finalised Mr Maddox's discharge report."

"Thank you," replied Joanne.

Joanne opened the door to Tom's room; he was asleep again.

"I'm back, Tom. Are you going to wake up now?" she said as she put everything down on a chair, walked over to the bed, took hold of his arm and shook him.

"Tom," she called. "Tom, can you hear me?"

At first there was no reply. Then he stirred.

"You know I was enjoying that sleep before you disturbed me."

"Tom, please don't do that. I thought there was something wrong with you!" cried Joanne as she punched his arm playfully.

"I have some clothes here for you now so you can get dressed. I think we may be allowed to go soon," added Joanne.

"Oh, I do hope so," replied Tom.

It wasn't long before the ward sister came into the room and gave Tom his medication and discharge letter. She also gave them a document that listed what Tom could and couldn't do while he was still in the recovery stage, and she also gave Tom a letter detailing his follow-up appointment in five weeks time.

"I hope that you continue to make a rapid recovery, Tom," said the sister. "And Joanne, if you have any problems or concerns, you just need to call us for advice. Other than that, if you are at all worried then make sure you call for an ambulance or bring Mr Maddox straight here like you did the first time."

"Thank you so much! We are both so pleased by how we have been treated, but we hope we never have to come here again," said Joanne.

She picked up the bag from the chair and offered it to the sister.

"This is just a small token of our appreciation for all that you have done for Tom. Maybe you could place them somewhere so that all your staff can help themselves."

The sister looked in the bag as she took it from Joanne.

"Thank you, thank you very much. I will make sure everyone knows where to find them," she said as she walked towards the door. Just before leaving the room, she turned back towards them.

"I'll be in my office so on your way out, make sure you stop and say goodbye."

"Thank you, we will do that for sure," replied Joanne.

She helped Tom get out of bed and to get dressed; then she placed everything in her bag and they made their way out of the room, stopping briefly at the ward sister's office to say goodbye before making their way down to the car.

As they walked out of the hospital, the heat took Tom's breath away.

"Oh, no, I think I need to go back to the ward," he said.

"Why, what's wrong?" questioned Joanne.

"Nothing, it's just much cooler there than out here," replied Tom.

"Don't worry, I'll put the fan on cold in the car, and once I get you home, I'll soon have you cooled down in a cold shower."

As soon as they got in the car and Joanne had started the engine, she immediately switched the fan to the full blower and placed the setting on cold.

"There, that should start to cool you down soon," she remarked.

"You know, I think that is why I love you so much, Joanne. You're so thoughtful."

"Really," remarked Joanne, "I do believe that's the second time you have told me you love me."

"Well, what could possibly be more loving than to put me in a shower of cold water to cool me down, other than stripping me naked and rolling me in snow," said Tom.

"Yes, I'd agree with that," replied Joanne, "but we don't have any snow now, so you will just have to wait to experience that joy."

CHAPTER NINETEEN

Joanne Aids Tom's Recovery

They continued the drive home in relative silence. They were both deeply engrossed in thoughts of what lay before them. The events of the last week had certainly been a shock and they would now need to re-evaluate their lives and learn to live together as partners do.

Tom was just pleased to be out of the hospital and going home, and, for the first time, he felt he could really begin to call it home. Living in the barn for what had been something over four years had had a certain effect on him, but it was something that he had become used to. However, that had all changed now, since he had met Joanne and she had invited him to 'move in with her'. His life was beginning to return to a kind of normality. He now realised how much Joanne meant to him and how quickly she was prepared to support him when he really needed it. However, he still had to overcome the deep-rooted scars of the accident which had killed his wife and son.

Joanne was also pleased to be able to get him home from the hospital in what appeared to be relatively good health, something she hadn't expected with the seriousness of his accident. Although two totally different men, Joanne was beginning to realise just how similar her current situation with Tom was to when she first met her ex-husband. The speed with which both relationships developed were pretty much in parallel, maybe that was just the person she was; she saw, she acted, she conquered, or something like that. However, the main difference was that with her husband she was too young, and she knew she should have listened to her parents, but she was headstrong and she knew best. Now she was that much older and wiser, or so she thought, and because of that she felt more able to deal with the situation and her lust for life, or what she expected from life. She too had learned a lot from the last week and she was now surer than ever that Tom was the man she had been looking for and she was determined not to let him go, or to let anything or anyone get in the way of what she wanted.

She pulled up on the gravel driveway outside the main door. As she put on the brake and turned the engine off, Tom leant over and kissed her.

"Thank you – it feels so good to be home."

"Hey, let's not waste time sitting here, we need to get you inside and then I will make you feel really good to be home," replied Joanne.

No sooner had Joanne closed the door behind them, than she was gently pushing Tom towards the stairs.

"Hey, where are we going?" he asked.

"Well, you, mister, are going to have that cold shower to cool you down a bit. I mean we don't want your temperature rising – or anything else rising, do we?"

"Can't I have a tea first?" he asked.

"No! Get your clothes off and get in the shower!"

"But my clothes are clean. I have only just put them on."

"Tom, you've been in hospital. Get your clothes off and get in the shower. I'll make your tea and bring it up to you."

Tom didn't reply; so he trudged off up the stairs and into the bathroom. Removing his clothes and throwing them on the floor, he got in the shower.

Joanne went into the kitchen to make Tom's tea and a coffee for herself. She took her phone out of her bag to check for any messages, but the battery was dead. She looked at Tom's phone, too. She had forgotten to give him the message about the pictures he had ordered but his phone's battery was also dead. The chargers were upstairs in the bedroom, so she put the phones in her pocket, picked up the drinks and then went upstairs. She placed the drinks on mats on her dressing table and then took the phone chargers out of the drawer and plugged both phones in to charge.

"I've put your tea in the bedroom, Tom, in a sealed mug to keep it hot," she said as she entered the bathroom. "How are you getting on?" she asked as she took her clothes off and threw them on the floor.

"I'm doing good. I'll be finished soon," he replied.

Joanne opened the door and got in the shower with Tom.

"How can you be nearly finished?" she asked. "I haven't even started washing you yet."

"Hey, what are you doing? Have you forgotten what the doctor said already? No excitement."

"So, who's getting excited? Not me, I'm only here to wash you, to make sure your whole body is clean after being in the hospital. You are the one that needs to control that thing between your legs," she said as she started to lather his back with copious amounts of soap.

"Do you have to be so rough?" he asked. "It feels as though you are using a scouring pad to get me clean."

"I am, and sensuous isn't allowed, remember? I am just trying to make sure you are clean. Okay, turn around, please."

Joanne continued to lather Tom's chest and arms, working her way down to his abdomen.

"You really ought to shave you know," she said as she started to lather between his legs. "Hey, I told you to control it."

"Well, I'm sorry, but it's pretty difficult with you doing what you are doing down there."

"Don't be ridiculous. Just forget about what I am doing and think of your worst nightmare; see, I told you it would work. Who were you thinking of then?" she asked.

"Boris Johnson."

"Oh my god, yes, nightmares don't come any worse than that, do they?" she replied. "Okay, all finished, you can rinse yourself off now, and make sure you get all the soap suds out of the nooks and crannies,"

"Are you going to stand there and watch then?" he asked.

"No, while you are doing that, I'm going to lather myself."

"Wait, that's not right. Surely that should be my job?"

"Maybe, but not now. You have at least a month to wait before you can even think about doing that, so just do what you are doing and forget I am even here," she replied.

"That is easier said than done with you standing naked right in front of me."

"Well, you've finished, so dry yourself off, then go lie on the bed and drink your tea."

"Seeing as you put it like that, there is not much else I can do, is there, so I shall leave you in peace," said Tom as he got out of the shower and picked a towel from the rail on the wall.

He dried himself off and then went into the bedroom to get a pair of pants. He then sat on the bed and drank his tea, waiting for Joanne to finish her shower. By the time Joanne had finished and walked into the bedroom, he was asleep. She dried her body and then sat on the stool in front of the dressing table where she dried her hair while drinking her coffee which was now barely lukewarm.

Hair dried and brushed, she picked up her cup and walked over to Tom's side of the bed. She picked up his mug of tea, which had only been half drunk and was now cold as he hadn't closed the lid properly. She went downstairs to the kitchen and switched on the kettle. Taking out some clean cups from the cupboard under the breakfast bar, she made him another cup and herself a cup of coffee. She took a couple of buns from the fridge, cut them in half and buttered them, just in case Tom was to wake up and feel hungry. Then she placed everything on a tray and took them up to the bedroom. As she walked in, she noticed that Tom was awake again.

"Sorry, I must have dozed off while I was waiting for you."

"That's okay, once I had finished, I went downstairs and made you another cup of tea as you hadn't finished the other one and it was cold. I also buttered some buns just in case you were feeling a little hungry."

Joanne placed the tea and a couple of buns on a plate on the cabinet by the side of the bed, then sat on the bed and moved closer to where Tom was sitting with his back supported by a pillow resting against the headboard.

He turned his head towards her. "You're naked," he commented.

Joanne looked at him, saying, "Well, we can certainly say one thing, Tom."

"What's that?" he asked.

"Your accident hasn't destroyed your power of observation," replied Joanne.

"Maybe, but I had to look twice to make sure," he replied as he started to laugh.

"Do you have a problem with me being naked then, Tom?" she asked.

"No! Not really, it's just that you've been downstairs so I thought you might have put some clothes on."

"Maybe if I had been planning on going somewhere, but what's the point in putting on some clothes to make a cup of tea, when I was coming straight back up here to take the clothes off again?"

"Point taken, and I must say you do look quite nice without clothes."

"Are you sure about that, only *quite* nice?"

"No! You look gorgeous, and I'd like to see you naked more often."

"Well, you'll be pleased to know then, that as long as you behave yourself, you will," stated Joanne.

"I think you should rest now, Tom. Put your pillow down and close your eyes. I'll cuddle you."

"Rest?" questioned Tom. "I've only just woken up."

"That wasn't proper sleep time. Did you not understand what the doctor said regarding sleep? He said you could expect to have sleep naps of anything from 30 minutes to an hour, at several times throughout the day, and that that feeling would continue for a week or two."

"Okay, yes, of course you are right, that's probably why I'm still feeling a little tired," he replied.

Tom removed his pillow from behind his back and placed it on the bed under his head. He turned onto his side and closed his eyes. He felt Joanne cuddle up close to him; the feel of her naked body next to his was electrifying. Her arm was straddled over his side with her hand gently resting on his chest. He was dozing off, but he felt Joanne move her hand slowly down over his abdomen to his stomach and then momentarily to his groin before she pulled her hand away again.

"Shave!" she said.

Joanne left Tom sleeping while she checked her laptop to see if there were any messages from work. As soon as she was logged on, she saw that she had three messages waiting to be answered. One was from Susan, but that was just referring to the conversation she had earlier with her, so no action was needed on that one.

The second one was from Warren. *'Sorry to bother you, Joanne, nothing work-related, just wanted to know how Tom is. If I haven't heard from you by tonight, I will ring you. Just worried about him and how he is responding.'*

The third one was from Jefferey. *'Hi Joanne, surprised you haven't tried to contact me, especially seeing that we are now socially active. Maybe we could meet up again. I can't wait for another session – you are really great. I could always come to you as long as you-know-who is out, and we can safely increase our socially active status; you really need to ditch him.'*

Joanne sat staring at the screen; she could not believe what she was reading and she knew that she dared not show it to Tom as he would freak out. She knew, though, that she had to share this with someone, if only to protect herself. She thought of Susan, but she didn't think she was ready for this type of involvement – after all, this had nothing to do with actual work. No! There was only one person she could share it with and that was Warren.

'Good evening, Warren, sorry, but I have only just seen your message as was busy at the hospital all day. Thank you so much for asking about Tom – I have some good news: he came home this afternoon. He is asleep on the bed now. He still gets tired at odd times, but they have told us that is all part of the recovery process. I will see how we progress over the weekend and then update you on Monday. One thing I can tell you is that he hasn't suffered any loss of memory which is a particularly good sign.

There is something else that is slightly worrying, though, and I'm telling you as I feel I must share this with someone. I can't tell Tom as he would seriously freak out. Below I have copied the message I received from Jefferey on my work laptop:

'Hi Joanne, surprised you haven't tried to contact me, especially seeing that we are now socially active. Maybe we could meet up again. I can't wait for another session – you are really great. I could always come to you as long as you know who is out, and we can safely increase our socially active status; you really need to ditch him.'

As I said in our meeting a while ago, he is up to something, but I am just not sure what yet. However, I intend to follow this through until I find out what it is. I will, of course, meet with him and see if I can find out any further information regarding his plans or what he is intending. I would like to thank you again for your concerns regarding Tom. I'll tell him you asked about him. I know you said to me that you passed by here the other weekend, and if you should come this way again, you're more than welcome to pop in. Take care, Joanne.'

Wondering what to do about Jefferey, she decided that she better reply to his message.

'Jefferey, I am not sure why you seemed surprised that I didn't contact you. As I saw it, you rang in sick, so no further action was required. As for us meeting, yes, of course, I am always willing to meet with colleagues out of hours to discuss private matters or to socialise when necessary. I am not sure what gave you the idea that you might come to my house, though. That's a non-starter – I have told you before never to turn up here and I expect you to honour that request. So, whenever you fancy meeting up, just let me know then we can arrange something. Hope you're feeling better soon.'

She logged out of her official site and left her laptop open; she would check later to see if there were any responses. Tom was still sleeping, but she guessed that he would be hungry when he woke up, so she went down to the kitchen to cook something.

Tom stirred and turned over. He opened his eyes, expecting to see Joanne there, but she had gone. He wasn't sure how long he had been asleep for. He turned back over and reached for the cup on the bedside cabinet; it was cold. Tom got up and, picking up his towel, he went to the bathroom. When he'd finished, there was still no sign of Joanne, although he was sure he could smell cooking. He picked up the dirty cups and plates and took then down to the kitchen.

"Hi gorgeous," he said as he entered the kitchen. He walked over to the sink and placed the dishes on the draining board. He then went over to Joanne who was standing in front of the cooker and put his arms around her waist, kissing her on the back of her neck.

Joanne stopped what she was doing and turning round, she flung her arms around Tom's neck and gave him a long passionate kiss on the lips.

"Thank you for bringing those dishes down. I forgot them earlier. I thought you might be hungry, so I cooked some food for us, just in case."

"Sounds good to me and smells even better. What have you cooked then?" he asked.

"There are some chops with sautéed potatoes and vegetables."

"Wow, thank you, that sounds just great," replied Tom.

Joanne finished cooking and then placed a plate of food in front of Tom who was already sitting at the breakfast bar in anticipation. Placing her plate opposite him, Joanne sat down and told him to eat.

"This is not right," commented Tom.

Joanne looked at him with a frown on her face. "What's not right?" she asked.

"This, me, us. Where do you want me to start? It's all wrong."

"Tom, will you please explain? You're not making any sense at all," said Joanne with an even bigger frown on her face.

"I need to pay you for this, for all of it. I feel really bad. I need to pay you for everything," replied Tom.

"What!" exclaimed Joanne. "So what am I? What do you think I am? Do you think I am some kind of proprietor who provides a twenty-four-seven service, along with sexual favours? A prostitute? Is that what you think I am? Did I ever ask you for money?" she asked him.

"No! Sorry, you misunderstood me! You are none of that," he replied.

"Well, I hope not for your sake because if I was, you couldn't afford me. I doubt you could even afford the sex part, let along anything else," replied Joanne.

"But we don't have sex," remarked Tom.

"Okay, my mistake, and if we did, from what I have seen so far, that would only be a very small part of the bill anyway, minuscule even," replied Joanne with a smile on her face.

Tom couldn't help but laugh too.

"You just wait … wait till I sort my head out, and the doctors give me the okay, then you'll see. What I was trying to say is that if we are going to be living here as a couple, then I must contribute, and I will."

"Don't worry about that at the moment, Tom. I am not asking for your money, all I want is your love, your total love, one hundred per cent, with no background interference, that is all I am asking," she stated.

He reached out across the breakfast bar and placed his hand over hers.

"And that is what you will get, I promise you that much."

"Thank you, Tom. I have been waiting to hear your commitment, but I won't rush you. I can wait for what I want, but for now let's take one thing at a time," replied Joanne.

"That sounds very good to me, Joanne," he replied.

They both sat there while they finished their meal, then Joanne got up and cleared the dishes away, placing them in the dishwasher and sat back down at the breakfast bar.

"Tom," she said. "I was thinking of inviting Aunty around tomorrow; what do you think?"

"I think that's a great idea," replied Tom, "as long as she won't get upset should I suddenly feel tired and need to sleep," he added.

"Don't worry, I've already explained to her about your naps and she understands that perfectly. It will also give you both time to get to know each other because should I have to go into the office then Aunty will be here to look after you," explained Joanne.

"That's perfect then, maybe we can actually use the dining room for the first time since I decorated it," replied Tom.

"Oh yes please! We can christen it with Aunty Matilda. We'll have a nice dinner. I am sure she would appreciate that very much. You know, she has told me many times that she cannot wait to see the place once you've finished all the decorating; she only remembers it as it was when she came to view the place with me," explained Joanne.

"I hope she'll appreciate all my hard work then," replied Tom.

"I am sure she will, Tom," said Joanne.

CHAPTER TWENTY

Close Times

Joanne and Tom were sitting in the lounge. It was early evening and still hot. Tom was looking at the bare walls and thinking of the photos that he had ordered; he was really hoping that Joanne would like them.

"Do you fancy going for a walk?" she said.

"What, now?"

"Yes, come on, instead of sitting here looking at the walls, why don't we go for a walk?" said Joanne as she got up from the sofa and held out her hand towards him.

"Okay, fine. You did say you had plans for the grounds and I would like to know what you have in mind," he replied.

"Come on then, Tom, let's go."

"Are you going to put something else on?" he asked, looking at her skimpy lace dressing gown.

"No! Only my trainers – is that okay with you?"

"Sure, no problem," he replied. "I'll just get my camera."

Joanne was already waiting outside when Tom came back with his camera.

"Where shall we go first?" asked Joanne.

"I'd like to go down by the stream first if that's okay," said Tom.

"Okay, the stream it is," said Joanne. "Actually that's a good choice. It's quite peaceful down there. I was thinking that maybe eventually we could put a small cabin down there if we level off the slope."

"That sounds a brilliant idea, but I don't think we need to level the ground off. We could leave it as it is but just build the cabin on stilts or lay down a small decking area with the cabin on that. That way we are protecting the stream and surrounding area. It also creates less of a disturbance to the nature that is there. What do you think?" asked Tom.

"You are so knowledgeable, Tom; I would never have thought of that. Is that something you would be able to do, or would we need to get specialist builders in?"

"I think with the slope it would be best to get specialists in; they will probably have built cabins in similar situations before. I could do it, but not sure if I would do it right."

They reached the stream; it was indeed a perfect setting for a summer cabin, and a prime location. On a warm evening it would be nice to sit there and relax after a hard day's work. Tom looked around; he could imagine just sitting there, with a lowering evening sun casting shadows through the trees, the stream babbling in the background.

"Can we sit here for a while?" he asked.

"Of course we can, Tom. Are you tired?" asked Joanne.

"No, definitely not, I just want to take some photos of you if that's okay?" he asked.

"If they are as good as the ones you took of me in the lounge, then click away to your heart's content, I love those photos," she replied.

"Okay, sit as you are now, but feet on the ground. Now, bring your knees up ... perfect. Now lean forward slightly and place your elbows on your knees; perfect, don't move, I just want to adjust your lace gown. Oh wow, that's brilliant. Just hold it there and look directly at the stream. Yep, and now look slightly to your right, great ... and now to your left. You're a great model! Every picture is perfect, every picture tells a story," remarked Tom as he kept clicking his camera.

They were there for almost an hour, with Tom taking photos of Joanne in different positions before she thought it was time to head back to the house. She wanted to see what Tom thought about putting a paved patio area outside the back doors. He was walking down along the stream when she called to him.

"Shall we go now, Tom? I want to show you what I thought we could do outside the back lounge."

"Okay, I'll meet you at the other end of this little pathway," he replied.

She continued towards the top of the slope and once back on even ground she heard Tom call out.

"Hey, Joanne! Come here a minute – look what I have found."

"What is it? What have you found?"

"Look, it's an apple tree and just look at all these apples," replied Tom as he reached up to pick one.

"Hey, you are not supposed to be reaching up or stretching; it places extra pressure on you," said Joanne as she walked down towards him. She too could not believe the amount of apples on the tree.

"We'll have to come back tomorrow with a basket. There must be at least a hundred apples here," she commented.

"Quick, I have an idea," said Tom. "Come and stand here under this branch while the sunlight is still strong." He pointed to the lowest branch on the tree. "Now reach up and let your hand cup the apple, that's it, stay like that." He walked over to where Joanne was standing and moved her lace top so that it appeared to be sliding down her back.

"Okay, hold it there … ready … good … just one more," he said as he walked towards her. He once again moved the lace top further down her back until it just showed the crease of her buttocks.

"Okay, hold it there, just one more," he said. "Now, let the top fall so it is hanging from one arm, and turn very slightly towards me. No, too far – go back again. I just want to show the mound of your breast without showing the nipple. Okay, perfect … hold it there, lovely … hold it. That's perfect."

He placed his camera down on the ground and walked over to Joanne.

"Okay, just one more," he said as he moved her slightly. "That's it, hold it there and do not move," he said as he picked up his camera and took a couple more shots of her, then put his camera back on the ground. Walking back over to where Joanne was still holding her position, he took hold of her waist, spun her around and gave her a long, lingering kiss on the lips.

"I love you so much Miss Webster. You are really quite special," he said.

"I love you too, Mr Maddox, and I want you so much. Why did you have to go and injure yourself like that? Now we have to wait to consummate our relationship and it is killing me more each day," said Joanne.

"Me too, Joanne, me too. I want you so much."

Joanne picked up the lace gown and carried it with her as they walked arm in arm back up towards the house. Tom was right about the light: it was a wonderful evening and still warm but the sun was dropping in the sky and the shadows were lengthening. As they approached the house, Joanne stopped and, turning to Tom, she explained where she would like the patio area to be.

"Do you think it would be too big if the patio area started from here?" she asked.

"Not at all; you could have it as large as you want it and here would be a good place to start it. You could split the area by having a sitting area and then a gazebo. Also, you could have a barbecue area and you could also have a spa or hot tub; the options are never-ending. You could even have a small swimming pool," he said.

"Oh, please Tom! Build it for me."

"Which bit?"

"All of it, Tom, all of it," replied Joanne. "I want it all, including the spa and hot tub and pool."

"Wait here a minute," he said as he went around to the side of the house and opened the side door leading into the kitchen. He picked up two stools and carried them through to the lounge. Opening the double doors, he placed the stools outside, and sitting on one, he beckoned to Joanne to sit on the other.

"Can you imagine sitting out here every evening during the summer and autumn, when the weather is warm enough? It will be the perfect location."

"It would be lovely," remarked Joanne, "but I would rather be sitting with you in a spa or hot tub! Can you just imagine those bubbles and what they could be doing to your body?"

"Oh yes, I can imagine you sitting there in a spa, and just the thought of it makes the mind boggle."

"Well, best you get on and sort it out, mister, because then you wouldn't have to imagine it, you could be seeing it every evening and what is even more important you could be having it every evening."

"Sorry to disappoint you, Miss Webster, but I think it's time for me to take that cold shower."

Joanne burst out laughing. "Yes, and I think I will have to join you."

They both went back inside. Tom picked up the stools and took them back into the kitchen, then went to join Joanne who was sitting in the lounge.

"Can I look at some of the photos you took please, Tom?"

"There you go. I think I took quite a few," he said as he handed her his camera.

"Oh Tom, you are *bad!* You've made me look so sensual," commented Joanne as she looked at the photos.

"No! You're wrong, you do that yourself. A camera can only duplicate what is in front of it, and you are a very sensual lady," he replied.

She picked up a tissue from the box on the coffee table and wiped the tears from her eyes. Tom felt guilty. What had he done? Maybe it was the photos?

"Joanne, I'm sorry if the photos upset you; you can delete them. I didn't mean to upset you by taking them, you just looked so beautiful, I couldn't stop myself. You had better not look at the photos by the apple tree; they are my interpretation of Eve."

He waited for an answer, but one was not forthcoming. He could see that she was still upset as she was still crying.

"I'm sorry, Joanne. I'd better go and have that cold shower," he said as he turned towards the hall.

"Wait," she called.

He turned back towards her and stood in the doorway, waiting for her to say something. Joanne got up and walked slowly towards him.

"Tom, the photos didn't upset me. They are the most beautiful photos I've ever seen. The apple tree photos were exactly how you described them. Your Eve photos and how you imagined she would have looked in the garden of Eden."

"Then why are you upset? Why? How did I make you cry? I didn't mean to do that! I had no intention of doing that."

"Tom, it wasn't your photos, it was something you said. No one has ever before said to me that I am a very sensual lady. Some have said I was very sexy, but no one has ever used the term sensual, and that makes me feel annoyed – all those wasted years. The way you referred to me as sensual proved to be the one thing in my life that I have been waiting for."

"Joanne, I don't understand."

"Tom, you are the only man I have ever known who has described me as being sensual and not sexy, and that proves to me your love for me, that is what made me cry. Thank you, Tom. I never want to lose you, I never want to leave you. Thank you so much."

He took her hand. "Come with me."

"Where are we going?" she asked.

"To bed."

He led her upstairs and into the bedroom, and standing by the bed, he removed her lace dressing gown and kissed her lips. He removed his shorts and placed her hand on his stomach, allowing her to move it down to his groin,

"You shaved," she said.

"For you. I will do anything for you," he replied.

"But Tom, we mustn't. I want it as much as you do, but it could set you back, it could cause you to have another bleed. I want you, Tom. Not your body, not sex, I want you and I can wait."

He turned and walked towards the bedroom door.

"Where are you going?" she asked.

"To get your coffee while you take a shower."

Joanne sat on the bed for a few minutes; she knew she had made the right decision, although she got the feeling that Tom didn't agree. What could she do? She was in a no-win situation, but as much as it hurt her, she had to wait and as much as Tom might have been hurt by her rejection, she had to wait until the doctors gave him the all-clear.

Tom came back into the bedroom and put her coffee on the bedside cabinet.

"I thought you were having your shower," he said.

"I was waiting for you, so we can shower together."

"But you said that's not allowed. You need to make your mind up."

"Tom, please, listen to me. I want you more than you will ever know, but I am not going to be the person who causes you to have another bleed on the brain and you heard the doctors the same as I did, so we'll just have to wait."

She got up and walked toward the bedroom door.

"I'm going to take a shower … are you going to join me?"

Tom sat on the bed, thinking that sometimes they seemed so close and then the next minute seemed so far apart; maybe that's just the way it was meant to be. He waited for Joanne to come out of the shower and then grabbed a towel and disappeared into the bathroom. When he walked back into the bedroom, Joanne was already in bed and asleep. He finished drying himself and then gently crawled into bed, trying not to wake her.

Joanne wasn't asleep; she had been waiting for Tom. She moved over closer to him, to cuddle him.

"Sorry, Tom, but this is just the way it has to be for the time being."

"Do you think I could cuddle you?" he asked.

Joanne thought about it but then gave her reply.

"I think not, Tom, it's just too much of a risk."

"Is that your final word on the matter?"

"Yes, it is and now you have to sleep and so do I."

Joanne woke and looked at the clock: five minutes past six. She turned over towards Tom but there was just a space where he should have been.

"Tom?" she called but there was no reply.

She got out of bed and went to the bathroom, then searched through her drawers for a lace bra and panties. She put them on and then went downstairs.

"Tom, are you there?" she called.

"I'm here, in the kitchen," came the reply.

Joanne walked into the kitchen.

"Tom, what are you doing?" she asked. "It's still early."

"Well, what does one usually do in the kitchen? First, I am preparing your breakfast, and second, it was early when I go up, but it isn't now," he replied. "Take a seat at the breakfast bar and your food will be with you in a couple of minutes."

"Thank you. I wasn't expecting this," replied Joanne.

"Okay, you can have croissants or toasted tea cakes, with butter and jam. I have used your oranges, which I've freshly squeezed in the jug, and you can have a cup of freshly ground coffee. Take your pick and enjoy."

"Where's your breakfast?" she asked.

"I thought I would eat what you're having this morning. I need to lose weight. I'm just making my tea, then I'll join you," he replied.

"How nice and thoughtful of you."

Tom sat there opposite Joanne, eating his breakfast which to his surprise he was enjoying; it certainly made a change to his usual egg, bacon, sausage, and a fried slice. Joanne sat quietly enjoying the fact that she did not have to prepare breakfast; it had all been expertly prepared by Tom.

"This fresh orange juice is so nice. Thank you."

She had noticed that Tom kept staring at her, and she was wondering why. However, she didn't want to ask him if there was a problem.

He finished his breakfast and sat there, both hands cupping the mug his tea was in, staring at her. Then the silence was broken by a question.

"Why?" he asked.

Joanne was puzzled by Tom's question. "Why what?" she replied.

"Why are you wearing a lace bra and panties?" he inquired.

"Ah, well, I know you don't like me walking around naked, so I put some clothes on, but quite obviously you are still not satisfied."

"But I was just wondering what they are meant to hide? They are pure lace, and I can see right through them, so they do not hide anything at all," he replied.

Joanne looked down at her breasts and the bra covering them, then looked Tom in the eyes.

"Yes, I'll give you that, but …"

"But what?" asked Tom.

"It's the thought that counts," replied Joanne.

At which they both burst out laughing.

Sitting there, Joanne suddenly remembered the message from the photo company.

"Tom, sorry, I forgot to tell you, a photo company rang on your mobile phone which I answered when you were in hospital. They said you'd ordered some prints and they'd be delivering them today."your phone is upstairs, I found it after the doctors asked me if I knew how you hit your head and I thought I would look to see if I could find the area where you fell, which I did and I saw your phone laying there on the ground near to the edge of the stream. Anyway, there was a message for you, some photo company, they said you ordered some prints, and they would be delivering them today."

Tom's face lit up.

"Really? That's great, I can't wait to see them. Maybe you can help me put them up when they arrive," he said.

"Okay, but how many photos and what are they of and where do you want to put them?" asked Joanne.

"Come with me and I will show you," he said as he took hold of her hand and led her into the front lounge. "I have three photos coming, one exceptionally large one, and two smaller ones. They are all the same theme, so I want to put the large one on the centre of the wall just there," he said pointing to the back wall. "The other two I want to place on either side of the main one and there is a special reason for that, which you will see later."

"Wow, that all sounds good, and it will break up the plainness of the wall. I did wonder why you left it like that, but I trust your decorating skills, so I didn't question it. Now I know the reason. And what are the photos of?" she asked again.

"Well, I'd rather leave it as a surprise if that's okay with you."

"That's fine with me. I like surprises, and something tells me I will very much like your surprise."

"I do hope so, Joanne."

"Sorry, but I need to go and get my laptop and see if there are any work-related problems that need sorting out."

"Of course, I know you must work while you are here. Could you bring my phone down too and the charger for it, please? I'll clear the breakfast things to give you room to work."

Joanne went to the bedroom to get her laptop and Tom's phone, while Tom did as he said and cleared away the breakfast things, leaving the area clear for Joanne's laptop as he knew that was where she liked to work.

"Here's your phone," said Joanne as she put it down on the breakfast bar, "and there are the login details for the internet in case you're not connected."

"Okay, thank you."

Tom opened his phone and checked for messages; there was only one: from Pixel to Canvas to say they would be delivering the canvas at ten o'clock. He looked at the time: nine-forty, only twenty minutes.

"I had a message from Pixel to Canvas. They will be here in twenty minutes, so you don't have long to wait for your surprise," he said.

It was just a few minutes after that when there was a knock on the door.

"I think this may be the prints. You need to stay here until they have gone."

"Why do I need to stay here?" asked Joanne. "I want to see the prints just as much as you do Tom!"

He turned and looked straight at her. "Well, for one, you're not exactly dressed for receiving visitors, are you? I'll call you when they have gone."

Joanne, couldn't concentrate; she wanted to know what Tom was doing but she had work to do, so she kept herself busy until he called her, which wasn't too long after.

"Okay, you can come and take a look now."

Joanne hurried through to the lounge where Tom was waiting for her in the doorway, but he wouldn't let her in.

"Right, close your eyes and keep them closed," he said Tom as he took hold of her hand and led her to the centre of the lounge, and turned her to face the wall where he had just hung the prints.

"Okay, you can open your eyes now," he said.

Joanne couldn't believe what she saw. She was totally stunned and she fell to her knees; she just did not know what to say. She had had no idea what he had done with the photos he took but now she knew. They were hanging on the wall in the form of canvas prints and they were just stunning.

"Tom, they are beautiful," she said as she got up from the floor and flung her arms around his neck, kissing him. I just had no idea you were going to do that. They're wonderful – thank you so much! I just don't know what to say … you have captured me perfectly. It's as though I am there in real life, hanging on the wall. I love you so much, Mr Maddox, thank you."

CHAPTER TWENTY-ONE

New Developments

Having got over the shock of seeing her true self plastered all over their lounge wall in three stunning canvas pictures, Joanne had work to do. She went into the kitchen, turned on her laptop and connected to the company web site. She had three new messages, which were from, Susan, Warren and, surprise, surprise, Jefferey.

Joanne decided to read Susan's message first.

'Sorry to bother you Joanne. I hope Tom is okay and that he will fully recover from his accident. Anyway, this is just an update that I thought you should know about. While I was taking my son to my mother's house this morning, I noticed that there was another van parked outside the block where the Saunders used to live, and Jefferey's car was there again. After leaving my mother's to get to work, I drove past the block and saw Jefferey getting in his car. I was in a queue of traffic and one of the cars had stopped to let Jefferey out. He was about three or four cars in front of me and hadn't seen me so, keeping my distance, I followed him to see where he was going. I thought he might be going straight to work, but I was surprised when he turned off and was then heading in the opposite direction. I kept following him and we ended up in Melbourne Road, where he pulled up in the middle of the road and at first I thought he had spotted me. However, the reason he stopped was to let someone out of the car and that person was Mrs Saunders. They kissed goodbye, not a friendly peck but a long lingering kiss. She went into a house there and he then continued driving. I'm not sure what's going on but I just wanted to update you. Speak soon, Susan.'

Interesting, thought Joanne to herself although, like Susan, she wasn't quite sure what to make of it all; however, it would appear there was something going on between Jefferey and Mrs Saunders. Joanne was confused; if that were the case, why the hell was he pestering her and leaving her oddly suggestive messages? She just could not fathom it all out. Joanne thought about Susan's message but decided not to respond straightaway. She needed time to try to work it all out, so she put it to one side and instead opened the message from Warren.

Joanne, I think you must try to meet with Jefferey as soon as possible. This has gone on too long and we both need to know what he is up to. I would love to sack him right now, but as you well know it is not as easy as that and I am certainly not going to give him any excuse whatsoever to sue me or the company. I think he is not right in the head, but before I can make a move to oust him, I need concrete evidence. Anyway, let me know if he wants to meet you and if you are happy and able to accept. I know it is awkward for you now with Tom not having fully recovered yet, but if there is anything I can do to help then just let me know. I am sure we will be able to work something out between us. Warren.'

The third and last message was from Jefferey.

'Hi Joanne, boy, you can be so awkward at times, I just do not know why I bother with you, but hey, that's me, after being socially active with someone! I'm not a person to just walk away. I think we need to meet again; can you make tonight? There's something particularly important I'd like to chat about and I hope you won't let me down. Please don't tell me you have to be with Tom! Surely he's man enough to take care of himself. Meet me tonight, please, and I will prove to you that I can give you so much more than him. Please don't let me down; I promise I'll be ready for you. See you about seven-thirty down by the pier where we can get incredibly close. I hope you will feel up for it because I will. Jefferey.'

Joanne knew that she had to act quickly. She decided that she had to ring Warren to help her sort this mess out. She picked up her phone and rang his number.

"Joanne. What can I do for you?" he asked.

"I've just read your message, thank you. I know you need concrete evidence and that is what I am trying to get, but it's difficult. Jefferey has also sent me a message – he wants to meet me at seven-thirty tonight down by the pier, but I don't think I will be able to make it."

"Oh no! Do you have to go somewhere?" he asked.

"No, it's just that it will be too late for my aunt to come and stay with Tom and I can't leave him alone, doctor's orders, so I can't go."

"Right, we need to find out what he is messing about at; his actions are affecting people's lives."

"Yes, and what's more, earlier today Susan saw something that has led her to believe there may be something going on between Jefferey and Saunders' wife."

"Look, enough is enough – we have to stop this man. I'm not doing anything important tonight, so if Tom doesn't mind, I could come over to your place and have a nice chat with him."

"Thank you, I am sure he wouldn't mind that, he likes you. I'll ask him as soon as we've finished, and I'll send you a message to confirm."

"Okay, Joanne. Did Jefferey say what he had in mind? Will you just be chatting in a bar somewhere, or will you go for a meal? I'm somewhat worried about your safety."

"He didn't say, just that I'm to meet him at the pier, so I guess I'll just have to play it by ear."

"Okay, well just let me know as soon as you can. As long as Tom would like me to come and chat with him while you are out."

"Alright, thank you. I will send you a message in a few minutes."

"Tom, where are you?"

"I'm in the lounge. Why?"

"Can you come to the kitchen for a minute? I want to show you something?"

Tom walked into the kitchen. "I'm here. What do you want me for?"

"Take a look at this message from Jefferey."

"The man's an idiot. Do you want me to go in your place and give him a slap?"

"Certainly not, we don't know what he is capable of and you could get injured."

"Well, if you have to go, I will be okay here for a couple of hours," replied Tom.

"No, that's out of the question too. If something should happen to you, I would never be able to forgive myself," she replied.

"So, what are you going to do?" he asked.

"Do you fancy some company tonight,"

"Oh no, Aunt Matilda? Are you sure? She is worse than you – she won't even let me go to the bathroom without coming and standing outside the door."

"No, not Matilda. But how about Warren?"

"Warren, your boss? Why not? He's an intelligent man, fun to talk to and really down to earth, just like me," said Tom, who was starting to look forward to some male company.

"That's it sorted then. I will message Warren to let him know," she said as Tom went back into the lounge.

'Hi Warren, Tom said yes. He's looking forward to having you for some company tonight, thank you.'

'Okay, I'll be at your place by seven. Warren'

Joanne was pleased that she had managed to get someone to stay with Tom while she was out; all that was left for her to do was to message Jefferey and let him know that she would meet him.

'Hi Jefferey, thanks for your message. I don't think I am being difficult, as I

have said before that I am always ready to meet whenever you feel it necessary. This message is just to let you know that I will be able to accept your kind request for a meeting and I'll see you later. Take care. Joanne.'

She had just finished catching up on work documents and was closing her laptop when Tom entered the kitchen.

"Would you like a drink?" he asked.

"Coffee, please."

"You know, having read that message from Jefferey, I am pretty worried about you meeting him tonight. Are you sure you will be okay? I mean, he seems pretty unstable judging by the language he uses," said Tom.

"Yes, Warren was worried too. I copied Jefferey's message to him, but I'll be careful. I'm going to pair my phone with yours so you can see exactly where I am by my signal."

"Alright. I've chosen some more photos to have transferred to canvas, if that is okay with you."

"As long as you have chosen your 'Eve' ones! They're beautiful."

"Yes, of course, they are included. And I have chosen another two from when we were down by the stream," said Tom.

"Your photos are so lovely; just looking at them, they exude such passion. I think you should quit decorating and concentrate on photography. You quite obviously have a gift."

"I think it is more about copying the work that Anne did, rather than a gift. She was a brilliant photographer. I'm not sure when she started but she was already a recognised photographer when we met; what I know now about photography, I learnt from her," explained Tom.

"I know how much you loved her and that is why I think you should concentrate more on what you learnt from her. What more fitting way could you have than to continue her legacy? She would be enormously proud of you," replied Joanne.

"Thank you, Joanne. That's why I love you so much. You are so understanding, and yes, I will certainly give your idea some thought."

"Right, I am going to get ready, Tom, so maybe you could look to see what we have in the cupboards in the way of snacks as I feel we ought to offer Warren something when he comes over tonight."

"Yes, I was thinking the same thing. I'm sure we must have something suitable in the cupboard but I'll check."

Warren arrived just before seven o'clock. Tom opened the door to him and led him into the lounge. He stopped and looked at the canvas pictures on the wall.

"What a statement they make! They are terrific! May I ask who took them?" said Warren.

"Me," replied Tom.

Joanne came down the stairs while Warren was still looking at the canvas pictures on the wall.

"What do you think, Warren? Would you say that Tom has a gift for photography?" asked Joanne.

"Oh, I think he has more than a gift, Joanne, and he should express it more, much more."

"I'm going now, Tom. I don't want to be late and don't forget I have linked my phone to you so you can see exactly where I am."

Joanne kissed Tom goodbye and then turned to Warren.

"Thank you, Warren. Be gentle with him."

Joanne got in her car and drove down to Eastbourne pier where she pulled into a parking space and turning the engine off. She sat there wondering what kind of evening was in front of her. She was early and still not sure if she had made the right decision by agreeing to meet Jefferey.

She looked at her watch again to check the time; it was still only ten minutes past seven and the hands on her watch had hardly moved since the last time she looked. It was still quite warm and she was beginning to sweat; she wasn't sure if it was the heat or just that she was nervous. She turned off the ignition and opened the window but that didn't help much as the temperature outside was still twenty-six centigrade.

She was getting fed up now; she waited and waited but still no sign of Jefferey and no messages. She got the feeling she was going to be stood up. Although it would end up being a waste of time, she felt as though being stood up on this occasion would be a bonus.

'Hi Jefferey, where are you? You said seven-thirty and it's now seven-fifty. I have moved heaven and earth just to get here to meet you and now you don't turn up. How on earth can we be socially active if one partner doesn't turn up? It takes two to tango, you know.'

She decided to text Tom while she was waiting as she knew he would be wondering what was happening.

'Hi, just in case you have been wondering why I have not moved it's because he hasn't turned up yet. I have sent him a message, but he hasn't replied. I'll give it another fifteen or twenty minutes and if he hasn't shown up, I'll come home. How are you getting on with Warren? Hope everything is going smoothly?'

Tom's reply came straight back.

'Don't worry about us, gorgeous. You just take care of yourself and don't wait too much longer for that toe rag. Warren was just about to tell me something when you rang, I'm not sure what it is but he said it was important and that he needed to tell me so I'll get back to him now. Okay, take care, love, see you soon.'

Joanne put her phone down and started to wonder what it was that Warren wanted to tell Tom; she was curious. Just then, a car pulled up in the space beside her; she looked across and saw that it was Jefferey. He wound down his window and beckoned to her to get in his car. She put her window up, removed her car key and got into his car.

"What's your problem?" she asked him. "You said seven-thirty and it's now seven-fifty-five."

"I know, I'm sorry. What more can I say?" replied Jefferey. "Seat belt," he added.

"Hang on, why? Where are you taking me?" asked Joanne.

"It's okay. I've a table booked for eight o'clock at Sovereign Harbour but it might be difficult to park there so no point in taking two cars. I can bring you back here later when you want to go home," replied Jefferey.

"You could have told me we were going there to eat; I could have gone straight there."

"Does it matter that much? I'm taking you there, so what is the problem?" he asked.

"It seems to me that for some unknown reason you just wanted to take away my freedom by getting me in your car. Can you explain that?"

"Hey, come on, Joanne, let's not argue about this. I mean, we're not even engaged yet, so why can't we just enjoy the evening now that we're together at last?"

"Jefferey! What are you on about? You are making no sense whatsoever! What's all this engaged business and on our own at last? Are you having an awake dream of some kind?"

"Okay, we're here now," said Jefferey as he pulled into a parking space right outside the restaurant.

"I thought you said it was going to be packed, and so there'd be no room for parking. That was your excuse, wasn't it? How many cars are here besides yours? I think I can count six and how many spaces are there? At least twenty I would say."

"Joanne, please, so I made a mistake. I'm sorry. What do you want me to do? Do I have to get down on my hands and knees and beg for your forgiveness?"

"That might work. You never know your luck. But as for a mistake, I think it was me who made the mistake by letting you talk me into meeting you like this tonight."

"Can we just eat and not argue?" said Jefferey as he opened the door to the restaurant for Joanne.

"Good evening, Madam, good evening, Sir. Do you have a booking?"

"Yes, the name is Jefferey and I asked for a secluded area."

"Yes, Sir, we have the perfect place if you would like to follow me. Sir, Madam, I hope this is suitable."

"Yes, thank you very much. This is ideal."

"Would you like to order drinks, Sir?"

"Yes, please, I'll have a dry white wine please," said Jefferey.

"And for you, Madam?" asked the waiter.

"A freshly squeezed orange juice for me please," replied Joanne.

"Thank you, Madam."

The pair sat there quietly until the waiter brought their drinks.

"May I take your order now, please?" he asked.

"Yes, can I just have the house grill please," replied Joanne.

"I'll have the same, please," said Jefferey.

"Thank you," said the waiter who then made his way to the order station.

"Are we going to sit here all night without saying anything, then?" asked Jefferey.

"Well, that depends on whether you have anything to say to me, doesn't it, Jefferey?"

"Tell me, why do you have to be so awkward? I am being nothing but nice to you and this is how you treat me."

"Excuse me!" she exclaimed. "Would you please like to explain exactly how you think I treat you?"

"Well, for a start, you seem oblivious to our relationship."

"Jefferey, we don't have a relationship."

"See, there you go again. We do have a relationship, you just refuse to admit it."

"Okay, clever boy, what does our relationship consist of then, can you tell me that?"

"Well, yes, of course, it is you and me meeting up and going out for chats and dinner, or maybe catching a film. It's a relationship that we are in together."

"Jefferey, this is not a relationship in the sense that you mean, it's a friendship brought about by working together, two vastly different things. You are always going on about us being socially active, and that is just a friendship. To be in the sort of relationship that you want would require more than just being friends, it would mean more than just being socially active. It would need a certain amount of sexual activity and that is *never* going to happen."

"See, there you go again! How do you know it will never happen? Why close an open door?"

"Jefferey, look, will you please understand that there is no open door, there never will be an open door, it's just your imagination. And as for any sexual activity between us, you stand more chance of becoming an overnight billionaire."

"I just don't believe how you can shut me out, just like that," Jefferey said and took a small box out of his pocket. He opened it before placing it on the table and pushing it towards Joanne.

"Are you trying to tell me, then, that you won't accept my ring? How could you be so crass?"

Joanne was aghast.

"Jefferey, no, I absolutely cannot accept your ring! I have nothing more to say, apart from the fact that I have to go now."

With that, she got up and walked towards the door. It was at that point that she realised that her car wasn't there – it was down near the pier where she had parked it. She walked through the harbour area, not sure of where she was going. She had only ever driven past Sovereign Harbour before, never actually stopping there and certainly never walking through there on her own at night before. With the help of directions on her phone, she found her way back to the main road where she hoped to hail a taxi, but in that respect she had been unlucky. After she had walked for some distance, she heard a car approaching from behind. It slowed almost to a stop as it pulled alongside her. She didn't dare to look as she thought it might be Jefferey. The driver's window opened and she heard a woman's voice.

"Would you like a lift? I am going towards the pier."

"Thank you. That's where my car is. I've had a disagreement with a work colleague which has left me without transport."

Joanne jumped into the passenger seat.

"Yes, I saw you storm off. Some men have trouble understanding the word *no*," said the woman. "Almost there. I'll just keep going until you shout stop."

"Okay, this is just fine. Thank you, my car is over there."

Tom checked his phone.

"Oh, Joanne is moving. It looks as though she has left the restaurant and is heading away from the pier. I think she should be home quite soon," he said.

"Tom, can you sit down please? There is something I have to tell you. I have been trying all night, but I'm just not courageous enough. I must tell you now."

"What is it, Warren? What's the problem?"

"Please don't say anything until I have finished."

"Okay," replied Tom.

"Tom, there is no other way to explain this. I don't know if you remember but when you were in my office, there was an enlarged photo on the wall. It was of my daughter, the best photo that was ever taken of her: your wife took that photo. We went to an exhibition on the pier where there were lots of photographers. Your wife was taking photos, too, so she took my daughter's photo and when we saw it, we couldn't believe how clear and life like it was. So I bought the digital print from your wife and had it enlarged. Now I can see your work reflects a certain technique acquired from your wife. I have bought some of her photos since and have them dotted around my house."

"That's okay. Why be worried about telling me that?"

"I've not finished yet, Tom, there is more, a lot more. You see, my daughter died five years ago and every time I look at her photo, I wonder how much more beautiful she would be now. But we cannot dwell on the past, we must move on and not live in the past. I can sympathise with your pain. Your wife and son both died in a car accident, and my daughter died in a car accident, too, the same accident as your wife and child, Tom. My daughter was a passenger, and her husband was driving. He had been drinking, as you know, and he killed my daughter and he killed your wife and son too, but more than that, he killed both of us and my wife as well. So, I am pleading with you, Tom, please leave the ghost of your wife as I have had to do with my daughter. I will help you, Tom. Whatever it takes, I will help you. Joanne is a good girl; she does not deserve to be burdened with your memories of the past."

Tom was shocked; he did not know what to say, but suddenly everything was becoming clear. He had thought it strange how Warren had taken to him and now seemed more like a father figure to him. He stood up and walked slowly over to where Warren was sitting and offered his hand to him. Warren got up and the two men hugged each other. There were no words, just some tears and hugs, but to both, in their own ways, it was a relief, a relief to know that someone else had been suffering just as they had been. The two were still hugging when Joanne walked in.

"Oh my, look at that! I leave you alone for a couple of hours and now look at you! The two of you can hardly be separated."

Tom and Warren smiled at her sheepishly. She didn't need to hear what had brought them to an embrace just yet.

"How did your meeting with Jefferey go then, Joanne?" asked Tom.

"It was useless, a waste of time. All he kept going on about was our so-called relationship. The man is crazy and then he produced what I think was an engagement ring, but I could not bear to look; it was at that point that I left. He is living in what would appear to be some imaginary world, where he thinks that we are in a relationship, a sexual one at that. I told him that he stands more chance of becoming an overnight billionaire."

"Joanne, we will talk about this later. I have heard enough about that man, but for now I am going to go home and leave you two love birds to enjoy each other's company," said Warren as he made his way to the front door.

They said their goodbyes, and Warren got in his car and drove off.

Tom closed the front door and, turning round to Joanne, he took hold of her around the waist and carried her up the stairs, taking her straight to the bedroom. He threw her on the bed and then started removing her clothes, one item at a time, until she was naked. He then picked her up again and carried her into the shower.

CHAPTER TWENTY-TWO

Broken Ties, Harmful Lies

After a restful weekend spent with Tom and Aunt Matilda, it was time for Joanne to concentrate on work and the problem of what to do about Jefferey. It was now obvious to her that there was no way she could ever work in the same office as him again although she still had not been able to work him out or what game he was playing.

Yes, it was obvious he had an infatuation with her, but why would he let that get in the way of his work and what was an excellent job with good prospects? Of course, she realised that he may be manufacturing a plot to get himself sacked and then sue for unfair dismissal, but that was a risky business anyway. Then there was the other theme – that he was jealous of her success and wanted to ruin it for her by causing a rift which would inevitably mean she would lose her job.

As much as she considered all of those scenarios, none held water, so she was still wondering what he was up to when her thoughts were interrupted by Tom turning over in bed. He was still asleep, so she edged her way out of the bed so as not to disturb him. She checked her phone: it was already twenty-six centigrade at this early hour. She had not slept well and she felt hot and sticky, so she decided to take a shower. She took out a towel from the wardrobe and went to the bathroom, her thoughts turning to Saunders and the reason why Jefferey would issue the incorrect information in the court sentencing procedure. If Susan was right and something was going on between

Jefferey and Lucy Saunders, then that would explain everything. However, it would also mean that Jefferey would have committed a criminal offence by falsifying evidence. She was hoping that her request for an urgent visit to Saunders would be granted as she felt it an obligation on her part to try to sort this mess out. Joanne stepped out of the shower and dried herself, then she placed her towel in the wash basket before heading back into the bedroom where she sat down in front of her dressing table to brush her hair. Her train of thought was disturbed by the sound of a clicking noise and looking around towards her bed, she saw Tom lying there with his camera, clicking away as he took more pictures of her.

"I didn't realise you were awake; did you sleep well?" she asked as she got up from the chair and crossed the room to the bed, leaning over to kiss him.

"Amazing," replied Tom.

"Wow, that's good," replied Joanne. "I'm glad you slept well."

"No," replied Tom, "my sleep was good, it's you who are amazing."

"And that, Mister, is why I love you so much. You never hold back on your compliments, thank you," she replied.

Tom reached out and taking hold of her waist, he pulled her towards him and gave her a lingering kiss before releasing his hold on her and allowing her to move.

"I am only telling the truth, Joanne, because you are the most amazing woman," he said as he got out of bed and went into the bathroom.

"What do you want for breakfast?" asked Joanne as she passed the bathroom on her way down to the kitchen.

"Can I have tea and toast, please, beautiful?" asked Tom.

"Okay, but don't be too long in there, or your breakfast will be cold," she replied.

Joanne continued down to the kitchen to prepare breakfast and when Tom appeared, everything was on the breakfast bar, ready and waiting. Joanne was seated at the bar in front of her laptop.

"Eat your breakfast, Tom. I just have to see if there are any messages from work."

"Okay, no problem. Do you think you will be here with me today, or do you have to go into the office for a while?" he asked her.

"I'm not sure yet, Tom. Obviously there is the problem of Jefferey to sort out, but I do not think that will require me to go into the office. I can control most of it from here. However, I am still waiting to see if I will be issued an urgent pass to visit Saunders in prison," replied Joanne.

"What prison is he in? Is he far away?" asked Tom.

"Not far at all. He's being held in Lewes Prison."

"At least that's good – you won't have too far to travel," commented Tom.

He sat there quietly eating his breakfast while Joanne was reading the new messages she had received from work. There was one message from Warren and one from Jefferey, which she had expected there would be. She opened the message from Warren first, to see if he had anything to say about his evening with Tom on Friday.

'Hi Joanne, we desperately need to chat regarding this business with Jefferey as this cannot be allowed to fester any longer. Please let me know as soon as you can if you will be able to come into the office on Monday. I want to bring this to a close now as the guy simply cannot take no for an answer. By the way, I had a heart-to-heart with Tom on Friday. He is a great lad, you really ought to tie him down as soon as you can. He's like the son I never had.'

Wow! Joanne was wondering what had happened between Tom and Warren on Friday evening for Warren to say something like that. Tom had not mentioned anything to her, but she knew that she had to ask him now.

"So, Mister, are you hiding something from me?" she asked him.

"Are you talking to me?" he asked.

"Well, I don't see anyone else here. I received a strange message from Warren. He was telling me you are a great guy, and that he considers you the son he never had," she said, looking enquiringly at Tom.

"That's nice of him," replied Tom.

"Nice of him? Is that all you can offer me? He hardly knows you, Tom, and yet he is likening you to a son he never had! There must be a good reason," she said.

"Maybe you should be asking Warren that question and not me," he replied.

"Perhaps I will do just that. He wants me to go into the office today to try to bring a close to the problem with Jefferey," she replied.

Although she did not want to, she knew she had to open Jefferey's message to see what he had to say, and perhaps find out what was going on in his head.

Joanne, why did you leave like that on Friday? I think you must have felt a little shocked at my proposal because you didn't even take your ring, but not to worry, I can give it to you later. I can't wait to see it on your finger and to know that you will be mine. We can tell everyone in the office later. I'm sure they will all be happy for us. I miss you so much, I just cannot wait to hold you in my arms and kiss you again. Ever since the first time we were together, I just knew the way you touched me and the things you did that you would always be mine. Have you told Tom that he will have to leave? Don't worry if you haven't, I can tell him, he doesn't frighten me, not the way he frightens you. See you later! Love you, sweetie. Jefferey'

Joanne was unbelievably shocked.

"What is wrong with this guy? He's crazy and he just won't stop," she said out loud. Having read his message, she was now even more worried and did not know what to expect next. She knew, though, that she had to show Warren Jefferey's message which she would do as soon as she got to the office. She had thought about replying but decided it was not worth the effort.

"Do you have a problem?" asked Tom.

Joanne turned her laptop around to face Tom.

"Read that message from Jefferey," she asked him.

Joanne sat there watching the expression on Tom's face as he read it.

"There is something seriously wrong with this guy," replied Tom, "and he needs to be sorted out."

Joanne quickly typed a reply to Warren's message, though not one to Jefferey.

Thank you for your message, Warren. Yes, I'll be in the office later today. By the way, I have had another strange message from Jefferey which I will show you when I get in, and yes, something will have to be done as this is betting beyond ridiculous and is no longer acceptable behaviour.'

She left her laptop connected in the kitchen and went back up to her bedroom, closely followed by Tom, to get herself ready for work. He sensed that Jefferey was driving her to breaking point, and her strong exterior was fast crumbling, but he felt helpless to intervene.

"Hey, beautiful, are you okay?" he said as he walked up behind her and placed his arms around her shoulders.

She turned around to face him and laid her head on his chest.

"Oh Tom, I am so worried. I just cannot fathom out what Jefferey is up to. His messages to me are so suggestive but there is nothing between us; it's all in his mind and it's getting worse all the time. At first, I thought, like you, that he may be annoyed at our relationship. I still do think that is part of the problem, it is pretty obvious he doesn't like you, however, it goes much deeper than that. I am sure now it is not just about you and me, it is about me and him. He sees me as an enemy, he thinks I stole his job, but in truth, Warren would never have made him an executive. I just do not know what to do."

Tom lifted her face towards him and kissed her lightly on the forehead.

"You'll have to wait and see what Warren suggests, but if he can't come up with an answer, then I think you may need to involve the police," suggested Tom.

Joanne moved slightly away from his body, and looking up at him she replied.

"I think you are right, but I think I have made the problem even worse now by making Susan my assistant, not because of the money side of it, as Jefferey earns much more than she does, it's the kudos that goes with the job and the relative closeness to me. That's definitely something that would annoy him. I'm now worried for her, too; she is a single parent who has a young son, and I may have put her in some sort of danger. Oh Tom, what can I do?" she asked him.

"Come on, you won't get anything done standing here worrying about it. You have to confront it head-on, you have to confront Jefferey, but not on your own, you have to do it when you are both in the office and there are people around you, preferably when Warren is there," he replied.

"Yes, you are right as usual. I think it wouldn't be wise to meet him on my own again. I need to get ready and then phone Aunty. I hope she's not busy today."

Tom picked up Joanne's phone.

"I'll ring Matilda while you are getting dressed."

Tom stood there next to Joanne, waiting for Aunt Matilda to answer.

"Hello Joanne," said the voice at the other end.

"Close, Matilda, but it's Tom actually," he replied.

"Oh Tom! What's wrong with Joanne?" she asked.

"There is nothing wrong with Joanne, please don't panic. She's here but she is busy getting dressed. She asked me to ring you to see if you were free this morning to babysit me as she has to go into the office?"

"Well, when you put it like that, Tom, how can I refuse, as long I you don't expect me to change nappies or anything like that," she replied.

"No, Aunty, I'm passed that stage now. However, I am still struggling with the tea bit," replied Tom jovially.

"That's not a problem, Tom, I can manage the tea bit quite easily. Okay, I'll phone for a taxi and come straight over. See you soon, bye."

"Thank you, Matilda, bye."

Tom placed Joanne's phone back down on the dressing table.

"You know I think she likes coming here, Joanne," he said.

Joanne turned towards him with a smile on her face.

"I think she likes you, Mister; I need to keep my eye on her."

Tom waited in the bedroom while Joanne finished dressing, then they both went downstairs to the kitchen.

"Would you like another drink?" asked Tom.

"Oh, yes, please. Can I have another coffee please?"

As Tom placed Joanne's coffee on the breakfast bar, there was a knock on the front door.

"I'll go," he said. "I expect that will be my new aunty."

"Good morning, Aunty," said Tom as he opened the door. "Go straight through, Joanne is in the kitchen."

"Good morning, Aunty," said Joanne as she stood up and kissed her aunt on the cheek. "Are you ready to babysit then?"

"It would appear so, dear, but I do hope he will behave himself," replied Matilda.

"I just need to check my emails and then I will go. Oh, I forgot to say I have had one from the prison service, Tom. I have been granted that visit today, so I'll phone them from the office to arrange a time. I will let you know later if I am going to be late," said Joanne as she closed her laptop and placed it in the hold-all. "Okay, I'm going now you two, behave yourselves. I'll see you both later."

"Bye, Joanne, take care," replied Matilda.

Tom followed Joanne to the door.

"Take care and remember what I said: don't get yourself in a situation where you are alone with Jefferey. See what Warren suggests and take it from there. I love you, beautiful," said Tom as he gave Joanne a lingering kiss.

"Bye, Tom," replied Joanne as she got into her car. Just before she drove off, she wound down her window and said, "Ring me later please. I love the sound of your voice."

Joanne drove into the car park. Warren's car was there, as was Susan's, but no sign of Jefferey's which was a relief as she was not looking forward to confronting him even if she did have backup.

"Morning, Therese," said Joanne as she walked into the office.

"Good morning, Joanne. Jefferey rang just now to say he won't be in again today as he is still not feeling well," replied Therese.

"Oh, is that so? He was not well all last week, but was okay on Friday evening and then not well again today. Just as well he does not have a case at the moment. Thank you for letting me know, Therese," replied Joanne.

She walked through the office to her desk just as Susan was leaving the kitchen, coffee in hand.

"Good morning, Susan," she said. "You can leave that on my desk if you want to. You will need a pen and note pad. We have to see Warren immediately. I'll just grab a coffee myself."

Susan was waiting for Joanne when she returned to her desk.

"Okay, Susan, I am going to ask you to describe to Warren the two incidents you relayed to me last week regarding Jefferey and Mrs Saunders. You have nothing to worry about, just explain to him what you saw, just as you did when telling me. While we are in Warren's office, some of what you hear may shock you, but it is all true. I also need to go to Lewes Prison today to see Mr Saunders and I want you to come with me as part of your training. Okay, let's do this," said Joanne.

Joanne knocked on Warren's office door and went straight in.

"Good morning, Warren. I hope you had a good weekend?" asked Joanne.

"Well, Friday night was excellent, much better than I had expected, but it kind of went downhill after that," he replied.

"I have brought Susan along. I hope that's okay with you?" said Joanne.

"No problem at all. Where do you want to start?"

"I would like you to listen to what Susan has to say as I think it is relevant to what's happening with Jefferey," said Joanne.

"Okay, fire away, Susan," replied Warren.

"Well, on two separate occasions last week I observed a van parked outside the flats where the Saunders live. On both occasions, Mrs Saunders was there and she was placing articles in the van, but she also had someone helping her – it was Jefferey Philips. I also saw his car parked just around the corner. These incidents occurred on consecutive days, the first one when I was taking my son to my mother's house, the second incident was the following day as I left my mother's house and was coming into the office."

Susan paused for a moment, picking up her cup. She took a few sips of coffee and then continued.

"I was waiting in a queue of traffic that had been caused by the van leaving the flats where the Saunders lived, and as it pulled away, I noticed Jefferey's car in front of it. He drove off at the same time. I was three or four cars behind him, he hadn't noticed me, but I could see he had a passenger in the car with him. I thought he may have been coming to the office, but he turned off, taking him away from town. I took it upon myself to follow him at a distance. He stopped in the middle of Melbourne Road, and I thought he had seen me, so I quickly pulled in, but Mrs Saunders got out, they kissed goodbye, she went into a house there and Jefferey drove off. I didn't see where he went because a car passed me as I was about to pull out and I lost him," explained Susan.

Warren sat in silent for a few minutes; he was obviously trying to take in everything that Susan had just told him.

"Of course, he could have just been helping her, maybe feeling guilty for the sentence that her husband had ended up with … but that wouldn't explain the kissing," he replied.

"Yes but there is something else, too. Joanne didn't have time to do it because of the Tom's accident so I carried out some checks that she had wanted to do herself. It appears Mrs Saunders has moved out of the flat she shared with her husband and moved into the house in Melbourne Road. She opened the front door with a key. So, I checked the owner of the house – it was recently bought by a Miss Sargent. Now, it may be a coincidence, but Sargent was the maiden name of Jefferey's mother," explained Susan.

"Well, I can see why Joanne wanted you as her assistant – you have certainly covered everything quite excellently," said Warren. "The problem now is, what do we do with Jefferey?"

"Did you see the message I sent to you this morning, which is the latest message that I have received from him?" asked Joanne.

"Yes, I did, and it is totally unacceptable, but my hands are tied without concrete proof which it looks as though we may be able to get. If not, all I can do is to reprimand him though I doubt that will stop him," replied Warren.

"I have been granted a visit to see Saunders, so I will confirm the time and take Susan along with me; I think we need to get Jefferey to break cover. It is quite strange how he was sick all last week but was okay on Friday when he wanted to meet me, but now, suddenly, he is ill again today. I was thinking of sending a company email to all staff, informing them that Susan and I will be out of the office this afternoon on a visit to Lewes Prison to arrange an appeal for a recently convicted client. Jefferey is bound to see the email and I would hope it may draw him out," explained Joanne.

"I think it could be quite risky though, Joanne, as none of us know how his brain is working; I think we should wait to see if you can find anything out from Saunders. Make sure you keep me informed of what happens," said Warren.

"Will do," replied Joanne.

They left Warren's office together and Susan went back to her desk while Joanne contacted the visitor service.

"That's fine, thank you," said Joanne as she ended the call and placed her phone in her jacket pocket. She turned off her PC and then placed her laptop in her holdall and went looking for Susan. She was not at her desk, nor was she in the kitchen area, so Joanne went to the reception desk.

"Therese, have you seen Susan?" she asked.

"Yes, Joanne, she is on her way back up now," she replied.

"Ah Susan, there you are. We need to go now – are you ready?" asked Joanne.

"Yes, Joanne, I just went to get my lunch, but I can eat it in your car if that's okay with you."

"Therese, Susan and I have a visit this afternoon with Saunders at Lewes Prison. If anyone should want us, please ask them to call back tomorrow or send an email," explained Joanne as they both left the office.

They were on their way to Lewes when Joanne started to explain to Susan the procedure on prisoner visits.

"As you haven't been on one before, I just want to make you aware that sometimes they can make you feel as though it is you who is the criminal. The prison officers may well stare at you and search you but don't let them worry you. When we see Saunders, some tough questions need answering, and he will probably lose his temper, he may well shout and swear, but don't worry, he's not a violent man, or at least he hasn't been in the past. However, there will be guards close by, so just try not to let it all get on top of you. Although we are going there to try to help Saunders, it's all down to mistakes that Jefferey Philips has made. Never forget that Saunders still committed a crime and has been found guilty – it is only the length of the sentence that is wrong," explained Joanne.

They pulled into the prison car park and then made their way to the entrance. After going through the obligatory security checks, they were directed to a room where they waited for Saunders; when he did eventually arrive, he was not at all happy.

"Who the hell are you two? Where's Philips?" he asked.

"I'm sorry, Mr Saunders, he wasn't able to be here today," replied Joanne. "I'm Joanne Webster, an executive in the company, and this is my assistant, Susan Caton."

"Just as well for him he's not here as he wouldn't have left here alive! What was he trying to prove? He's ruined my life and he's going to pay for it," said Saunders.

"We are aware that mistakes were made, Mr Saunders, which is why we are here now trying to make amends. We have applied for an emergency hearing and intend to get your sentence reduced," explained Joanne.

"Yeah, well, don't let that Philips anywhere near me or else I'll be serving time for murder," shouted Saunders.

"I would suggest you keep your voice down, Mr Saunders. As much as you may have a bone to pick with Philips, that's not going to help you get out of here; so, let's get down to business, shall we, as we don't have long," replied Joanne.

"Why is your sidekick here if she isn't going to speak?" he asked.

"She will speak, Mr Saunders," replied Joanne, "but you seem to prefer the sound of your own voice. We are here to try to help you, so if you would just control your temper for a while and let us ask the questions, we might get somewhere."

"Mr Saunders, did you have a problem with Jefferey Philips?" asked Susan.

"What? Apart from the fact that I just did not like him? No, not really," replied Saunders.

"Any particular reason for not liking him, then?" asked Joanne.

"He came to visit me with my wife once, when I was on remand. I got the impression he was more interested in her than he was of handling my case, or maybe I was just jealous because he was sitting next to her, and I wasn't," he replied.

Susan picked up on Saunders' reply. "So, did you mention that to your wife?" she asked.

"You bet I did, in the very next phone call, but she told me she had no interest in him and that she didn't even like the man, but he was doing everything he could to get me out on a suspended sentence," he replied.

"Did you doubt her reply to you?" asked Joanne.

"Not then, no."

"Not then?" questioned Joanne. "Meaning that you did later?"

"Well sort of. My wife was always very non-committal, so being in here, I had to play it cool, well, to her anyway; but I still wasn't sure … it was something he said." Saunders stopped mid-sentence; he looked down at his hands which were on the table and started clicking his knuckles, as if he was getting ready for a fight or something.

"What did he say, Mr Saunders?" Joanne asked.

"It was on another visit, when he was on his own and we had been talking – he told me not to worry," Saunders explained.

Joanne continued her line of questioning. "So, was that it? Is that what made you doubt your wife, nothing else?" she asked again.

"He just made some comment," replied Saunders.

Susan took over from Joanne who was now becoming impatient with Saunders.

"Mr Saunders, we know this is not easy for you, but we really are here to help you. You will not see Philips again, he has been removed from your case, but unless you can tell us everything, you will make things harder for yourself, and then it's going to be harder for us to help you," explained Susan.

Saunders placed his hands flat on the table and looked across the table at them both.

"Look, I know I did wrong, and I know I am guilty as charged, but five years, come on, I don't deserve that! Something is going on. I hate it in here and I never want to see the inside of one of these places again."

Looking across at Susan, he continued. "You have an incredibly soft but convincing voice, just like my wife, but I hope you are not lying to me like her. I asked Philips before the trial if he would get me out and his exact words were, 'Leave it to me, I am sorting everything out with your wife, and she will get what she wants.' That played on my mind, so I got someone to check, and I was told that Philips had been staying at the flat with her." At that point, the tears started rolling down his cheeks and he lifted his arm and used the sleeve of his shirt to dry his eyes.

Joanne looked across the table to Saunders. "I am so sorry and as for Susan, she is nothing like your wife and she certainly will not lie to you. Susan and I, we will sort this mess out for you but unfortunately we cannot give you a time scale. It will be down to the court but as soon as we know more, we will be in touch with you. Thank you so much, Mr Saunders, and again, I'm sorry this has been so upsetting for you, but the truth usually pays off," said Joanne.

At that point, they were interrupted by the prison guard telling them that their time was up. Saunders stood up to leave and looked across the table towards Susan.

"Thank you very much, Susan" he said before turning and leaving the room.

Joanne and Susan sat there for a while, waiting for their escort out of the prison.

"Well, at least that answers one question, Susan," said Joanne.

"Which is?" she asked.

"You were right about Jefferey and Mrs Saunders – they are clearly having an affair," replied Joanne.

They were interrupted by the door opening.

"Okay, ladies, if you would like to follow me, I will escort you both back to relative safety," said the guard.

"Come on," said Joanne as they got in her car, "let's get you back to the office, you need to pick your son up."

"Don't worry, Joanne, I phoned my mother earlier to tell her I might be late tonight. Do you honestly believe you will be able to get his sentence reduced?"

"Me?" asked Joanne. "No, but *you* may be able to; this is your case from now on, Susan. I will help you, but you will be doing the majority of the paperwork. I need to deal with Jefferey, so I won't be able to give Saunders one hundred per cent which is what his case now requires. As for Saunders' reduced sentence, we should be looking for a suspended sentence now and nothing less."

"What about Jefferey?" enquired Susan. "If all that Saunders said is true, then surely Jefferey is in deep trouble?" she added.

"Deep shit, I would say," replied Joanne. "Not only will he lose his job without any compensation, but he could also end up in prison himself."

CHAPTER TWENTY-THREE

Troubled Emotions

When Joanne pulled into the office car park, Warren's car was still there which pleased her as she wanted to update him on her findings from the meeting with Saunders. Susan went straight to her car and then drove off to her mother's house to collect her son.

As she went into the office, she noticed Warren was on the phone, so she put her bag on her desk and went to the kitchen to make herself a coffee. Standing there as she took a couple of sips, she began to realise the enormity of the problem with Jefferey; she was now under the impression that their only course of action would be to fire him, something that she wasn't sure Warren would agree to, even if push came to shove. Joanne tipped the rest of her coffee into the sink, placed the empty cup in the dishwasher, and went to see Warren.

Knocking on his office door first, she walked in.
"Ah, Joanne, I didn't see you come back in," he said.
"You were on the phone, so I went to get a drink," she replied.
"How did everything go with Saunders?" he asked.
"I think I would have to say it went as well as could be expected under the circumstances," she replied with an air of trepidation in her voice.
"As bad as that, eh? I was hoping for a somewhat better response," said Warren, tapping his fingers on his desk in a somewhat agitated fashion.

"Sorry," she replied. "I'm just telling it as I saw it. I got the impression that he doesn't trust us and under the circumstances, who could blame him? We have a mountain to climb to rebuild his trust."

"That man … he makes my blood boil. He's become a real liability," said Warren, his elbows on his desk and his forehead resting on his hand.

"Yes, but I think all is not lost with Saunders. I'm going to give Susan the responsibility of overseeing his appeal and of conducting any subsequent meetings with him."

"What?" Warren raised his voice somewhat. "Have you lost your mind? She isn't qualified enough to cope with something like that."

"On the contrary, I know she has what it takes and I will guide her from the office. I think she should be the one who has face-to-face contact with Saunders, she's more than capable," replied Joanne.

"Preposterous idea!" exclaimed Warren in a fury.

Joanne took a step back. It was the first time that she had seen Warren lose his temper, but she believed that she was right.

"Warren, please. May I explain my reasoning?" she asked.

Warren looked up at her. "Sorry for my outburst, Joanne. I'm just so stressed with all of this. Yes, of course, please do explain," he replied.

"Do you recall the Cannon-Vickers case a few years ago?" she asked.

"Why, yes, but what has that got to do with this case?"

"Well, it was handled by Johnson & Johnson, my previous firm, but it wasn't Johnson himself who did all the leg work, it was me, although I never got the recognition for it. Susan is every bit as good as I was then, in fact, she may even be better. This afternoon with Saunders, she asked some very probing questions, but did Saunders get annoyed with her? No, and in the end she got him to open up to her. It wasn't a good sight – the man was in tears. I could tell at that moment that Susan was the one who could rebuild his trust in us; as I sat there listening to her, it took me back to that case at Johnson & Johnson and how I carried out all the leg work for that case. Honestly, Susan is perfectly capable."

"But Joanne, you are a special entity. That's why I made you an executive."

"You know, there is nothing special about me or the way I operate – I just try to do what is right," replied Joanne before turning and leaving Warren sitting there. She collected her things from her office and then went straight down to her car.

Joanne took out her mobile and rang Tom.

"Hi, how are doing, beautiful?"

"Not feeling that beautiful at the moment," she replied.

"Then get yourself straight home. I will soon change that for you," replied Tom.

"That sounds very promising. I was just wondering what you wanted to eat as I don't really feel like cooking tonight."

"That's already sorted. Aunty had a rummage through the freezer and she already has something in the oven. So, you can have dinner and then a long soak in the bath while I drive Aunty home," replied Tom.

"Oh, Tom, you make it sound really wonderful! Thank you. I'll be home in fifteen minutes," said Joanne as she put her phone down and started her car.

When dinner was over, Tom directed Joanne and Matilda to the lounge while he cleared away the things from the dining room and stacked everything in the dishwasher.

"You know, Joanne, I just cannot get over these pictures of you! They look so real … it's almost as if you are going to jump down from them any minute."

"I know, Aunty, they are amazing, aren't they? Tom has captured every detail which is what makes them so life-like," replied Joanne.

Having cleared up in the dining room and kitchen, Tom made his way to the lounge just as Joanne was replying to her aunt.

"Makes what so lifelike?" he asked.

Matilda turned to look at Tom. "I was just saying to Joanne that your pictures of her are so lifelike."

"Yes, I'm quite proud of them. I reckon I've captured Joanne's outstanding beauty," said Tom.

"Not forgetting her sexiness," added Matilda.

"Oh Aunty, surely you mean her sensuality?" responded Tom.

Joanne opened her mouth and feigned putting her fingers into her mouth, pretending to be sick.

"Oh, excuse me," said Joanne. "I'm here, you know! Maybe I should go to bed and leave you two to talk to the wall. At least you won't get any contradictory answers."

Tom leant towards Matilda and whispered in her ear, "I think we should sit down; the lady of the house is not pleased."

Tom sat on the sofa next to Joanne, leaving Matilda standing in the middle of the room, staring at the pictures, as though she was glued to the spot.

"What did you whisper in my aunt's ear just then?" asked Joanne.

"I suggested we sit down because I thought you weren't pleased," he replied.

"Well, you're correct about that, but your concerns in telling my aunt were wasted," said Joanne.

"Excuse me?"

"Try the other ear; she's stone deaf in her left ear," replied Joanne with a broad grin on her face.

Tom rushed over to where Matilda was still standing. He took her arm and as she turned to look at him, he said, "I think we should sit down now, Aunty."

"Oh, but not for long. I should be getting home," she replied.

"If you're getting tired, Aunty, Tom will order a taxi for you to take you home," said Joanne.

"Well, I am feeling tired; it has been a long day, so if you don't mind. Tom, I would like to go now," she replied.

"No problem aunty, I'll get your coat for you and order a taxi. Thank you very much for babysitting me, and for stopping me from getting into any further trouble," said Tom as he went into the passage to get Matilda's coat. Reappearing a couple of minutes later he passed Matilda's coat to her saying, "your taxi will be here in ten minutes."

"It was my pleasure, Tom, and anytime you need a babysitter, just call me."

"How about tomorrow, Aunty?" asked Joanne.

"Oh, that would be lovely, dear," she replied.

As soon as Matilda had left Joanne went to have a bath to relax her aching body; it had been quite a stressful day and she was beginning to feel very tired. After she'd had her bath, she dried her hair and then got into bed. She picked up her phone and sent a text message.

Tom went into the kitchen to tidy up and to make himself a cup of tea. He then checked to make sure the windows and door on the ground floor, before going up stairs to check on Joanne. Walking into the bedroom, he saw Joanne sitting there with her phone in her hand, but she was fast asleep. He took the phone from her and, looking at the screen, he noticed a half-completed message still there. It was to him but she had obviously fallen asleep before sending it.

Tom went back downstairs, made two drinks, and then took them with him back up to the bedroom. He placed the drinks on the bedside cabinet before removing the pillows from behind Joanne's back and tried to lay her down in the bed, covering her naked body with the duvet cover. Then he picked up a towel and went into the bathroom to have a shower. He dried himself and shaved before going back into the bedroom.

He was surprised to see Joanne had woken up; she was lying on her side, facing the dressing table.

"Hey, beautiful, you're awake," he said as he sat at the dressing table, looking at her reflection in the mirror.

"Sorry, Tom, I fell asleep while waiting for you. I need to talk to you about today."

"Why? What happened?"

"I went to see Saunders. I took Susan my assistant with me, and she managed to get Saunders to open up. He thinks that Jefferey may be having an affair with his wife."

"Did you confirm that with him, then?" replied Tom.

"I wasn't there to confirm or deny it, I just wanted to find out what he knew."

"How does that change things, then?" asked Tom.

"It may complicate things as now we must include Lucy Saunders in our plans. The thing is, we don't know whether she is acting voluntarily or if Jefferey has a hold over her," she replied.

Tom got up and lay down next to Joanne on the bed. She sat up and leant her head on his shoulder.

"I'm sorry, Tom, but the next few days are going to be very busy. I was thinking of asking Aunty to stay. She can sleep in the spare bedroom. What do you think?" she asked.

"It's okay with me, beautiful, although there is one slight problem," replied Tom.

"And what would that be?" asked Joanne.

"You won't be able to walk around naked while she is here," replied Tom.

"Then maybe it would be best if she didn't stay overnight after all," replied Joanne.

Tom turned towards Joanne, giving her a lengthy kiss.

"I am sure you could manage the clothes thing for one or two nights," he replied.

"I suppose I could manage that, if I really have to."

Tom rose from the bed and looking at her, he said, "I want to check some of the photos I have of you. I won't be long and you need to sleep, miss, as it looks as though you are going to be busy again tomorrow."

"Okay," replied Joanne, "but please don't be long. I want you to cuddle me until I fall asleep. I feel so safe in your arms."

Tom went back down to the lounge and, picking up his camera, he sat there looking at all the photos he had taken of her. He hadn't realised there were so many. He wanted to choose some more photos to use as wall art, but he just couldn't make his mind up on which ones. As he sat there, he could feel his eyes getting heavy and then realised he was repeatedly looking at the same photo. He stood up, taking his camera with him, and slowly climbed the stairs to the bedroom; Joanne was already asleep, and as usual she was taking up most of the bed, leaving him just enough room to squeeze in beside her.

Joanne woke early and picking up her phone, she checked the time: it was only four-thirty but she got out of bed and went into the bathroom before going downstairs to make a hot drink. She placed the two cups on a small tray and then carried them up to the bedroom. She sat on the edge of the bed drinking her tea and then lay back down beside Tom and cuddled up to him; that was where she wanted to be, and she never wanted to lose him. She lay there like that until he woke about an hour later.

"Morning, gorgeous," he said as he turned onto his side to cuddle up to her. He slid his hand over her bottom, allowing his fingertips to make intermittent contact with her body. He let his fingers continue up over the stomach until reaching her chest where he traced a circle around her nipple before cupping her breast, while all the time planting kisses on the back of her neck.

"Ooh, that is so nice, Tom, thank you."

"Thank you for what exactly?"

"For loving me, Tom. You're great, but I hope you're not getting a little bit too excited, are you?" she asked.

"No! Of course not," he replied. "Why do you ask?"

"I just thought I felt something moving down there."

"No, definitely not," replied Tom.

"Are you sure?" she asked.

"Well, maybe just a tiny bit," he admitted.

"Tom, I was thinking, when you are given the okay by the doctors, I was thinking of taking a week off."

"A week? I was thinking more like a month – we have a lot of catching up to do."

"Tom, I am going to call Aunty to ask her what time she'll be coming this morning as Warren sent me a message last night – he wants the business with Jefferey sorted out now."

"That's okay, it needs to be sorted out, it's gone on far too long without anything being done," said Tom.

Joanne turned over to face Tom and kissed him.

"I'll have to get up now as I need to ring Aunty."

"Okay. What do you want for breakfast?" he asked.

"Oh, can I have coffee and cereal, please?" she asked.

"No problem. I'll call you when it's ready."

Tom went down to the kitchen to prepare Joanne's breakfast and to make his tea and toast. He picked up a bowl from the cupboard and placed it on the breakfast bar along with a spoon. He also set out an assortment of cereals as he didn't yet know what her favourite was; he still had a lot to learn about her. He found a card in one of the drawers and took it out of the envelope to see if there were any words printed on it. As luck would have it, it was blank, so he picked up a pen and proceeded to write a little verse for her.

Then he placed the card in the envelope and wrote 'To Joanne' on the front with a hastily drawn heart and some kisses. He was just about to call her when she walked into the kitchen.

"Thank you, Tom. I spoke to Aunty and she has already booked the taxi. She's waiting for it to arrive, so she shouldn't be too long."

"Okay, I had better go and put some clothes on, then. I wouldn't want to shock her."

"I think it would take more than that to shock her," replied Joanne with a smile on her face.

As Tom disappeared up the stairs to the bedroom, there was a knock on the door.

"Good morning, Aunt Matilda, thank you for coming. I'm so pleased you were able to get a taxi straight away as I need to get into work as soon as I can – we have a problem that needs sorting out today and I can't do it from home."

"That's okay, dear, you get off to work. I'm here to make sure Tom doesn't do anything that he shouldn't be doing."

"Thank you," said Joanne as she leant forward and kissed her aunt on the cheek. "Hopefully I won't be too long. I think once our decision has been made, Warren will be the one to see it through and I should be able to leave."

"Tom, where are you? I'm going now."

"I'm here," said Tom as he ran down the stairs.

"I have to go now. I'll try not to be too long," said Joanne as she kissed him.

Tom walked into the kitchen to find Aunt Matilda sitting at the breakfast bar.

"Good morning, Matilda. Have you had breakfast and something to drink?"

"No, I haven't eaten yet as I was too busy getting ready to come here. I would just love a cup of tea though."

"Okay, and what would you like to eat?" asked Tom.

"I'd like a bacon sandwich if that's at all possible," she replied.

"No problem, one tea and one bacon sandwich coming up."

While he was waiting for the bacon to cook, Tom cleared away Joanne's breakfast things. It was then that he noticed she hadn't even opened his card; maybe she had other things on her mind. He picked it up and placed it on the cupboard.

"There you are – a bacon sandwich and a cup of tea, as requested."

"Thank you, Tom," replied Matilda.

Joanne pulled into the office car park. The traffic had not been good, and it had taken her almost thirty minutes. *That's unusual*, Joanne said to herself when she saw that the car park was almost full. She noticed that both Warren's and Susan's were amongst the cars there, but no sign of Jefferey's yet again. Joanne made her way into the office but as she said good morning in her usual manner, there were very few replies.

When she reached her desk, Warren knocked on his office window and beckoned for her to go straight in to see him.

"Have you seen this?" he said as he turned his laptop around to face her.

"What is it?" she asked.

"I thought you would have known! It's your engagement."

"What? I haven't got engaged, not yet anyway, and should Tom and I take the plunge you will be the first to know," replied Joanne.

"I wasn't referring to your engagement to Tom – I was referring to your engagement to Jefferey! Look at the video," he replied.

"What?" exclaimed Joanne. "Where did you get this from?"

"It's not just me; everyone has been sent a copy."

"But this isn't true, it's fake! I wonder who would have done something like this?"

"Look at the photos in the video. They are all of you and Jefferey," said Warren.

"It's fake, you know it is! Surely you don't believe this?" asked Joanne.

"What am I to expect? Look at the video, look at the photos, all thirty-five of them. There is even a voice recording of you telling him you want to be sexually active with him. Tell me, what do you expect me to say?" asked Warren. "Look at this one – there is a photo of him removing your dress and undoing your bra! How do you explain that? It looks pretty explicit to me."

Joanne was speechless. She just didn't know what to say. She was in tears at what she had seen but she just couldn't explain how it had happened.

"I want to know what you are playing at, Joanne, and I want to know pretty damn quickly!"

"But surely you don't believe this? It's fake! I would never agree to get engaged to Jefferey. He is the last person on earth I would get engaged to. As for kissing him and letting him remove my clothes, the thought sickens me."

"You say that now, Joanne, but how you do explain the photos, the video, the voice recordings? Are you trying to tell me that you have a double? How unlikely is that?" asked Warren.

"Please, believe me, this is all part of Jefferey's plot to discredit me. I should have stopped this from the start. I was stupid to believe that I could talk to him to find out what he was up to."

"Joanne, I want to believe you but look at the photos. Are they not photos of you, your clothes? You have worn those same clothes to the office. Your voice – it is all concrete stuff, listen to your voice, it's you no one else. You even say how much you enjoy having sex with him. You say you want to be sexually active with him at lunchtime as it would help to ease the stress! For God's sake! Tell me how you can do all those things with Jefferey and then say you love Tom. Why? Why would you do it?" he asked.

"But it isn't me, Warren, I wouldn't lie to you. I don't know how he has done it, but somehow Jefferey has altered the photos, and I wasn't even aware that videos were being taken. Please believe me, those videos taken in compromising act with him are not of me, I can guarantee that."

Joanne took out her laptop and connected to the company website then she went straight to her emails and checked for one from Jefferey. There was nothing there, so it looked as though he had deliberately sent the email to everyone but her.

"I did not receive that email; he sent it to everyone but me. Now, why would he do that?" asked Joanne.

"I'm not sure what is happening, Joanne, but at the moment things do not look good on your part," he said.

As Joanne searched through company files, she remembered seeing something that she could use and, if she were right, she had every intention of acting upon it.

"Joanne, what are you doing now? I want answers and I want proof of what you are saying."

"Yes, I know, and I will give you answers and I will get proof that what I am saying is true, but I just need twenty-four hours."

Warren slumped back in his chair. "Joanne, I am putting my trust in you, so don't let me down. You have twenty-four hours in which to sort out this mess."

"Thank you. Can I take it that I am not under suspension at the moment and can take whatever action is deemed necessary according to my contract?"

"No, you are not under suspension and your contract stands to the letter," he replied.

"Thank you. Could you just confirm that to me in an email, please?" asked Joanne.

"Is that really necessary?" asked Warren.

"Yes, it *is* necessary. I wouldn't have asked if it wasn't."

"There – sent. Is that okay?" he replied.

"Perfectly. Thank you."

That was what Joanne had been waiting for and now she could fire off an email to all staff and put in place her first line of defence that would give her some breathing space.

To all staff. Please read now. *Important*

Dear staff members and colleagues,

You will all have received an email sent this morning (I am the only person not to have received that email) which was sent by Mr Jefferey Philips, the contents of which are substantially inaccurate, twisted and false. To issue such photos to any member of staff or colleague renders the issuer liable to instant dismissal seeing that the content portrays images which are sexual and demeaning to another member of staff or colleague.

The company has, effectively immediately, issued a notice of instant dismissal against Jefferey Philips. This action has ramifications for you all and you should, therefore, consult your terms of contract, which as of now forbid anyone of you to contact or receive contact from Jefferey Philips, either in work or during your non-work social hours. You are all to immediately block Jefferey Philips. This action is not taken lightly nor is it taken without foundation. This company will always protect any employee from vitriolic attacks such as this one.

Joanne Webster (Executive)

Warren read the email that appeared on his laptop and immediately leapt to his feet. Crossing his office and opening his door, he called out.

"Joanne, my office – now!"

Joanne had been waiting for that. She got up and walked casually to his office and closed the door behind her.

"What do you think you are playing at? Who permitted you to issue the email that you just sent?"

"I didn't need permission."

"What do you mean, you didn't need permission?"

"It's in my contract of employment – as Executive, I can act unilaterally when a colleague or member of staff has been placed in an intolerable situation by another colleague or member of staff. Furthermore, where such an act is deemed to refer to or be sexual in nature, an immediate notice of instant dismissal may be issued." Joanne stopped and took a breath, expecting an immediate reply from Warren but there was none.

"I am doing exactly what you employed me to do, to protect our clients and our colleagues and staff members."

Just at that point, Joanne's phone rang – it was her aunt Matilda.

"Aunty, what can I do for you?"

"It's Tom – he's gone."

"What do you mean, he's gone?" she asked.

"There was a package delivered this morning addressed to him. He opened it and then put everything back in the envelope and said he had to pop down to the barn, which was two hours ago. I have just been down there to see where he was, and he wasn't there. What should I do?"

"Aunty, did you look at what was in the package?"

"No, dear, I didn't."

"Okay don't. It's not nice. Where is the package now, Aunty?" asked Joanne.

"It's in the barn where Tom left it with the card."

"What card, Aunty?"

"Tom wrote you a lovely card and left it on the breakfast bar this morning, but you didn't read it. After he looked in the package, he picked up the card and took it all down to the barn. When I went down there to look for him, I noticed he had taken the card out of the envelope and left it under the package. The writing on the card said:

To my gorgeous Joanne,
Who could fill a book of dreams?
or poems of love,
who came into my life,
on the wings of a dove,
today I give you cereal,
tomorrow, maybe croissant,
but one day I hope I can give you,
what you really, really want.

It was signed *love Raymond* and in brackets *Tom* but underneath the last line, in red he wrote, *there's no chance now."*

"Okay, Aunty, there is nothing you can do. I'll get home as soon as I can," said Joanne.

She put her phone down and looked at Warren.

"Tom has disappeared," she said.

"Well, can you blame him?" asked Warren.

"If that were me in those photos and videos, then no, I couldn't blame him, but it is not me," she said defiantly.

"Do you remember what I said to you about Tom? That still stands. If he has disappeared, you had better go and find him."

"With all due respect, Warren, I fear I have already lost him, but through no fault of my own. I am now concerned about saving the reputation of this firm and curtailing Jefferey's vitriolic lies. He has acted in a quite disgusting manner, one which you fail to see as quite deceptive. I can do nothing about your ties to Tom, whatever they may be because he hasn't confided that much in me. But what I can do is try to trace Jefferey and compile the truth that I need to save my job. Goodbye, Warren."

With that, Joanne collected her things and left the office, not knowing if she would ever return.

CHAPTER TWENTY-FOUR

A Rushed Plan

Joanne got in her car and drove down to the seafront, it was the only place that she could think of to start looking for Tom. A feeling of déjà vu came over her because this was exactly where she was when Tom had his accident. She parked her car, got out and walked along the front. She wasn't expecting to find Tom there at this early stage, but she just wanted to see if there were any homeless or rough sleepers who Tom may have joined.

She walked from the Lifeboat Museum down to the pier, took a walk along the pier itself, and then down onto the beach. She counted maybe ten people who looked like being rough sleepers and she hated the thought that Tom might be joining them.

After a fruitless search, she walked back towards her car and took a few minutes just to sit on a bench and watch the world go by. She hadn't been there long when a woman who was passing stopped in front of her.
"Hi there! How are you? Did you get home okay on Friday?"
"Excuse me?" replied Joanne.
"You were at Sovereign Harbour on Friday; I gave you a lift back to here."
"Oh, sorry, was that you? I didn't recognise you! Yes, thank you very much – you got me out of a hole."
"That's okay. Us women have to stick together," she said.

"Yes, I think you're right there," replied Joanne.

"So, what are you doing here then? You look lost – and sad. I'm Sonia, by the way."

"I'm Joanne. My partner has disappeared and I don't know where to start looking for him."

"Another woman's house or flat is usually the first port of call."

"Probably, but not with Tom. He wouldn't do that."

"He must be a very special man then," remarked Sonia.

"He's exceptional," replied Joanne.

"So, do you want to talk about it? It can sometimes help,"

Joanne moved along the bench, giving the woman room to sit down beside her.

"There's this man, one that I work with, who does not understand the meaning of the word *no*. I was meeting with him on Friday, our second meeting like that, just to get to know what makes him tick. It was part of the requirement of my promotion to get to know everyone in the office, but he confused that with thinking I fancied him. He's the guy I was with on Friday."

"What happened to make you walk out like that?" asked Sonia.

"He completely misread the situation; he knows that I have a partner, but he insisted that I should kick him out and get engaged to *him*. So, next he pulls out an engagement ring and expects me to say yes! So, I stormed out."

"But don't you think you made it worse by going back? Perhaps going back encouraged him?"

"What do you mean?" asked Joanne. "I didn't go back! I started walking and almost got as far as the main road when you came along and I am incredibly grateful that you did."

"Hang on a minute … after I'd dropped you at your car, I went back to the Harbour restaurant as I know the manager there and he'd text me to ask me to join him for a nightcap. I was sitting at the bar on the other side of the room. As you know, I had been watching the two of you earlier out of boredom; saw you storm, then I left, then I picked you up to take you for your car. Anyway, I went to the ladies as the manager, Ian, hadn't quite finished his shift, and when I came back, you were back in your seat. He took the ring out of his pocket again and placed it on your finger and then he gave you a lingering kiss. You accepted the ring *and* the kiss!"

"No! That isn't how it happened! I didn't go back after I stormed out and we never got engaged!"

"In that case, what the hell was I watching then? I would swear that was you: same look, same clothes, same hair. I was convinced it was you," said Sonia.

"I knew it! He had someone dress up like me. He even sent an email to my office today, with an attachment, supposedly showing the two of us getting engaged. There were photos of us kissing and whatnot, and even a video of our encounter at the Harbour. What is worse, there was even a video clip of someone like me sitting on a bed in a hotel room having her dress and bra removed."

"What! That's shocking!" said Sonia.

"He's also sent my partner copies of the photos so not only am I in danger of losing my job, but my partner has left me."

"That's bad. Have you been back to Sovereign Harbour? I think they'll have CCTV there, so you might be able to see what exactly happened."

"Would you be prepared to tell my boss what you saw?"

"Yes, of course, but it would not be worth much without CCTV footage from last Friday. Look, what are you doing now? We could go there. As I said, Ian the manager there is a friend. Maybe he could help you get a video clip."

"Okay, my car is just here. Could you come with me?" asked Joanne.

"Sure, come on, let's go there now."

Joanne drove the short distance to Sovereign Harbour as quickly as she could. They approached the restaurant car park and Sonia pointed towards a space.

"Park there," she said. "That's it, come on, just follow me."

They went into the restaurant where most of the staff there

appeared to know Sonia. She and Joanne went straight through to the manager's office.

"Sonia, what can we do for you?" asked the manager.

"It's not for me, Ian, it's for my friend, Joanne. She has been the victim of a very nasty scam, and she needs your help."

"So, what are you after, Joanne?" asked Ian.

"I was wondering if you keep CCTV recordings and if so, would you have one from around eight o'clock last Friday evening?"

Ian got up from his chair and opened a cupboard on the wall and turned some buttons to activate a computer screen.

"Okay, let's try this section of footage. There, I think that's you arriving, so we'll just run this through a little. Okay, one argument, yep, and there you go storming out … is that what you wanted?" he asked.

"Sorry, but can you run it on a little more, please? There! That's not me!"

Ian stopped the video. "No, that can't be you because you stormed out the front door and that will be recorded on the external CCTV surveillance there. This person on the video now, although dressed in the same clothes, isn't you because there's no way you could have come from that direction after going towards the front of the restaurant.

"Can you keep that video for me?" asked Joanne, "and, if possible, get me a copy of that section and the camera from the front? No matter how much it costs, I need them urgently," she added.

Ian looked at her. "If you only want those sections, then I can get them for you. Just give me twenty minutes."

"That would be great. Thank you very much! You have no idea how much that means to me. Can you email me the clips, please?" said Joanne as she wrote down her email address.

"Thank you so much, Sonia. Can I give you a lift back to the pier?" asked Joanne.

"No, I'm fine. I was coming up here anyway. You go and sort out that horrible man, and if you get a chance, give him a slap from me too," replied Sonia.

"Thank you, Sonia. You have been a great help, thank you so much.

You, too, Ian."

Joanne left the restaurant. She hadn't realised the time and it was getting late. She needed to get back home. Her aunt was still there and would be worrying. As she pulled in through the gate and up the drive, she saw a car parked outside the front door. As she got closer, she could see it was Warren's. Joanne parked, got out of the car and opened the front door.

"Aunty, I'm home," she called.

"I'm in the kitchen," replied her aunt.

Joanne entered the kitchen and saw Warren sitting there with Matilda. She ignored him.

"Sorry Aunty, I had some business to sort out and the battery went on my phone," said Joanne as she opened her laptop and connected to the company website. She went straight to her emails and opened the one from the manager of the restaurant.

Joanne pushed the laptop along the breakfast bar towards Warren.

"When you are ready, play the clips and watch carefully, watch very carefully," she said. "Aunty, I'm going to get changed before I go back out to look for Tom. Would you mind making me a cup of coffee before I go, please?" she asked.

Before Joanne went upstairs, she spoke to Warren.

"Warren, you will see me storm out of the restaurant in the first clip, and in the second clip you see what appears to be me approaching from the rear of the restaurant. However, having gone out the front of the building there is no way I could have got to the rear without appearing on the CCTV video again. In the third clip, you will see me leave the restaurant and continue walking down the harbour area. Look at the time of the recording, then go back to the second clip and look at the time of that recording. It's impossible for me to be in two separate places at the same time."

She left him to it, went up to change her clothes and went downstairs again where she switched on her phone and checked for messages; there was one from Jefferey, one from Warren and another one from Tom.

She opened the message from Jefferey.

'Finding it tough, now, are we? You should have accepted my offer.'

She replied straight away.

'Jefferey you're an idiot. You really should check there is no CCTV surveillance when you are trying to stage an event. I'm just wondering how Saunders will feel when he finds out you falsified evidence deliberately to get him a longer sentence just so you could screw his wife. Goodbye, Jefferey. Oh, by the way, I dismissed you for malpractice. You no longer have a job. Have a nice day.'

She then opened Warren's message.

'Joanne, I'm not sure what you're doing. Your phone has been off, so I'll come to your house to see if you need help.'

She looked at Warren.

"How do you have the nerve to send such a crap message? Why would I want to accept help from someone who doesn't even trust me? Well, you can stuff your help and you can stuff your job, too," she said.

She picked up her coffee and took a few sips.

"I am going now, Aunty; I'd appreciate it if you could stay here tonight, just in case."

"No problem," replied her aunt. "I'll be here if you need me."

Before she left, Joanne opened the final message which was from Tom.

'Why?'

She was upset; what type of message was that, she thought to herself before replying.

'My dearest Tom, how can you ask that? I have done nothing wrong. You are just like Warren, blaming me for something that is of Jefferey's making and born from his imagination. After not trusting me and giving me just twenty-four hours to prove I did nothing wrong, Warren then offers to help find you. Well, I told him to stuff his help and to stuff his job too. I wish I could do the same with you, but I can't because I love you. Even the fact that you too do not trust me cannot diminish my love for you. I have left Aunt Matilda and Warren at home; what Warren does is up to him; I can live without him *in my life*. With you it is different because I cannot live without you, so I will look for you every night for the rest of my life and, if I don't find you, I will die a withered old divorcee who found love once but whose love walked out the door. It doesn't have to be this way, Tom. Our love doesn't have to end like this. You have a choice. Come home! All my love forever!'

Joanne put the phone in her pocket and drove down into town. She parked down by the Wish Tower – there always seemed to be spaces there, especially later in the day. She sat in the car for a while; it was still very warm. She picked up the bottle of water she had brought with her and put it in her shoulder bag. She got the feeling it was going to be a long evening.

She got out of the car and walked up towards the Wish Tower and then along through the Western Lawns, past the statue of Spencer Compton, the Eighth Duke of Devonshire. She stopped there for a while, remembering the day she'd looked out from her window at The Grand Hotel where she had been staying – such a lot had happened since then and she was still trying to piece it all together.

She carried on through the gardens down to the where they joined the Eastbourne Promenade, all the way to the Holywell Tea Chalet at the end. It was still open so she stopped for a drink and a rest for ten minutes; she wished the little train were running, she could have taken it back to the pier which would have been a lot quicker, but then she thought she might have missed Tom if he were sitting somewhere; so, she started her long walk back towards the Wish Tower.

There weren't many people on the beach along that stretch, but it was slow going as she had to make sure Tom wasn't sitting close to the wall or sheltering under any of the stairs leading down to the beach. As she approached the main beach leading from the Lifeboat Museum to the pier, the number of people still on the beach increased substantially. She was frantically searching everywhere but it was so difficult as there were the two pathways where people would sit and then the beach itself. She wished that she had someone to help her but giving up was not something she even contemplated. As she continued towards the pier, she was surprised that almost every seat on the benches was taken.

She stopped at one of the refreshment huts to get herself a drink, then continued along to the bandstand area where she sat drinking her tea. It was while sitting there that she suddenly realised the enormity of her predicament; even at that late hour in the afternoon, there were still all the comings and goings of people on the beach. Joanne continued along to the pier, looking at all the people sitting on the seats, predominantly elderly people. She thought that most looked as though they were locals, but there were also some she thought to be day trippers, noticeable by their bags, now packed and ready for their trip home. There were a few vacant seats next to some homeless people – clearly nobody wanted to sit near them. Joanne looked carefully at everyone she saw as she didn't want to miss Tom, however, she did realise that it was a bit like looking for a needle in a haystack.

Finally reaching the pier, it seemed to her as though she had been walking for ages, something she was not used to doing. Although she now felt rather tired, she decided to walk to the end of the pier where she knew there was an area reserved for sea fishing and thought it was a place where Tom might try to mingle in without being conspicuous; however, having reached the end of the pier, it was obvious to her that he wasn't there.

Joanne found an empty seat and took a few minutes out to rest her weary feet; taking her phone from her pocket, she looked to see if there were any messages. There was another message from Warren.

'Joanne, what can I say apart from sorry? I was wrong and I should have trusted and supported you. I really do want to help. I'm parked near the seafront. Please let me help you. Where should I start looking?'

Joanne typed a quick reply to Warren's message and hit the send button.

'Warren, if you want to help, you could message Tom and tell him that he needs to come home. If he won't, then I will have to report him as missing because he should be in the hospital. He shouldn't be out on his own.'

Sitting there, Joanne was beginning to get seriously worried about Tom. She didn't really want to accept Warren's offer of help, but she knew if she was to even stand a chance of locating Tom, then she could not do it alone. It was getting late, and the light was fading fast. She opened her phone and highlighted Tom.

'To my dearest Tom / Ray – whatever you want to call yourself is not important to me. What is, though, is your health. I am worried about you; I need to be looking after you, not wasting time trying to locate you in a busy town. Please come home, Tom.'

She then clicked on the four dots at the end of the message bar, allowing Tom to see her location, then she pressed send.

Joanne made her way back down the pier, stopping at the end to get fish and chips. She took them onto the beach and sat halfway down, eating her food and listening to the waves lapping against the pebbles at the water's edge. Several people walked past while she was sitting there. She looked to her left and noticed there were still quite a few people walking along the pier. There was still no sign of anyone who looked remotely like Tom. She had almost finished eating when her phone rang: it was Warren.

"Joanne, I was just wondering if you had heard from Tom? I have left him messages and just rang him, but he's not answering his phone."

"No, I haven't heard from him or seen him. I really don't know where to start looking for the best," she said.

Warren was worried, not only for Tom, but also for Joanne. He knew that he had to help and felt that they needed to work together in their efforts to find him.

"Where are you now?" he asked. "We really need to sit down together and work this out, to come up with a plan."

Joanne still wasn't happy with the way that Warren had treated her earlier, but she guessed that was because of whatever it was between him and Tom. She knew how serious Warren had been when he told her that he considered Tom to be the son he never had and she knew that she needed Warren's help.

"I'm sitting on the beach, about halfway down towards the sea in front of the first lot of beach huts," she replied.

"Okay, thank you. Sit tight, I'm coming to find you and I won't be long as I'm in front of the Queen's Hotel."

Joanne sat there staring at her phone. It was as though she thought that might help to get some sort of acknowledgement from Tom, but it didn't work. In all reality, she knew in her heart it was already a lost cause. She was still looking at the inactive screen in front of her when she heard footsteps from behind getting closer, then she heard a voice call.

"Joanne, is that you?"

She turned her head in the direction of the voice and saw Warren approaching.

"Yes, it's me," replied Joanne.

Warren noticed straight away the sadness in her voice; it was so different from the usual exuberant voice she was known for. He continued the last few steps down the beach to where she was sitting and then sat down next to her. Instinctively, he put his arm around her shoulders and pulled her towards his chest.

"Don't worry, we'll find him for you," he said.

"Do you think so? Do you really think so?"

"Hey, what happened to your positive attitude? Of course we can find him, but we need to work together, and we need to work fast; he should still be under supervision."

Joanne looked at him with tears running down over her cheeks.

"That is what worries me most of all. Do you think we should notify the police?"

"Maybe, but would they look for him? I know he is carrying an injury and was only released from the hospital under your care, but will the police care that much about that? If he's not a danger to anyone else, they will just look at him as an adult who has walked out after a dispute at home. I think for tonight at least we would be better off looking for him ourselves rather than spending the time in a police station filling in forms," explained Warren.

"I think you could be right."

Warren placed his hand on her shoulder. "Joanne, I'm here for you and for Tom and I will do whatever it takes to help you find him and to get you two back together again," said Warren.

"Thank you so much. I'm sorry I shouted at you earlier. I hope you can forgive me," said Joanne as she looked towards Warren, tears streaming down her cheeks once more.

He pulled her towards him in a sudden moment of compassion, something that he was not usually noted for.

"Hey, we are never going to find Tom if you are going to sit here crying all night! He could walk right past you and you wouldn't see him through those tears," said Warren.

Joanne gave a little giggle. "Thank you, Warren, thank you so much," she replied as she leant towards him and gave him a peck on the cheek.

"Hey, that's enough of that. Don't you think you're in enough trouble with men at the moment? Let's go and find Tom," he said as he stood up.

"I know you want to find Tom as much as I do, albeit for different reasons," replied Joanne.

"Come on then, let's go find him before it gets dark."

With that, Joanne got up and, pointing towards Beachy Head, said, "I'm going to walk up towards the Lifeboat Museum and then back along the pathway to the Holywell Tea Tooms."

"Okay," said Warren. "Then I will walk along past The Queen's Hotel again and if I don't see him, I will cut up towards the town. Stay in contact; either text or ring me. And if I hear from him, I'll let you know. And you do the same," he added.

"Okay, will do," replied Joanne as they separated on their chosen routes.

Reaching the museum, Joanne sat down and sent Tom another text message and then rang Warren.

"Hi, I'm at the Lifeboat Museum but there is still no sign of Tom anywhere. I'm going to walk along the lower pathway down towards the Holywell Tea Chalet at the end," she explained.

"Joanne, I know you want to find Tom, but is that wise? It's getting dark now and that's a long walk on your own," remarked Warren.

"I'll be okay, there are still quite a few people walking along the pathway."

"Alright. I'm going to try to ring Tom again and then I'll call you."

"Okay. Where are you now?"

"I'm heading up towards the town; I should be there in a few minutes."

"Okay, call me in fifteen minutes, please."

Warren detected a nervousness in her voice.

"Joanne, are you okay?"

"I'm just so worried about Tom, but I'm okay, just keep calling me," she replied.

Joanne's explanation was not good enough to quell Warren's concerns, so he decided that he would have a quick look around town before ringing her again to make sure that she was okay. He waited fifteen minutes and then tried ringing her, but all he got was a 'no signal' message.

CHAPTER TWENTY-FIVE

A Painful Experience

Joanne was tired; it was now quite dark and looking around she suddenly realised there was no one else there, only her. She looked towards the pier in the distance, now lit up, and although she thought it looked nice, it now seemed so far away. She gave a glance back towards the cliff face and to the Tea Chalet which was also now in darkness. The walk back to the main sea front seemed to her much further away now that it was dark. She was distraught: she had failed and it was now time for her to give up her search and start the long walk back to the Wish Tower and to her car. She took out her phone to call Warren to let him know what she was doing.

"Oh no! Shit! No battery!" she said as she looked at the blank screen. Then she heard a voice.

"Hi, beautiful."

She looked around but couldn't see anyone. She was just about to keep walking and then she heard it again.

"Up here, beautiful."

The voice seemed to be coming from above, where there was a pathway, but she still couldn't see who was calling her. She thought it could be Tom because he often called her that, but she wasn't sure. She hurried up the pathway and then caught a glimpse of a figure, but when she reached the top, it had gone.

"Tom, is that you?" she called out ... then everything went blank.

When she woke up, she didn't know where she was. Her head was aching and she couldn't see anything: it was pitch black, she was cold and she appeared to be lying on a floor. She was tied up and couldn't move. She found it hard to breathe as she had been gagged. She was alone and frightened and then she began to feel dizzy again.

Jefferey looked at his watch as he drove through the town at speed; he had promised to take Lucy out for a meal and he was late. He knew that she would be angry, and he was trying to think of an explanation; he pulled up outside the house and rushed in through the door.

"Where have you been then?" asked Lucy when Jefferey walked through the door and joined her at the kitchen table.

"I'm sorry," he said as he leant across the table and kissed her. "I was unavoidably delayed."

"Can we go and get something to eat now, please, I'm getting hungry," she said.

"Okay, come on then, let's go to Sovereign Harbour and have something there," replied Jefferey.

"Can I drive?" asked Lucy.

"You sure can," replied Jefferey as he handed her the keys.

"Okay, Sovereign Harbour, here we come," said Lucy as she got into the car and switched on the ignition.

"Drive carefully. You've only just passed your test," said Jefferey as they pulled out of the parking space and drove off.

Warren was getting worried; he had tried several times to ring Joanne, but it appeared her phone was off, or had no signal or maybe the battery had gone. He had continued to look for Tom but with no joy, and, as it was getting late, he decided to walk up towards the Lifeboat Museum as he remembered Joanne had mentioned that she'd parked near there. He looked all around but he couldn't see her car anywhere. Maybe if her battery had gone on her phone, she had driven straight home. He decided to go back to his car and drive up to her house. As he approached, he could see that Joanne's car was not there.

What is going on? he thought to himself. He got out of his car and knocked on the door.

"Who's there?" asked the voice from inside the house.

"Matilda, it's me, Warren Fredericks. Can you let me in, please?"

Matilda opened the door to let him in.

"I thought you might have been Joanne; I cannot get in touch with her and I don't know what's going on and I am worried," she said as Warren walked past her into the kitchen.

"I'm sorry, Matilda," said Warren, "but this isn't looking good. I have been trying to call her for the last hour, maybe more, but she hasn't answered. I thought her battery may have run out, but I didn't know where she was. I was looking for her car but couldn't find it. I thought that maybe she'd have driven home, so that's why I came back here," he explained.

Matilda sat down and, taking a tissue from the box in front of her, she started dabbing the tears in her eyes as she looked towards Warren standing by the sink.

"May I make myself a drink?" he asked, pointing towards the kettle.

"Yes, of course," replied Matilda. "Would you like me to make it for you?"

"No, you sit there. Would you like me to make you a drink?" he asked her.

"Tea, please," replied Matilda. "You know, I am very worried about Joanne. If, as you say, the battery in her phone had run out, I would've thought that she'd come straight home, too. And if her car is not where she parked it, what's happened to her?" asked Matilda.

Warren placed Matilda's tea down in front of her and sat down opposite.

"I wish I knew, Matilda, I really do, but I do not have the answer you are looking for. And what about Tom? Where is he?"

"I'm here," interrupted Tom, walking into the kitchen. "Where's Joanne?"

"Good question," replied Warren, "to which I just do not have an answer."

"Why? What has happened to her?" asked Tom.

"Well, maybe if you hadn't walked out, if you'd trusted her, then we wouldn't be having this conversation now, and Joanne would still be here," said Matilda, raising her voice. "So if you want to know what has happened to her, best you get your ass into the town and look for her."

"Well, what was I expected to think? Maybe you should have looked at those photos and videos!"

"Stop right there unless you want to wear this hot cup of tea," shouted Matilda. "And believe me, that is not a threat, it is a promise. You come into this house, you say you love Joanne, but all the time you are comparing her to your dead wife! You even use your dead son's name, don't you, *Raymond*? You're a fraud. If it weren't that I know how much Joanne loves you, I'd kick you out of this house right now and out of the barn, too. And before you utter another word about those photos and videos, sit there and look at them and then try to tell me that the woman in them is Joanne," said Matilda. She turned the laptop around and pushed it towards Tom.

Warren was shocked as he listened to Matilda; he felt he should interrupt.

"I know you are upset, Matilda, but I think you are being a little bit too harsh on Tom," he said.

"Is that right? Don't think *you're* getting away scot-free because you're not. You made the same mistake as he did, and you should be ashamed of yourself too, threatening my niece when all she had been trying to do was to save your company from embarrassment. You should have sacked that Jefferey guy straight away but no, you were too worried he might sue you or your company. Well, how could he do that? He lied and sexually harassed and goaded Joanne," added Matilda, "so you owe her a massive apology."

Matilda turned her attention to Tom next. "Well, young man, what did you see?" she asked.

Tom gave her a puzzled look. "I'm still studying them, but I find it really hard and upsetting," he replied.

"So, you don't really love my niece then, do you, because if you did, you would have noticed that the woman in the video and photos has a tiny star tattooed between her thumb and forefinger on her left hand – that woman is *not* Joanne. The best thing you two can do is get your arses out there and look for my niece, and don't dare come back until you have found her."

Tom was shocked – he couldn't believe what an absolute fool he had been.

"I'm sorry, Matilda, I've messed up, I realise that now. Do we know where Joanne is likely to be? Where should we start looking?" he asked.

"When she left me on the beach, she was going to walk down to the Holywell Tea Rooms," said Warren. "The last time I spoke to her she sounded nervous. It was getting dark and she asked me to ring her again in fifteen minutes, which I did but there was no connection. I looked for her car, but I didn't see it there, so I thought she must have gone back to it before I got there and driven somewhere else or come straight home" he added.

Tom knew they had to act quickly as they had wasted too much time already. He was becoming increasingly anxious wondering what had happened to her.

"Warren, will you drive me, please? We have to go into town and along the seafront. We have to look everywhere. Matilda, will you report Joanne missing, please? The police probably won't do much tonight, but they may at least put out an APB out for her car," said Tom. They both went straight out to Warren's car and he drove them down to the seafront; it was late now, and they were both very worried about Joanne.

Jefferey had finished his meal. He was sat waiting for Lucy, becoming increasingly agitated by the length of time she was taking to finish her dinner.

"How much longer are you going to be? I've never known anyone take so long over fish and chips," said Jefferey.

Lucy looked across the table at him. "Well, so sorry to keep you waiting but I didn't realise it was a race. Maybe you should have told me that before we started eating," she replied.

"Look, I'm sorry. I've had a bad day, I'm tired and just want to get home," replied Jefferey.

"Well, sit tight, I've nearly finished," replied Lucy.

It was almost thirty minutes before Lucy finally finished her meal. Jefferey was becoming increasingly frustrated by her and the time that she was taking to finish her meal.

"Okay, I've finished now, Jefferey, are you ready?" she asked.

"Ready? I've been ready and waiting for the last thirty minutes," he replied irritably.

Jefferey pulled up outside their house and, turning to Lucy, he said, "You go in. I have forgotten something. I was meant to go into the office tonight to collect some papers referencing the new case that I'll be working on."

"Why now, Jefferey?" she asked. "Can't they wait until tomorrow? I mean, what is so urgent that you have to go back to the office *now* to collect them?"

"I'm sorry, love, but I have to get them tonight as I need to start work on reading through the papers. It is a complicated case and I know that bitch Joanne will be looking over my shoulder, just waiting for me to make a mistake," replied Jefferey.

Lucy looked puzzled. "But I thought you told me you were leaving as there was no way you could work with Joanne constantly picking on you?" she asked.

"Well, yes, I was, but when I spoke to Fredericks about it, he persuaded me to take this one last case to see if things improved as he didn't want to lose me," replied Jefferey. He didn't even know what he was saying; he was just making up any excuse to get away, but the meaningless words were flowing freely from his mouth.

"Okay, if you really must go now, Jefferey, go, but don't be too long. I'll be ready and waiting for you when you get back."

Joanne was drifting in and out of consciousness; she was cold and thirsty and feeling hungry after realising all she had eaten that day was the fish and chips. She was confused and she had no idea when or if she would eat or drink again. She didn't know where she was or who had taken her there but that was about to change. Her eyes were closing again, not that it made much difference as it was pitch black so she couldn't see a thing. She could feel herself drifting off to sleep again when she heard footsteps approaching. They got closer until it sounded as though they stopped directly outside wherever she was.

She was already scared and frightened, but the level of fright she was feeling suddenly increased tenfold. She heard sounds: someone putting a key into a lock and then turning the key. It sounded to her like the door was opening and although it was already cold, when the door opened there was a sudden rush of fresh chilly air which only added to her shivering and intensified her level of fear once more.

From lying down on the floor, she was now being pulled into a sitting position; she could feel pressure on the tape covering her mouth. She was hoping whoever was there was going to remove the tape but no, that wasn't their intention. She could feel something being forced into her mouth.
"Drink," said the person in what seemed to be a rattled voice. She guessed it was a man's voice, but not one that she recognised. As the person withdrew the straw from her mouth, Joanne tried to speak but she couldn't, the tape was affixed too tightly. With her hands and feet tied and with a blindfold covering her eyes, she was helpless; she had no idea of why she was there, or what her fate was going to be. She heard movement and then the door opened and closed followed by a key turning in the lock.

She was alone again; she had no idea of when or even if the person would return, but he had left her sitting up at least, her back resting against something. She knew that she couldn't stay like that, but what could she do? Her hands were tied behind her back which made it more difficult. She tried to shuffle her body along the floor, but she only managed to move a short distance before she found herself stuck. She tried again, but it was then that she realised that she had something tied around her waist.

She realised the severity of the situation that she found herself in. She wasn't exactly sure where she was although she guessed it was near the sea as she was sure she could hear the waves crashing against the shoreline. She didn't know who had kidnapped her or for what reason, but if she were being honest, she guessed it could either be something to do with her recent meeting with Saunders, an opportunist attack, or maybe even something to do with Jefferey as after seeing the photos and video he'd compiled she would not put anything past him.

Joanne was struggling to come to terms with her thoughts; she didn't think that even Jefferey would stoop to these depths to make his point. As for Saunders, there was no reason for this; she was trying to help him, and he needed her to be alive. She was cold and tired, hungry and thirsty, and she was trying to stay awake, but it was a battle that she could not win. Her thinking was becoming fuzzy: she wanted to sleep but she was frightened and cold. She kept dozing off, but she found it was an impossible task trying to keep herself awake.

Tom and Warren had been searching for hours. Not only had they not found Joanne, but they hadn't seen any sign of her car either.

"Tom, we have to stop now. This is serious, and we need expert help," said Warren.

Tom agreed in principle but he wasn't prepared to give up at that point.

"I think you need to get a drink and some food, Warren; you can go back to the house if you want to, but you'll have to leave me here. I will keep looking for a while yet and I can get a taxi home. I'm very worried, this can't be right," replied Tom.

It was at that point that Tom got a call on his phone; he looked at the screen, then pressed the accept button.

"Hi Matilda, are you okay?" he asked.

"Tom, the police are here. I rang them; they want a photo of Joanne and the registration of her car and things like that. Can you come home, now, please?" asked Matilda.

"Okay, we're on our way now, see you soon," Tom ended the call and placed his phone back in his pocket.

"Matilda wants us to go back to the house – the police are there," explained Tom.

"Okay, let's go then," replied Warren. It was only a short walk back to where Warren had parked his car.

"Do you think the police will do anything?" asked Tom.

"I wouldn't bet on it, Tom," replied Warren. "They will try to help but I doubt they will do anything tonight and that could be important lost time. They will want to see the video and photos that Jefferey sent, and they will probably want to wait 24 hours to see what happens. Try not to lose your temper, Tom, as that will not help, but you have to be prepared for them to suggest that Joanne has run off with Jefferey. After all, she is an adult, so it won't be top of their to-do list," replied Warren.

"You're kidding me! I hope, Warren, you don't really expect me to stay calm if they suggest that, do you?" asked Tom.

"I'd say that's a worst-case scenario, Tom, one you have to be prepared for, but whatever happens, do not lose your temper with them, that won't help at all," replied Warren.

They pulled up outside the house and walked towards the main door. Warren placed his hand on Tom's shoulder, forcing him to stop.

"The one thing you must do, Tom, is to give them all the information they ask for. They will probably want to look in her wardrobe to ask you if any clothes are missing but stay calm; you must offer up anything they ask for," said Warren.

Tom and Warren went straight to the kitchen where he guessed Aunt Matilda would be waiting with the police officers; he wasn't wrong. Matilda was sat one side of the breakfast bar while two officers were sitting on the other side. He walked towards Matilda and kissed her on the cheek.

"Matilda, sorry, we got back as quickly as we could. There was a lot of traffic in town as the pubs and restaurants were just closing," he explained.

"That's okay. I've been chatting to these two police officers," she replied, pointing towards them both.

"I'm Tom," he said, looking towards the officers. "I am Joanne Webster's friend."

The younger of the two men stood up and offered Tom his hand.

"Detective Sergeant Field," he said. "Sorry, Tom, can I have your family name please, for our records?" he asked.

"Certainly," replied Tom. "It's Maddox, Tom Maddox."

"Sorry, Mr Maddox, can I just check something with you? You introduced yourself as Miss Webster's friend, but I was under the impression that you are her partner?" asked Field.

Tom picked up the kettle from the breakfast bar and, walking over to the sink, he filled it with water before returning it to its base and switching it on.

"Tea, Warren?" Tom asked.

"May I have a coffee please, Tom?" Warren replied as he moved closer to where Tom was standing.

"Remember what we spoke about," he whispered in Tom's ear before saying aloud: "I'll make the drinks, Tom, while you concentrate on giving the police the information they require," added Warren.

"Where were we?" asked Tom, looking towards the detective. "Oh yes, friend or partner, well, both, I guess. Does that satisfy your curiosity?"

"I guess it will have to," replied Field. "Do you have a recent photo of Miss Webster?" he asked.

"Yes, I do," replied Tom as he searched his phone and gave it to Field for him to copy.

"Thank you," replied Field as he returned Tom's phone to him. "Mr Maddox, I feel as though we are not on the same side here; we really are trying to work *with* you, not *against* you."

"Really," replied Tom. "I am sure that Joanne's aunt has told you everything you need to know. So, if there is anything else you need, why not just come straight out with it and then start looking for Joanne, which is what Warren and myself have been doing for the last six hours. We could really do with your help."

"All in good time, Mr Maddox, all in good time, but first I need to know what makes you think Miss Webster is missing?" asked Field.

"Okay, some freak sends me a video and photos which are meant to portray Joanne and like an idiot I fall for it and walk out. She finds out about it and comes looking for me with the help of Warren, her boss, but they don't find me. Then no one knows where Joanne is; she doesn't answer calls or messages, her car isn't where she said she'd left it in town, she's gone, disappeared. I have probably told you the same things that her aunt has told you, so please tell me why you are wasting time here?" asked Tom.

"Mr Maddox, the thing you don't seem to grasp is that Miss Webster is an adult, who is free to make up her own mind and to choose her own friends and partners. From what I have seen, it looks very much to me as though that is what she has done. No matter what you say, the woman in that video and the photos I have been shown is the same as the woman whose photo you showed me from your phone. It looks to me as though she has left with a lover; it's not uncommon," explained Field.

"Are you kidding me? What about the star tattoo on the woman's hand? Or the fact that she hasn't taken any clothes with her? And why wouldn't she tell her aunt what she was doing?" asked Tom, but his questions were ignored.

"The best I can do is to read through all my notes, and if she hasn't turned up in twenty-four to thirty-six hours, I will start looking more deeply into this case for you," Field replied.

Tom was reaching boiling point; he recalled Warren's words and didn't want to make the situation worse.

"You just do not get it, do you? This isn't about me or you, it's about Joanne, whom we believe is missing and you are not prepared to do anything! You fail to accept the fact that Joanne was in the beach area with Warren Fredericks, looking for me. She was in phone contact with Warren and then all of a sudden, without warning, she stopped answering his calls. Why would she even be at the beach looking for me if she were planning to walk out on me the same evening?" asked Tom.

"Mr Maddox, I think we are finished here, we have all the information we need for the moment. When you hear from Miss Webster, please don't forget to let us know so that we can put this case to bed," replied Field.

Turning to Joanne's aunt, Field asked, "Should you need to contact us again, then please do so. Would you show us out, please?"

Matilda walked back into the kitchen where Tom and Warren were sitting at the breakfast bar.

"So, will someone please tell me what we do now, and how on earth are we meant to find my niece without police help?" she asked.

"I need to get back out there and keep looking. I must find her," said Tom.

"Wait," interrupted Warren as he picked up his phone from the breakfast bar.

"I'll see if I can contact Susan Caton, Joanne's assistant. She's close to her so there may be something that she can tell us that might be able to give us a lead."

Warren held the phone to his ear, waiting for an answer.

"Susan, sorry to disturb you at this hour, it's Warren Fredericks. We have a problem: Joanne Webster has gone missing. I know it's the middle of the night, but can you recall anything strange over the last few days which could help us?" he asked.

"Wait, what do you mean, Miss Webster is missing?" enquired Susan Caton. "I was talking to her yesterday."

"I know, we all were. Look, I need to talk to you. We don't know what to do – can you think of anything strange, or has Joanne been acting differently over the last few days?" asked Warren.

"There was nothing wrong with Joanne, she was fine until the video photos arrived, then when she heard that Tom was missing, she just dropped everything. What's happened to her?" she asked.

"We don't know, that's why I was wondering if you could add anything that might help," replied Warren.

"I can't do anything at the moment, I have my son to look after, but I can take him to my mother's in the morning and then meet with you," she suggested.

"That would be great, Susan, the earlier the better. Can you meet us at the office at nine?" asked Warren.

"No problem, I'll see you there," she replied and put down the phone.

"Tom, Susan will meet us at the office at nine. I'm going home to get a couple of hours sleep and a shower. I think you need to do the same," said Warren as he put the phone back in his pocket. "I'll be back here to pick you up at eight-thirty," he added.

"Thank you, Warren. I'm not sure I can sleep, but I certainly need a shower," replied Tom.

"Tom, we'll do everything we can to find her, even if we have to do it without the help of the police," said Warren as he turned to leave.

CHAPTER TWENTY-SIX

Serious Times

Tom got out of the shower and went into the bedroom to dress; he hadn't slept properly, maybe thirty minutes and a few shorter naps. As he went down the stairs, he smelt cooking – that could mean only one thing: Matilda was up and cooking breakfast.

"Matilda, what are you doing awake?" he asked.

"Like you, I couldn't sleep. I heard you go into the bathroom for a shower, so I came down and cooked you a bacon sandwich. You need to eat if you are going to be out all day," she replied.

"Thank you," replied Tom. "Yes, we have to speed things up today, but I'm not sure how. We need to find Joanne, time is running out."

Their conversation was interrupted by a knock on the door. Tom suspected it was Warren and got up to see.

"Good morning, Warren," he said as he opened the door.

"Hi Tom, are you ready?" asked Warren.

"Come in for a minute, I'm just finishing a bacon sandwich. I think Matilda may have made one for you too," replied Tom.

"Good morning, Warren," said Matilda as they entered the kitchen. "Take a seat. Would you like a bacon sandwich?" she asked.

"Ooh yes please, I would love one thank you," replied Warren. "However I don't really have time to eat it here as we have to leave now to meet Susan Caton at the office; may I take it with me?" he asked.

"But of course. I'll wrap it for you," replied Matilda.

"Okay, I'm ready now, let's get started," said Tom as he put his plate in the dishwasher.

"Matilda, make sure you keep all the doors locked, and don't answer the door unless you know who is there. You have our phone numbers if you need us, and I'll check with you throughout the day. Try not to worry too much, we will do everything we can to find Joanne," said Tom.

"Thank you, both of you. Just bring her back home safely, she is the only family I have left and I love her dearly," replied Matilda.

Tom got into the car and sat quietly for a few moments while Warren headed off towards the town.

"What are the plans for today then, Warren?" asked Tom in a rather sad voice.

"Well, let's start with meeting Susan," replied Warren.

"What if Joanne has had an accident, or worse? Or what if that nutcase Jefferey just drove her too far and she has …" before Tom could continue, he was interrupted by Warren.

"Don't even think about it, Tom, she would never do that!" said Warren.

"I hope you are right, Warren, I really do," replied Tom.

As Warren drove in through the gates of the office car park, he could see that Susan Capon was already there waiting for them. He pulled up by the side of her car and wound down his window. Susan got out of her car, locked it and walked round to Warren's car and got in the rear seat, behind Tom.

"Good morning, Susan, thank you very much for coming," said Warren.

"Good morning, Warren, morning, Tom. So, what the hell is going on?" she asked.

Tom looked towards Warren. "Could you explain because you were with Joanne when she disappeared?" asked Tom.

Warren turned the key in the ignition and reversed out of the parking space as he started to explain.

"After the photos, which everyone saw, Tom left the house. Joanne's aunt rang to let her know what had happened, so she went straight home. After she had left the office, I sat thinking and I knew that I hadn't handled the situation well, so I drove to Joanne's house to apologise, but she was not in the right frame of mind for apologies and she stormed out. Anyway, I met her later by the pier; she went to Holywell to search for Tom, and I looked around the town. That was the last I saw of her. I tried ringing her but was getting no answer. I walked back to where she had told me she had parked her car, but I couldn't see it there. I thought maybe she had driven back to her house, but she wasn't there either. So now no one knows where she is and the police appear not to want to look for her until she has been missing for at least 24 to 36 hours," explained Warren.

"What!" exclaimed Susan. "Then we need to find her, and quickly at that," she added.

Warren nodded his head in agreement. "Susan, did you say that you know where Lucy Saunders has moved to?" asked Warren.

"Yes, I do, and I think that Jefferey might be living there with her, although I can't confirm that. I can direct you there, it's not far from here."

They pulled up a few houses back from Lucy Saunders' on the opposite side of the road and sat discussing how to handle the situation. They needed to find out if Jefferey was there, and if so, they would ask him if he had seen Joanne. Susan Caton was chosen to approach the house while Warren and Tom would keep a careful watch. Susan walked in through the gate and pressed the doorbell; there was no immediate reply, she waited a few moments and then pressed the doorbell again. Tom had been watching carefully from the car.

"Maybe there's no one in," said Warren and as he looked, he saw Susan turn to walk back towards the gate.

"No, tell her to go back," said Tom. "Quickly, ring her, tell her to wait. I saw a shadow in the upstairs window and then the curtain moved – tell her to go back."

Warren rang Susan and waited for her to reply. "Susan, go back and ring the bell again, Tom saw a shadow behind the curtains in the upstairs window, and then he saw the curtain move!"

Susan turned around and went back to the door, this time leaving her finger on the bell until she heard a noise coming from behind the door. It was opened and she was confronted by Lucy Saunders.

"Oh, Mrs Saunders, sorry, I thought this was Jefferey Philips' house, I do apologise," she said, the only thing she could think of.

"Why? Who are you and why do you want to see Jefferey?" asked Lucy.

"I'm Susan Caton. I work with Jefferey at the solicitors. I just needed to ask him something about one of the cases we have been working on together," replied Susan.

"Okay, that would explain it then but he doesn't live here. He just helped me move my things into this place," replied Lucy.

Susan looked enquiringly at Lucy Saunders before replying. "Sorry, there must be some mistake as this is the address that Jefferey gave when we made changes to our system at work. Anyway, is he here or have you seen him because I really do need to speak to him?"

"Well, I'm sorry, but I can't help you as I haven't seen him since last night. He took me for a meal and then dropped me back here, saying that he had to go to his office to collect some papers that he had forgotten, but he never returned," she replied.

"Don't you find that rather strange?" asked Susan.

"Not really. I'm not his keeper. Maybe he succumbed to that tart in your office who keeps trying to seduce him. I had better not bump into her or she'll be in trouble," replied Lucy in an angry tone.

"Do you know who that person is, Mrs Saunders?" asked Susan.

"Oh, come on," replied Lucy. "Are you trying to protect her too? Jefferey told me everyone was against him because that tart had made it difficult for him because he ignored her advances. I think he said her name is Joanne."

"I'm sorry, Mrs Saunders, but I hadn't heard about that so I can't really comment," said Susan.

"No, I bet you can't comment! Is that's what you've been told to say? Well, I know the truth and you can't fool me! Wait, I want to show you something," said Lucy as she turned and disappeared into one of the rooms off the hallway.

Susan stepped inside the door where there was a small cabinet sitting on a table. She quickly opened the cabinet door and saw a couple of keys hanging there. She picked them up and put them in her pocket before closing the cabinet door and stepping back outside the doorway, just in time as Lucy reappeared from the room and walked towards the door.

"Look at this," exclaimed Lucy as she held out a piece of paper towards Susan.

Susan took the paper from her; it was what appeared to be a handwritten letter to Jefferey from Joanne, although on studying it Susan wasn't convinced. She knew Joanne's handwriting and it was nothing like what she was looking at on the piece of paper she was holding, and it certainly wasn't Joanne's signature.

"Did Jefferey give you this?" asked Susan.

"No, he didn't," replied Lucy. "I told you I haven't seen him since last night, he didn't come home. I was getting suspicious, certain things, certain happenings over the last few weeks, have not been right. He told me he loved me, and I believe him, but I think he has been tricked by that tart. I was looking through some of his papers that he'd left here and came across that letter which proves what I was saying about her trying to seduce him and it proves what Jefferey told me about her. He told me that if he didn't do as she wanted, she would expose him as a liar and a cheat and she would make sure that he never worked again."

Susan needed to gain Lucy's confidence although she knew the letter was fake; she needed to find out more of what was going on.

"I can certainly see why you are upset. This letter is so wrong and totally out of order," replied Susan. "Would you mind me taking a photo of it, as this kind of coercion has got to be stopped," she added.

"No, it's quite okay. Do you think you can do something about it then?" asked Lucy.

"I would hope so," replied Susan. "Tell me Mrs Saunders, are you sure you and Jefferey aren't living here together?"

"Why do you need to know that?" asked Lucy.

"Well, it would give credence to the content of the letter from Joanne. I mean, if she has designs on Jefferey and she found out that you and he were living together, it would probably have made her even more determined to get what she wanted," explained Susan.

"Yes, I see, and yes, we are living together. You know, Jefferey is such a nice man, so different from my husband. *He* is certainly where he belongs now and I'm pleased about that," replied Lucy.

"Okay, I will make sure that the boss sees the copy of this letter. Have you found anything else that's a bit odd in Jefferey's paperwork?" asked Susan.

"Well, there was a letter a couple of weeks ago from the local council. I didn't see it but when I asked Jefferey what it was about, he said that he had rented a garage and had to pick up the keys, which was quite strange."

"Why's that?" asked Susan.

"Well, I asked him a couple of days later if he had collected the keys for the garage and he told me he had, but he hasn't once used it," replied Lucy.

"Yes, that does seem a little strange," commented Susan. "So there was more than one key?

"I don't really know that" replied Lucy. "I didn't see the letter but when I asked him about it, he said *keys*. Look I am sorry, but I must go into town now, but thank you for trying to help," added Lucy.

"No problem," replied Susan. "I'll let you go now, you've been a great help. As soon as Jefferey gets home, would you tell him I called and ask him to contact me? It's especially important that I speak to him before Monday."

Susan walked slowly back to the car, but Warren beckoned to her to keep walking as he noticed that Lucy Saunders was still standing in the doorway of her house. Susan continued to the end of the road and waited there until she received the call from Warren telling her to walk back to the car.

"Wow! You had a long conversation! Did you get anything?" asked Tom.

"You might find these handy," said Susan as she reached into her pocket and took out the keys, which she gave to Tom.

"What are these?" he asked.

"I think they're the house keys and I think you might find something in there which will help us find Joanne," replied Susan.

"What!" exclaimed Tom. "Do you think Joanne is being held in there?"

"No, but you may find a key or keys and a letter from the council; a couple of weeks ago, Jefferey received a letter which Lucy said was from the council and when she questioned him about it, he said he was going to rent a garage and he had to go to the council offices to collect the keys. However, she said that since picking up the keys, to her knowledge Jefferey has not used the garage which I think you would agree is rather strange."

Tom looked towards Warren and then at Susan. "So you expect me to break in and search the house?" he asked.

"Well, I can't do it, and neither can Warren, we'd lose our jobs, but you could do it and you wouldn't actually be breaking in as you have the keys," replied Lucy.

With that, Tom looked back towards Warren for his opinion.

"Well, Susan does have a point, not a cast-iron one but you just might get away with it," said Warren.

Susan interrupted them both. "Look at this," she said as she gave Warren her phone showing him the letter supposedly to Jefferey from Joanne. "That is not Joanne's handwriting and neither is it her signature. Lucy Saunders found the letter and asked Jefferey about it; he told her that Joanne was trying to seduce him and threatened him if he didn't do as she asked."

"The man is deranged," Warren uttered as he handed the phone to Tom for him to read the letter.

"Well, that's definitely not Joanne. So, what do we do now?" asked Tom.

"Susan, you were the one who confronted Lucy Saunders; what course of action do you think is required?" asked Warren.

Susan sat there for a while before she replied.

"Joanne is missing, Jefferey hasn't returned home after supposedly going to the office last night to collect some papers he was supposed to be working on over the weekend. By his own admission, he has rented a garage but hasn't bothered to use it for his car. He has shown his married lover a letter which he says is from Joanne, but which is a lie. We need to find that letter from the council and they garage keys and if we don't, then another day might be too late for Joanne."

"So, you want me to go and search through the house to see what I can find?" asked Tom.

"I think that is the first thing we need you to do," replied Susan.

"I am not sure about this," replied Tom. "As much as I dislike Field, don't you think it might be better to contact him first?" he asked.

Warren looked at Tom. "Do you want to find Joanne or not?" he asked.

"Yes, of course I do," replied Tom before being interrupted by Warren.

"Well, it looks as though your time has come, Tom. Mrs Saunders is just leaving the house."

They sat there and watched as she started walking towards the end of the road leading towards the town centre. While they were still watching, a car drove past them and pulled up just in front of where she was walking. A man got out of the car and walked towards her; he obviously said something to her because she pulled away, but he grabbed her arm and pulled her towards the car and then drove off.

"Well, what was all that about?" wondered Warren.

"I have no idea, but I got a photo, although it's not clear and no faces are visible," replied Susan.

"And you two want me to go into the house when that just happened?" asked Tom.

"Well, neither of us can, so it has to be you, and they've gone now, so it will be quite safe for you," replied Warren.

"Okay, so I'm looking for a letter from the council and hopefully keys as well; is that all?" asked Tom.

"Yes," replied Susan, "unless you come across anything else that you think may be of importance."

"Okay, call me if I'm about to be interrupted," said Tom as he got out of the car.

Tom felt nervous as he walked down the street towards the house. His feelings were telling him that he was being watched but he tried his best to look natural and stay calm. As he approached the gate, he took the door keys out of his pocket, making sure that if anyone were watching him they could see that he had a key, however, he still wasn't sure if the keys that Susan had picked up were for Lucy Saunders' house.

Placing a key in the lock, he tried to turn it. "Damn!" he said, dropping the keys as he did so, to make it look an accident that he couldn't open the door. He picked up them up and tried the other one. *Bingo*, he thought to himself as it turned and he opened the door. He went straight to the room where Susan had told him Lucy Saunders had got the letter from and looked through all the drawers and cupboards but found nothing.

Having got this far, Tom was not about to give up. He systematically went through every room but found nothing; walking back down the stairs towards the front door, he was about to leave when he noticed a man's coat hanging just inside the door. Tom riffled through the pockets of the coat and came across a piece of folded up paper: it was the letter from the council. He gave it a quick look and then put it in his pocket. He felt it was time to leave, so taking out his phone he rang Warren.

"I'm ready to leave now, Warren. Is the coast clear?" he asked.

"Yes, get out of there now," he replied.

Tom left the house and walked slowly back to the car, getting in the front seat next to Warren. They both looked at him.

"Well, did you find anything?" asked Susan.

Tom turned round to face her, took the keys out of his pocket, and gave them back to Susan, followed by the letter from the council which he opened and handed to her.

"Only this letter, showing that Jefferey had asked for a duplicate key, but there was no sign of the key. I found the letter in the pocket of a coat hanging next to the front door. Maybe that was why he hadn't used the garage; he has misplaced the original key," said Tom.

"Shit!" exclaimed Warren. "I thought we may have been onto something there, but we are just back to square one," he continued.

"Worse than that," replied Susan. "Because Jefferey is now missing too, and I was hoping that he would be our lead to Joanne. But now we have nothing, and time could be running out."

Tom sat there, not knowing what to think, but his thoughts were interrupted by his phone ringing. Taking it out of his pocket he saw that it was Matilda.

"Hello, Matilda," he said.

"Tom, I have been out of my mind waiting for you to call, but I just couldn't wait any longer. Please tell me you have some good news," she said.

"Sorry, we've been a bit busy. I was just about to ring you. No, nothing concrete for now, but we have a couple of leads to follow up. Just make yourself another strong cup of tea and sit down and rest. I don't suppose the police have been back in touch?" asked Tom.

"No, no one has been here at all. I would have rung you if they had called," replied Aunt Matilda.

"Okay, try to rest, I will call you soon. Bye," said Tom as he ended the call.

Warren looked across at Tom. "Interesting conversation, Tom. Do you mind telling us what the leads are that you mentioned?" he asked.

"Sorry, just a figure of speech," replied Tom.

"Was that helpful then, Tom?" asked Susan.

"Probably not," replied Tom, "but do you think I should have told her that not only is her niece missing but also Jefferey, our only lead? And that we also sat and watched as Lucy Saunders was stopped on the street and put in a car? I could hardly tell her that we were up the creek without a paddle, the boat had sprung a leak, and we didn't even have any life jackets."

"Good point," said Warren.

"So, what do we do now then?" asked Tom.

"Tell me, Tom, are you a religious man," asked Warren.

"Why? Does that make a difference?" asked Tom.

"Yes, because as I see it, all we have left is to pray and you better mean it when you do," replied Warren.

The three of them spent the rest of the day walking along the beach area, speaking to anyone they came across, showing them a photo of Joanne, and asking them if they were in the area on Friday afternoon or evening, and if they remembered seeing her anywhere, but they were out of luck. Not many words were spoken between the three of them and Susan had noticed that none were spoken between Warren and Tom; a friendship that appeared to have been cemented by one meeting now seemed to have made them almost total strangers.

Tom was feeling guilty; if he hadn't acted so rashly and had waited to let Joanne explain, they wouldn't be where they were now, and she wouldn't be missing. Warren was also blaming himself; he knew too that he had let Joanne down. He hadn't believed her, and his actions had left her feeling alone and broken. Yes, he had tried to make it up to her, but he should never have let her walk down the far end of the beach on her own, bearing in mind that the sun was going down and the light fades very quickly once it starts to get dark.

Susan was stuck between the two of them; she had to find a way to bring them back together and get them working as one and not blaming themselves because she felt it was affecting all of them in their search for Joanne.

"Look, you two, enough of this, stop feeling sorry for yourselves because it's getting us nowhere. What is done is done, you can't change the past, but if we are all working together, we can change the future. Just think about Joanne instead of thinking about yourselves; she is somewhere, maybe cold, hungry and thirsty, so please just concentrate on her," said Susan, making sure they knew she was not happy with either of their attitudes.

Tom stood there, Susan's words shocking him to his senses. "Sorry, Susan you're right. What do you think we should do now?" he asked.

"Well, I want to go back to the house to see if Lucy Saunders is there or if Jefferey has reappeared; I just feel we are wasting valuable time here," replied Susan.

"Come on then, let's go," added Warren.

"That doesn't look good," commented Tom as they pulled up outside the house. "No sign of any lights."

"I'll go and check," replied Susan as she got out of the car. She rang the doorbell and knocked a few times but to no avail; it was obvious to her that there was no one home. She walked back to the car, her head down. The events of the day were getting to her, but all she could think of was Joanne and what had happened to her.

"Do you think we should call the police?" asked Tom as Susan got back into the car.

"Well, under normal circumstances I would say yes, but they weren't very accommodating last night. Field was convinced that Joanne and Jeffercy were having an affair and that they had run off together, so in that respect, nothing has changed," replied Warren.

"What about the business earlier with Lucy Saunders and the men in the car?" asked Susan.

"So, what could we tell the police if we called them? All we can do is confirm that Jefferey has now disappeared, something that they probably already believe to be the case if he's allegedly run off with Joanne? As for Lucy Saunders, well, she already told you she was going out when you were talking to her and it would appear she knew the man whose car she got in as she didn't appear to struggle or try to get away. And, once again, she's an adult," replied Warren.

"As much as it hurts me to say this, but I think we should go home, get some food in our bodies and get a good night's sleep if there is such a thing at a time like this," said Tom.

"I think you're right, Tom," replied Susan. "Tomorrow is going to be a make-or-break day and we all need to be fresh and full of energy."

"Will you be able to help again tomorrow, Susan?" asked Tom.

"I wouldn't be seen anywhere else," she replied.

"I will be here too," added Warren, "but I'll bring my wife with me if that is okay. She can keep Matilda company."

"That's a really great idea, Warren. I have a feeling that she will need a lot of support tomorrow," said Tom.

Warren took Susan back to the office car park to retrieve her car and then drove Tom up to the house.

"Do you want to come in?" asked Tom, "or would you prefer to go straight home?"

"I'll get straight off if that's okay, Tom, it's getting late and I want to get some much-needed rest. I know you're worried and I know how much you love Joanne, even though you still find it hard admitting it to yourself. Tomorrow we will find her; we *must* find her; goodnight, my friend," said Warren and then he drove off.

Tom opened the front door of the house and found Aunt Matilda sitting in the lounge, staring at the photos of Joanne that were hanging on the wall.

"She is very beautiful, isn't she," remarked Tom.

"Yes, she is, Tom. You know, the first time I saw those photos hanging there I was shocked," replied Matilda.

"Why were you shocked?" asked Tom.

"It was the first time since she was a young child that I had seen her with so few clothes on for one thin! She is an incredibly beautiful woman and you have captured her perfectly. Could you get me a smaller one of those, the centre one? I would like to hang it on my wall at home."

Tom could hear the upset in her voice, and he knew she was awfully close to breaking down.

"You need to sleep, Matilda. I'll make you a hot chocolate and then you have to go to bed," said Tom.

"The hot chocolate would be very welcome, but what makes you think I could sleep at a time like this?" she replied.

"Okay, point taken. I'll make you a chocolate and then I'll join you in here. You can have the sofa where you are and I'll take the one over there," said Tom.

Joanne regained consciousness. She had no idea how long she had been out for, she didn't even have any idea of what day it was or the last time that she had had food or drink; all she knew was that she felt sick with hunger, and she was so thirsty that she couldn't even form spit in her mouth. She couldn't understand why she had been left there, tied up and helpless, and she wasn't even able to call for help. Although she was confused, she had accepted the thought that whoever had placed her in that situation intended her to die, as if not, then they would have been back by now. She was frightened and exhausted but there were no tears. Her body was almost out of fluids and her only consolation was that she felt she would drift off to sleep or unconsciousness and that would be it. Joanne did try to keep her eyes open in the hope that somehow she would be rescued, but no one knew where she was apart from the person or people who had put her there and it seemed obvious to her now that they had no intention of coming back.

CHAPTER TWENTY-SEVEN

Disturbing News

Detective Sergeant Field walked into the office, got a coffee from the machine, and headed towards his desk. It was Sunday, there were very few people in the office and he was looking forward to an easy day.

"Morning all," he said as he sat down at his desk. "I do like Sundays and I'm looking forward to a nice easy day. Okay, Roberts, fill me in on what's happened overnight."

"An attempted stabbing, theft of a vehicle, theft of petrol, a fight outside a pub at closing time, the perpetrators are still locked up, sleeping it off I think," replied Roberts.

"Did you not understand my point about a quiet day?" asked Field.

"That's not all, Sir," said Roberts.

"What, you mean there's more? You have got to be kidding me," replied Field.

"I'm afraid not. There was a suicide too – the report is on your desk," replied Roberts.

"Why me? Tell me who is working with me today?" asked Field.

"Anne Green; she's in the canteen having breakfast sir," replied Roberts.

"That's where I'm going then, breakfast," replied Field as he got up and walked towards the door.

"Sir, before you go, what was the name of that missing person you had a call about yesterday?" asked Roberts.

"Umm, Webster, I think, Jane Webster or was it June? No, Joanne, that's it, Joanne Webster. Why is that?" he asked.

"Wasn't there someone else involved?" asked Roberts.

"Yes, one of her colleagues where she works, Jefferey Philipps, I think, why? What has he been up to?" asked Field.

"Well, maybe nothing, Sir, it could just be coincidence, but I think you might want to ditch the idea of breakfast and look at the other folder on your desk. A car was found at the bottom of the cliffs early this morning," explained Roberts.

"Why should that stop me from having breakfast? If there was anyone in the car, then nothing I can do is going to help them. They need a clergyman not a copper," replied Field.

Roberts hadn't finished, so he continued to inform the detective sergeant of the information to hand.

"Sir, the car was partially burnt out and one of the number plates was missing, but a number plate was found a little way from the crash site. When they checked it, they found it belonged to a car registered to a Jefferey Philipps. They weren't sure about the occupants because of the force of the crash but the fire brigade is on the scene now and they intend to let us know as soon as possible if there was anyone inside the car," he explained.

"Shit!" exclaimed Field on hearing the full details from Roberts.

"Exactly, Sir," replied Roberts.

"Please tell me this is a wind-up, Roberts?"

"I wish it was, Sir, but no, it's no wind-up, I'm deadly serious," replied Roberts.

"Double shit!" exclaimed Field just as Anne Green entered the office.

"Come on, Detective, we have work to do," said Field to Green.

"Where are we going, Sir?" asked the detective.

"To the bottom of Beachy Head. It's a shame you've just had your breakfast as this will not be nice, I can guarantee that," replied Field.

They got into the car and headed down towards the seafront. As they approached the pier, Field pulled into a parking bay and placed his police 'on duty' sign on the dashboard and got out of the car. He walked around to the entrance of the pier and then stopped; turning back towards the car, he shouted to Green.

"Are you coming then or are you going to sit there all day?"

She got out of the car and quickly followed, trying to catch up with him.

"I thought you said we were going to Beachy Head, Sir," said Green.

"That's exactly right, we are," he replied.

"But why are we on the pier then, Sir?" she questioned.

"Well, we can't get to the bottom of Beachy Head by road, so unless you fancy jumping over the edge, we have to go by boat," he replied. "I've already alerted someone to pick us up."

Green became noticeably quieter as they continued along the pier and then down the steps to the boat which was waiting there, manned by a police officer.

"Come on then, Green," he said as he looked up towards her. He was already on the boat while Green was still at the top of the steps.

"I don't like boats, Sir," she replied as she trod cautiously down the steps towards the boat.

"You'll be fine, it's not far," replied Field.

"Okay, are we all in?" asked the officer at the wheel of the boat. "Hold tight. It's okay here but it's a bit rough the further out we go, and we have to give the rocks a wide berth."

The officer was certainly right about it getting a little rough, and unfortunately for Green she was unable to keep her breakfast down for long.

"Do you have a bottle of water," Field asked the officer. "Unfortunately the detective has just fed the fish."

"There's some in the box you are sitting on, Sir," replied the officer.

The detective took out a bottle of water and took it to Green who was still leaning over the side of the boat.

Handing her the bottle of water he said, "Here, rinse your mouth round with this and then drink the rest slowly; at least it's better to be sick here than when we get to the bottom of the cliffs."

He walked back up and stood next to the officer. "How much longer?" he asked.

"Not long at all. As soon as we get around this point, we can start moving back in towards shore, so it won't be as rough. Do you know exactly where you want to go?" asked the officer.

"Not exactly," replied Field, "but we are looking for a wrecked car, not just bodies, and the fire service are already there so it should be a lot easier to spot."

"If you open that small cupboard door just in front of you, there are some binoculars in there, so you may be able to spot it easier using those," said the officer.

Field took the binoculars out of the cupboard and started scanning the shoreline; it wasn't long before he thought he saw something.

"Well, it looked as though they definitely meant it: that must be the highest part of the cliff where they went over," commented Field.

"Okay, yes, I see them now," replied the officer. "I will get in as close as I can, but you may get your feet wet."

Detective Green heard them talking and as she was feeling a little better now that the ride was not as choppy, she got up and walked up to join them.

"Are we nearly there now?" she asked.

"Not far," replied Field, pointing to an area of the shoreline where they were heading to. "Can you see the car there?" he commented.

"Oh no, that looks really bad," said Green as she moved her position in the boat to try to get a better view.

"Here, these may help," said Field as he handed her the binoculars.

"Surely there can't be anyone alive?" she asked.

"I wouldn't have thought so. The fire service is trying to recover the bodies now, but the tide has already turned and is on its way back in, so it'll be a race against time," replied Field.

"This is about as close as I can get," said the officer. "You'll have to transfer to the small boat but you're going to get wet feet."

"That's okay, all in a day's work. I take it you will wait for us and take us back to the pier?" asked Field.

"As long as you're not going to be too long," said the officer.

"Thirty minutes maximum," replied Field.

They reached the beach just as the recovery crew had retrieved the body of the driver from the wreckage of the vehicle. Field climbed over the stones and fallen rocks to the car.

He showed the crew his ID.

"DS Field and Detective Green. We need to take a look," said Field.

"If you want to, but it's not a pretty sight," came the reply.

Field approached the body laid out on the stretcher. He pulled down the cover to see a barely recognisable face. He took the photo out of his pocket and could see a couple of similarities that allowed him to take a rough guess that the body could quite possibly be that of Jefferey Philipps.

The fire officer walked over to where Field was standing by the stretcher. "My team are just going back to look for a second body," he said.

Field looked back towards the wreck of the car, lying on its roof and crushed against the rocks underneath it.

"What makes you think there is someone else in the car, then?" asked Field.

"One of the team thought he saw what looked like a burnt part of a woman's shoe; he wasn't one hundred percent sure, but better to be safe than sorry," replied the fire officer.

"So, you think there is the body of a woman in the car too then?" asked Green.

"No, that's not what I said," replied the officer. "What I said was, one of the team thought he saw what appeared to look like part of a woman's shoe, so not necessarily the same thing. However, we never leave anything to chance, so we need to take another look, which is what they are going to do now."

"That car looks pretty flat to me, so if there is another person in the vehicle, how long is it likely to take before you can get the body out of the wreckage?" asked Field.

"As long as it takes. Sorry but I can't be more specific than that, and it looks as though we may have to lift the car to get a clearer view. But if there's a chance that there is another person in there, that's what we have to do," replied the officer.

"Okay, thank you. I guess we'll just hang around for a while, but don't worry, we won't get in your way," replied Field.

"Don't worry, you won't get in our way because we won't let you, so if you and your colleague would kindly move back to those rocks over there," he said, pointing to an area of rocks about 30 metres away near the water's edge, "then we can get on with our work unhindered, and if we have any news for you, I will call you."

Field and Green moved back to the rocks and sat there, rather impatiently waiting for the fire officer to call them.

Green got up from the rocks and walked slowly down towards the water's edge.

"Feeling a little queasy again are we, Anne?" Field asked.

"Not really, Sir," she replied and turned back towards him. "I'm just trying to figure all this out. If there is another body in the car, are you thinking that it will be Joanne Webster?"

"Well, I would have thought that is quite a good supposition, wouldn't you?" he asked.

"Maybe, but I wouldn't be convinced, not just yet, Sir," replied Green.

Field was surprised by her answer and shaking his head, he replied: "You have a lot to learn, Anne. It seems quite open and shut to me. You have two work colleagues, one single and one with a partner; we see a video and photos of them together out of work hours in what can only be described as a compromising situation. Then the female colleague is reported missing by her aunt and her partner, and then the very next day a car registered to the male colleague is found crushed and burnt out at the bottom of the cliff with a male inside. So, if the fire department now find the body of a woman in that same car, you don't have to be Einstein to work out who that female is."

"But, Sir, if, as you think they were about to run off together, why would they then drive the car over the cliff resulting in their deaths?" asked Detective Green.

"Have you ever been in love, Anne?" asked Field.

"Sorry, Sir, but what has whether or not I have been in love got to do with this?" she questioned.

"Well, quite simply, if you had ever been in love, real love, you would know that love can have a strange effect on people and they can sometimes take rash actions for which there is no explanation," he replied quite confidently.

"Maybe, but I would still need something more concrete than that to convince me," she replied.

"Believe me, if they find a woman's body in that car, then the disappearance of Joanne Webster is solved, case closed," he stated.

The ongoing conversation between Field and Green was interrupted by the fire office calling to them. They both walked back over to where the wreck of the car was precariously positioned on the rocks.

"Sergeant Field, I'm sure you will be interested to know that there *is* another body in the car, though we do not yet know the sex of the person, but we are in a race against time to get the body out from the wreckage," explained the officer.

"Thank you, thank you very much," replied Field looking at the officer; turning to Green he added with a grin on his face, "I think we can safely say case closed, Detective; let's head back to base, where you can write this one up."

Field took a card out of his pocket and offered it to the fire officer. "Would you please call me as soon as you know the sex of the second body? Thank you."

The fire officer watched as Field and Green made their way back across the beach and out to the boat that had brought them there.

Tom had been awake for a couple of hours; he couldn't sleep. He knew that it was going to be a make-or-break day and he was fearful of the outcome. He had started to cook breakfast but then grew bored and turned the cooker off. He heard Aunt Matilda go to the bathroom, so he started cooking again. He had to try to hold his nerve and act as though he was still in full control, which was extremely difficult when he was suffering from his internal turmoil.

"Good morning, Matilda. I'm cooking some breakfast, what would you like?" he asked as she walked into the kitchen and sat at the breakfast bar.

"Thank you, Tom, but I don't think I could eat anything. Whenever I see food, all I think of is Joanne and I start wondering where she is and how she would be feeling, whether she's eaten or had anything to drink," she commented.

"I know, I do understand that," replied Tom. "You know, I started cooking at four am, and then I stopped and then tried again but I had the same feelings as you. It was only when I heard you in the bathroom that I thought I must try; we both need to eat, or we will only make things worse."

They were interrupted by a knock on the door.

"I'll see who it is," said Matilda.

Tom continued cooking as he knew that he had to try to get Aunt Matilda to eat something, even if it was only some toast or cereal. He heard her coming back into the kitchen and turned around to see Warren and his wife.

"Good morning, Warren," said Tom. "Food is ready if you're hungry."

"Thank you, Tom," replied Warren. "We tried to eat at home but couldn't manage anything, maybe we can get something later."

Warren's wife nudged him and looked at Tom as if to remind him of something.

"Tom, I do apologise, this is Patricia, my wife," said Warren.

"Good morning, Tom, I'm very pleased to meet you. I've heard so much about you," said Patricia.

"The pleasure is all mine. I did see you briefly at the firm's dinner, but we weren't introduced," replied Tom.

"Warren tends to forget the intricacies of meeting new acquaintances where I am concerned," she replied.

"I'm sure it was just a slip of the mind! He's a very busy man, and it was such an important evening for him," replied Tom.

"I can see why my husband likes you so much, Tom, you have a certain way with words."

"Thank you, Mrs Fredericks, I …" but Tom was interrupted before he could finish.

"Please don't call me that," said Patricia. "Patricia will be fine, as long as I may call you Tom."

"But of course, Patricia," replied Tom.

Warren watched in awe of the way his wife and Tom were interacting with one another; it was as though they had known each other for years. He was so surprised that his wife had carried out his wishes to the letter, doing exactly as he asked in trying to gain Tom's confidence as he was worried about the outcome at the end of the day if they had still not found Joanne.

"I hate to interrupt you two, but I was hoping, Tom, that my wife could stay here today with Matilda, and they could keep each other company. What do you think?" asked Warren.

"I think that is a wonderful idea. What do you think, Matilda," asked Tom as he turned to look at her.

"I could certainly do with the company," she replied, then turning to Patricia, she said, "I can show you around the house and all the decorating that Tom has been doing and then maybe we could go for a walk around the grounds."

"That sounds great," replied Patricia.

"Well, tuck in," said Tom as he pointed towards the food. "It'll be getting cold."

"I think we are all in the same boat, Tom, and food is probably the last thing on our minds at the moment," replied Warren.

Tom was surprised by another knock on the door.

"I don't know who that could be. I wasn't expecting anyone else."

Warren was standing by the kitchen door so he was the nearest to the hallway.

"I'll go," he said and turned and walked towards the front door. He opened it and was startled to see Detective Sergeant Field standing there with a colleague.

"Can I help you?" asked Warren.

"I would like to speak with Tom Maddox if he's available," replied Field.

"Yes, of course, please come in," replied Warren.

Tom was shocked when he saw Field following Warren into the kitchen.

"Tom, Detective Field would like to speak with you," said Warren.

"Well, to what do we owe this pleasure, Detective Field?" asked Tom.

"It's Detective Sergeant, actually. and I'd like to speak with you in private, if I may," said Field.

"Okay, fire away, I'm all ears," replied Tom.

"Umm, this is not really private," said Field.

"Well, maybe not but it's as private as you are going to get," replied Tom.

"I am sorry, Mr Maddox, but it's a private matter regarding Joanne Webster."

"Well, I'm sure you remember Aunt Matilda here, she is Joanne's only living relative so whatever you have to say to me you can say in front of her, too," replied Tom in a slightly raised voice.

Warren could see Tom was getting annoyed by Field's continuance to demand a private conversation.

"Detective Sergeant Field, I hate to interrupt you, but I am Tom's legal counsel, Jefferey Philips is one of my employees and my wife here is director of employment, so I believe we are all entitled to be here," said Warren.

"This isn't easy, but Detective Green and I here have just come from Beachy Head where we had the unfortunate business of seeing a car at the bottom of the cliff. The driver of that car I believe was Jefferey Philips," he explained.

The room fell immediately silent, with looks of exasperation on their faces.

"What! Are you sure?" exclaimed Tom.

"Well, we have to wait for formal identification, but the car in which the bodies was found was registered to Philips and I used this photo from our records to try to confirm my belief that a body we found was him," stated Field as he took the photo of Jefferey Philips out of his pocket and showed it to them all.

"I am sorry to hear that, but how does that help Joanne? You haven't even asked if we had managed to find her. I thought maybe that was why you had come here," replied Tom.

"Mr Maddox, there were two people in the car, a man and a woman. The car had caught fire and the woman's body and face were badly burnt, so I couldn't make an identification."

Aunt Matilda immediately let out a loud scream and slumped into the chair behind her. She was straight away attended to by Patricia who was trying to calm her down.

"So, what are you implying?" asked Tom nervously.

"I'm sorry, Mr Maddox, but you have to be prepared for the fact that the woman in the car might have been Joanne Webster," said Field.

"No, no, *no*! I won't accept that until you give me proof. Don't come here without one iota of proof!" replied Tom angrily.

"Mr Maddox, I know it is upsetting for you, but you have to listen to reason," replied Field.

"No, you listen to me Detective *Sergeant* Field! When you can come back here and tell me you are trying hard to find Joanne, then and only then can we continue this discussion. Until then, our conversation is over, and you need to leave," replied Tom.

"Mr Maddox, if–"

"No, stop right there. I am not interested in your ifs! Do you not understand English? I asked you to leave, so will you please do so? Now! Goodbye!" said Tom furiously as he walked out of the kitchen and stormed upstairs.

Warren took over where Tom had left off. "Detective Sergeant

Field, my client has asked you and Detective Green to leave, so I suggest that as you have no further business here you should do so immediately."

Detective Sergeant Field stood there in shock, not really knowing how to respond. Detective Green stepped forward and nudged Field's arm.

"I think we should go back to the station now, Sir, we have paperwork to complete," she said.

"Yes, of course, you are right," he replied to the detective.

Turning to Fredericks, Field said, "We will leave now, please tell Mr Maddox that we are sorry to have brought this news to him, but we are only doing our job. However, if the results of tests that will be carried out show that the woman in the car is not Joanne Webster, then the police force will do all we can to find her."

"But how long will that take?" asked Warren.

"We hope to have a formal identification by tomorrow," replied Field.

"Well, I'm sorry, Detective, but that's not good enough. Joanne has been missing since around three pm on Friday afternoon and it is now Sunday, and in approximately five hours she will have been missing for forty-eight hours. If she has not been given water, the next few hours are critical, and we cannot wait until tomorrow for you to act. We need you to take action now. If you are not prepared to do that, then please do as you have been asked and leave these premises now," said Warren angrily.

Tom came back down the stairs just as Warren was closing the front door.

"So, how do we find Joanne now? The police think she is already dead and by the time they find out the body in the car is not her, it will be too late," said Tom.

Warren wasn't ready to give up. "Come on, Tom, we can't give up now, we're going to find Joanne. We will stop everyone we see, but we're going to need help."

They went back into the kitchen where Warren picked up his phone and called Susan.

"Susan, good morning, are you still able to help us today?" he asked.

"Of course, it's the only place for me today, and for as long as it takes," she replied.

"Thank you so much. Can we meet you at King Edward's Parade near the Wish Tower? I am already with Matilda and Tom and we will be leaving Joanne's house in about fifteen minutes," said Warren then finished the call.

"Okay, I'm taking charge today," continued Warren. "Matilda, Patricia, get your coats – you're going to the beach."

"Warren, what are you talking about? I am meant to be staying here with Matilda," remonstrated Patricia.

"Well, not anymore. I'm afraid we need your help and it's non-negotiable, so get your things because we're leaving in five minutes," replied Warren.

Tom turned to Warren. "I am sorry Warren, I just cannot think straight at the moment, everything seems to be a muddle."

"That's why I am taking control, just trying to relieve the pressure on you; have you got the photographs of Joanne?" asked Warren.

"I have them here in this holdall," replied Tom.

"Right, then, let's go then," said Warren.

CHAPTER TWENTY-EIGHT

Loose Ends

Warren drove down to the seafront and parked near to the Lifeboat Museum, just a short walk from the Wish Tower where he had asked Susan Caton to meet them.

Tom got out of the car and looked up at the Wish Tower.

"I think Susan is already here. I'm sure that's her sitting on the seat up there," he said.

Warren looked towards the seating area and waved at the woman sitting there. She got up and started walking towards them.

"Yes, that's Susan," he said.

Susan hurried towards them. "Did you hear the news on the TV this morning?" she asked looking anxious.

"What news, Susan?" asked Tom.

"Someone drove over the cliff at Beachy Head last night and two people are dead," she replied.

"Yes, we heard," remarked Warren. "The police came to Joanne's house this morning and–"

Susan interrupted him. "Why, what did they want?" she asked.

"The car, Susan – it was registered in Jefferey's name," replied Warren.

"What?" shouted Susan. "What do you mean? Do they think it was Jefferey?"

"Yes, they do, but the detective is of the opinion that should the other body in the car be that of a woman, he expects it to be Joanne," replied Warren.

"No, it can't be!" screamed Susan. "It can't be Joanne, it just can't be her!"

"I told them the same thing," remarked Tom, "and then I asked them to leave."

"Look, we can't let this revelation distract us. Jefferey was the driver of the car and there is nothing we can do about the fact that he is dead. And after what he has done, he doesn't deserve our thoughts. We don't know who the woman in the car was and until we do, we can't change anything. We must believe it was not Joanne and we have to keep searching for her," said Warren.

Tom gave out photos of Joanne to Warren and Susan, and some small posters to Patricia and Aunt Matilda.

"Patricia and Matilda, if you two could work together and hand out one of the flyers to each shop, tea stall, burger bar or whatever, and ask if they could place it where their customers can see it, please. Warren, Susan and I will ask people to look at Joanne's photo and see if they remember seeing her. We all have each other's phone numbers so we can stay in contact in case we get any positive responses. In any case, I think we should meet back here in three hours," said Tom.

"Okay," said Warren, "if we are all happy with what we are going to be doing, let's get started. See you all in three hours," he added.

Susan, Tom and Warren split up. Tom walked along the beach while Susan took the lower pathway and Warren the upper pathway next to the road. They covered the area from the pier to the Hollywell Tea Rooms, where the three of them met up. Tom had kept a flyer back and went into the tea rooms while Susan and Warren waited outside.

"Hi, I wonder if you could put one of these up for me? It is a photo of my partner. She has been missing since Friday and I believe she may have been in this area or close by at the time she disappeared. If you have any information or someone thinks they may know something, then I'm Tom, and they could ring me on this number," he said as he handed over a card with his contact details.

"Okay, the boss is out at the moment, but I'll show this to him. I'm sure it will be okay to put it up in the window, though, so I'll put it right here next to the till to make sure everyone sees it," she replied.

"Thank you, thank you very much," said Tom as he turned and joined Susan and Warren who were sitting outside.

"What now?" asked Susan as Tom stood by the wall where they had been waiting.

"I think we should get the train back to the main beach and get something to eat and drink," suggested Warren.

"What do you think, Tom?" asked Susan.

"Although it hurts me to say it, I'm not sure there is anything else we can do apart from treading grounds we have already been over," he replied. "I'll ring Matilda to let her know we are on the way back to them. I think we should meet them by the Beach Club Tea Tooms," said Tom as he picked up his phone.

"Matilda, we're on the way back now. We'll meet you at the Beach Club Tea Rooms. We are just getting on the train now. See you soon, bye."

They joined the two women at the tea rooms and Tom took their orders. He then went to place the order. Luckily, there was only a short queue, so he was soon on his way back to the table. It was then that he heard someone calling.

"Raymond, Raymond, is that you?"

Tom looked around but wasn't sure who was calling him, or where the voice came from, so he continued back to the table where the others were waiting for him.

"Ray," he heard the voice call again, "over here by the beach huts."

Tom looked towards the huts and saw a face from the past.

"Simon! Long time, no see. Hang on, I'll come over there," he said as he picked up his tea. "I won't be a minute, Simon is an old work colleague," he explained to the four of them.

"How are you Ray? You just disappeared after your terrible accident. People were asking after you, but no one could find out where you went to. It's really good to see you! How are you doing?" asked Simon.

"I am okay, but it's a bad time, Simon. I have recently been piecing my life back together after all this time but now my new partner has gone missing, so I'm here with friends, asking around if anyone has seen her," replied Tom.

"Sorry to hear that Ray. Lucky I saw you; I was just going to lock up," said Simon as he took a key out of his pocket. "Maybe we can meet up some time and have a chat? Alan, my son, is running the business now, and he needs a good chief designer. We have had a few since you left but none were up to scratch compared to you, but then it was difficult for them, following the shoes of someone of your calibre," said Simon.

"Wait, sorry, Simon, can I look at that key?" asked Tom.

"Ye,s of course, why? What's the problem?" asked Simon as he handed Tom the key.

"Can I just borrow this for two minutes, please? I just want to show it to someone," asked Tom.

"But of course," replied Simon.

Tom walked over to the table where Warren and the others were sitting. "Susan, do you have the keys with you that you took from Lucy Saunders' house, and the letter?" he asked.

"Yes, but why?" asked Susan.

"I just want to compare one of the keys with this one," he said as he held out the key towards her.

"Here they are," said Susan as she handed Tom the keys.

"Bingo!" shouted Tom in a loud voice. "What number is on that letter from the council, Susan?" he asked.

"EBH 7241," replied Susan.

"This is that key, the numbers match and it's the same make as this man's beach hut. Jefferey hired a beach hut, not a garage, which is the reason he didn't park his car in it. That proves he was planning something, and I guess if we find this beach hut, we will find Joanne," said Tom with a new level of excitement in his voice.

Warren jumped up out of his chair. "Tom, that's great but there must be at least a hundred beach huts! Which one is it?" he asked.

"Well, we will just have to check every single one until we find the lock that the key fits," replied Tom.

Simon was still standing there next to Tom. "Hang on, Ray, what's going on here? What's this about a beach hut and who is Joanne and why did he just call you Tom?" asked Simon.

Tom looked at his old friend. "It's a long story, Simon, which I haven't got time to explain now, but I told you my partner is missing and there's a chance that she is being held in the beach hut that this key belongs to," said Tom as he returned Simon's key to him and showed him the key he was holding. "She has been missing for two days so we haven't got long," explained Tom.

"Sorry, Ray, but I think you might find yourself in trouble if you go to every beach hut and try your key in the lock. The owners here are quite protective of each other and you can be sure someone will query what you are up to and call the police," explained Simon.

"I think he has a point, Tom," said Warren, "so maybe it's time to call in the cavalry."

"Maybe you can call the police and wait for them to turn up. Don't forget they already think it was Joanne who was in the car at the bottom of the cliff," replied Tom.

Tom was interrupted by his phone ringing. He looked at the screen: unknown number. He clicked the accept button and held the phone to his ear.

"Hello, who is this?" asked Tom.

"Is that Tom Maddox?" asked the person calling him.

"Yes, this is Tom. Who's calling please?" he asked again.

"Okay, I am the owner of the Hollywell Tea Rooms. You popped in earlier and left a flyer here about a missing person," said the caller.

"Yes, that's correct, my partner is missing. Do you have any information about her disappearance?" asked Tom.

"Well, I'm not sure, but I just want to tell you about something I heard on Friday. I had locked up and was just about to leave when I heard a woman's voice in the distance. All she said was, 'Is that you, Tom?' which was followed by an undistinguishable noise, which was again followed by the woman asking, 'Is that you, Tom?' I waited a few minutes but that was it, that was all I heard, then nothing,"

"Okay, thank you, that sounds very helpful. Tell me, was that right by your tea rooms?" asked Tom.

"Yes, it was, but I'm not sure where exactly the woman was as I couldn't see her, but she couldn't have been far away," replied the caller.

"Would you know if there are any vacant beach huts in that area?" enquired Tom.

"As it happens, yes, there have been a few recently, but I think most of them have been let now," he replied.

"Okay, thank you, that's great," replied Tom. "I'm at the Beach Club Tea Rooms, so I'll come straight down there now. Could you wait for me, please?" he asked.

"No problem, I'll be here waiting for you."

"Sorry, Simon, it's been great to see you, but I have to get down to Hollywell right now. Here, take this, it has my number on it, so give me a call some time, please," said Tom.

They left in a hurry and drove the short distance along to Hollywell. Leaving their cars in King Edward's Parade, they made the short walk to the tea chalet at Hollywell. As they approached, Tom noticed a man sitting on the wall outside where Warren and Susan had sat earlier. He was holding the flyer that Tom had left there earlier.

"Hi, are you the owner of Hollywell Tea Chalet?" asked Tom as he walked towards him.

"Yes, and I take it you are Tom?" he replied.

"That's right. Tell me, was it around here that you heard the woman's voice last Friday?" Tom enquired.

"Well, I was walking to my car, that's it parked just there, so yes, I had just locked up and was walking towards my car and I was about here when I first heard her voice. I didn't take much notice and then as I was about to get into my car, I heard it again, so I stopped and waited and then nothing. I just assumed that the woman had found whomever she was looking for. The light was fading fast, and I couldn't actually see anyone. It was difficult to pinpoint exactly the direction the voice came from," he said.

"Okay, more importantly, you said there were some vacant beach huts in this area. Could you show me where, please?" asked Tom.

"Yes, head straight down the pathway behind the metal screen, which is where the chalets are. I think there were a couple that were vacant, but I think they have recently been taken," he stated.

Tom, Warren and Susan continued down to the huts while Patricia and Aunt Matilda sat down and waited at the tea chalet. Tom was feeling excited but also nervous as he approached the huts. He felt very apprehensive; what if he was wrong and Joanne wasn't in any of the beach huts? Maybe she was in one but dead – what would he do? His emotions were getting the better of him. He was fumbling with the key, trying to get it in the lock of the first chalet, but it didn't fit. The next hut was open and a man was walking back up the beach towards it.

"Hey, what are you doing? That hut isn't yours!" he shouted.

"No, sorry, I'm trying to find the beach hut that this key belongs to. Do you know if any have been let recently?" asked Tom.

"Why should I tell you that?" asked the man.

"You don't have to, but I will just keep trying each hut to see if the key fits any of them," replied Tom as he continued towards the next hut.

"Okay, try the first red one just there and then try the second orange one towards the end of the row; they are the only two that have recently been let," replied the man.

The three of them hurried up to the red-fronted chalet, but the key didn't fit. Tom was becoming increasingly anxious as he approached the second orange one.

"Here, let me do it," said Warren as he took the key from Tom. Warren placed the key in the lock, and there was a click as he turned it; he tried the handle and the door opened. They had found the chalet. Susan pushed past Tom, who seemed rooted to the spot, and followed Warren inside.

"Tom, she's here!" shouted Susan.

Warren tried hard to stay calm, but he could see Joanne was unconscious.

"Quickly!" he shouted. "Unresponsive female – we need a doctor and an ambulance … and someone call the police!"

Tom rushed in and seeing Joanne there on the floor, tied up with tape over her mouth and blindfolded, he feared the worst.

"Is she still alive?" shouted Tom. "Warren, is she still alive?" he immediately repeated.

"I don't know, it's too noisy in here, everybody out!" shouted Warren who was busy removing the tape from Joanne's mouth. "Susan, come here, help me, I can't feel a pulse."

Susan looked around the sparse chalet. There was a small mirror on the wall. She pulled it off and placed it just above Joanne's mouth.

"Is she breathing?" asked Warren.

"I can't say for sure, no change in the mirror, but if she is then it's very weak. I still can't feel a pulse. I think she could be in a coma," replied Susan.

They could hear the sirens getting closer, but they feared they would be too late.

"I think we should turn her on her side," said Susan.

"Why, will it help?" asked Warren.

"It's the recovery position, stops people from swallowing their tongue," said Susan.

"Okay, let's try it, gently does it," said Warren. "There's no movement, she's not showing any signs of life," said Warren just as the paramedics burst in.

"Okay, can we all move out of the way please? Who found her?" asked one of the paramedics.

"We did," replied Susan. "She was tied up with tape across her mouth and a blindfold over her eyes; I couldn't find any pulse, so I put a mirror above her mouth but there was nothing."

"Do you know how long she has been like this?" asked the paramedic.

"She went missing on Friday afternoon, about five o'clock, I think," replied Tom.

"Okay, can we have everyone outside, please?"

Warren got up and followed Tom outside. "They are doing everything they can, Tom," he said as he placed his arm around Tom's shoulders.

"If this was Jefferey's doing, I would kill him, but he has even taken that away from me now," replied Tom.

Susan was still in the chalet with the paramedics, answering their questions.

"Could you hold this saline up for me?" asked one of the paramedics. "We have to get some fluid running through her body and we need to give her oxygen too, but there is still no response. Was she already collapsed when you found her?" he asked.

"Yes," replied Susan. "She was just lying there, not moving. We tried to arouse her but there was no response."

"She's breathing but we need to get her to hospital as soon as we can. Where's the ambulance?" he asked his colleague.

"Two minutes," replied the other one.

"Oh, I thought you two were in an ambulance?" Susan said.

"No, we're on motorbikes. We can get here quicker than an ambulance and start emergency treatment," he replied.

Susan was frantically looking at her watch; it seemed longer than two minutes when the ambulance crew arrived. She thought the awkward part was going to be getting Joanne onto the trolley. There wasn't a lot of room in the chalet but with the four of them there, they managed it quite easily. Susan walked along with them as they wheeled Joanne along to the ambulance. Tom and Warren were a little way behind them.

"Which one of you is her partner?" asked one of the medical crew.

"I am," replied Tom.

"We need you to come in the ambulance with us as we have some questions to ask you and they will need to speak with you at the hospital," said the paramedic.

"Can her aunty come with us to the hospital?" asked Tom.

"Yes, of course. Is she here now as we have to go? There is no time to lose," replied the paramedic.

"Come on, Matilda, you can come with us," said Tom.

"I'll wait here with my wife for the police to arrive, Tom," said Warren, "and then we will come to the hospital."

Warren stood and watched along with his wife and Susan as the ambulance drove up the slop towards King Edward's Parade; they were talking to the two paramedics outside the chalet when the police arrived.

"Detective Sergeant Field, how nice to see you again so soon," said Warren.

"Mr Fredericks, isn't it? May I enquire why you are here? Were you at the tea chalet when the woman was discovered?" he asked.

"Well, it seems that you have a habit of making the wrong assumptions, Detective Field," replied Warren.

"It's Detective *Sergeant* Field, actually, but I am not here to argue with you. I have to investigate the discovery of a collapsed woman, so if you will excuse me, I need to talk to the paramedics," said Field as he turned and entered the chalet.

"I'm Detective Sergeant Field. What can you tell me about the woman that you found?" he asked.

"Sorry, we can't tell you much apart from the fact that she appeared to be in a coma. She had been tied up with tape covering her mouth and a blindfold over her eyes. It appears she had been here since Friday, which would explain her near-comatose appearance," replied the paramedic.

"Okay, so, if you didn't find her, do you know who did?" asked Field.

"What?" asked the paramedic as he looked at Field. "I thought you would have known that as you were just talking to him outside," he replied.

"Oh, really, thank you," replied Field.

Field walked back outside to where Warren was sitting. "Well, Mr Fredericks, it would seem you failed to inform me that you found the body of the woman in the chalet."

"I didn't fail to do anything – you didn't ask me if I had found her, you just assumed that I was a bystander. Anyway, now that you have asked, I was here when the chalet was opened, but it was Susan Caton, Joanne Webster's assistant, who opened the chalet and I followed her in. Tom Maddox was also here with us," replied Warren.

"So, where are they now as I need to speak with them?" asked Field.

"Susan Caton had to go to collect her son from her mother's and Tom Maddox has gone to the hospital, but I can answer any questions you may have," replied Warren.

"If you don't mind me asking, Mr Fredericks, I am intrigued as to why the three of you would be here together anyway? Does the chalet belong to one of you and if so, why was a woman inside it, apparently tied up?" asked the detective.

"We had been searching for Joanne, who has been missing since Friday," Warren replied.

"But why were you wasting your time? I told you this morning that we believed Joanne Webster to be the woman who was in the car with Jefferey Philips," said Field.

"Yes, you did, Detective Field, but I think that is highly unlikely because Joanne Webster was the woman we have just found tied up and dumped in that chalet."

"What? Are you sure?" exclaimed Field.

"One hundred percent, Detective Field, one hundred percent."

Field turned and went back to the chalet to speak to the paramedics.

"What are her chances?" he asked.

"Difficult to say now. She was unconscious, probably without water since Friday, locked up in a small space like this, with the sun shining, it gets pretty hot in these chalets, which increases the speed with which dehydration takes place. Hopefully, she'll recover, but it's dependent on several factors, not just rehydration," replied one of the paramedics.

Field asked more questions of the paramedics and then moved everyone out of the chalet and sealed it until the fingerprint team arrived. He walked back to where Warren was waiting and checked with him once more exactly where Joanne was when they first found her, how she had been restrained and if she had been unconscious.

Warren was getting extremely impatient with Field's line of questioning; he kept going on and on, repeating the same questions as though he was trying to catch him out.

"Detective Field, if you are finished now or unless you have any questions to ask me that you have not already asked several times, I would like to go now," said Warren in a rather stern voice.

"Ah, okay, Mr Fredericks. Am I worrying you with my line of questioning?" he asked.

"Not really, but it is getting very, very boring, and I am not going to change any answers, no matter how many times you ask me the same questions," replied Warren.

"Okay, you can go now but I'll need to speak to you again later," said the detective.

"Thank you very much, Detective," said Warren.

As he was walking away, Field called to him.

"Mr Fredericks!" he shouted.

Warren turned to face him. "Yes?"

"It's Detective *Sergeant*, actually," he said.

"Really?" replied Warren. "A fancy title doesn't prove you know what you're doing."

"Don't leave the country," shouted the detective.

Warren ignored him and turned around and kept walking. Taking his wife's arm, he whispered to her.

"What a waste of space, a complete idiot! Let's get out of here before he changes his mind," he said.

Warren pulled into the carpark at the hospital and they quickly made their way to A&E, where they saw Tom and Joanne's aunt who were still waiting for news of Joanne.

"Any news yet, Tom?" asked Warren.

Patricia sat down next to Matilda and took hold of her hand, squeezing it gently as she did so.

"It will be okay, your niece is a very strong young lady, she won't let this beat her," said Patricia.

Just then someone came out of the treatment area and walked towards them.

"Are you with Joanne Webster?" he asked.

Tom stood up in front of him.

"I'm her partner, and this is her aunt," replied Tom, beckoning to Aunt Matilda to come and join them.

"Would you both come with me, please? I just want to have a chat with you both and explain what we are doing," he said.

Tom turned to Warren and his wife and asked them to wait there. He followed the doctor to a small room just off the treatment area.

"Please take a seat, I won't keep you long. I am Dr Selway, one of the team looking after Joanne. I still have nothing concrete to tell you apart from the fact that we are currently doing everything we can for her. Were either of you present when they found her?" asked the doctor.

"Yes, we were both there," replied Tom. "She had been missing for over forty-eight hours and we were just following a couple of leads as to where she might be. It's a long story but we knew she'd been abducted and we'd worked out that it was highly likely she'd been taken to a beach hut. It took ages to find the right chalet."

"Was her disappearance reported to the police?" asked Doctor Selway.

"Yes, the evening she disappeared but they weren't interested as she's an adult and they didn't think there was anything suspicious."

"Typical," commented the doctor. "So, when you found her, how was she? Did she move when she heard you?" he asked.

"No, there was no movement from her, not even when we were freeing her; removing the tape covering her mouth must have been painful, but there was no movement at all from her," replied Tom.

"Okay, thank you. All I can say is that she is young and appears strong so we should be able to bring her round, but until we can do that we will not know if she will have any lasting damage," replied the doctor.

"How long do you think it will be before she comes round?" asked Matilda.

The doctor looked at them both; he had done this many times before, but it never got any easier, something most people would never be able to understand.

"I am sorry, I do not know the answer to that question. All I can tell you is that we are doing all that we can, and when she comes to, we will be ready and waiting," he replied.

"What about me? Can I sit with her? I want to be there when she wakes up," asked Tom.

"Yes, of course, but only one of you at a time, please," replied the doctor. "We just have a couple more tests to carry out, then we will call you and you can sit with her."

"Thank you," replied Tom.

"If you'd both like to go and wait outside again, I'll call you when we are ready."

On seeing Tom and Aunt Matilda reappear from the treatment area, Warren stood up and walked towards them.

"So, what is the news?" he asked expectantly.

"There isn't any," replied Tom glumly, "apart from the fact that they are still fighting for her and doing all they can to help bring her around. The doctor pointed out that as she is young and fit, then she should pull through, but it's just a waiting game for that moment to happen. I asked if he had any idea how long it would take but he said he couldn't answer that as he didn't know. They have another couple of tests to carry out and then either Matilda or I can go in and sit with her, but only one at a time," said Tom.

Warren could see the hurt in Tom's eyes. He put his arm around his shoulders and pulled him closer, giving him a hug.

"Come on now, Tom, you have to stay strong. You owe it to Joanne to be there for her. She is going to need you more than ever now," he said.

Patricia and Aunt Matilda joined Tom and Warren in their huddle, and that is where they stood, giving each other much needed support until the doctor reappeared and told Tom that one of them could now go and sit with the patient.

Tom looked at Matilda. "Do you want to go first?" he asked her.

"Thank you for asking, Tom, but no, you go. If these lovely people will take me home, I would like to get some sleep. You go and sit with Joanne; she will be expecting you to be there when she wakes up. I will come back in the morning and relieve you for a few hours," replied Matilda.

"Thank you very much, and thank you all! None of this would have been possible without your help; I will contact you all as soon as there is any change in Joanne's condition," said Tom as he turned and headed towards the treatment area.

CHAPTER TWENTY-NINE

Waiting Time

Tom sat there, focusing constantly on Joanne, afraid even to blink in case he should miss any slight movement from her. He was fighting a losing battle with his eyes, though, as sitting there watching Joanne was making him feel ever more tired. His eyes were closing again, but he soon sprang to life as two nurses entered the room who had come to check on Joanne.

"Any movement, Tom?" asked one of the nurses.

"Not that I have noticed but I do keep dozing off. It's been a long day," he replied.

"Don't worry. We will be alerted if she should wake up. Her signs are improving, but I think we need her white cell count to drop before we can hope for any further improvement."

"How long will that take?" asked Tom.

"Her body has suffered stress and trauma, both of which can cause the white blood cells to increase, but now that she is more stable and receiving oxygen they should start returning to normal very soon. We'll be here for another few minutes yet if you want to stretch your legs or get a drink," suggested the nurse.

"Thank you," replied Tom as he got up from the chair. "I'll visit the bathroom and grab myself a tea if that's okay, try to wake myself up a little," he added.

"No problem at all. There are some biscuits and cakes in the kitchen – if you fancy any of those, help yourself," replied one of the nurses.

Tom returned to Joanne's room just as the nurses were finishing their checks. "How is she?" he asked as he sat back down in the chair with his cup of tea.

"She is responding well, Tom, although rather slowly, but that is to be expected. Her body has suffered a significant trauma," replied the nurse.

As they were leaving, the junior nurse turned to Tom. "Don't worry, Tom, she will be okay. You know you can move your chair closer to the bed if you want to? You are allowed to hold her hand and it may help you relax, too," she said.

"Thank you," replied Tom as he got up and moved the chair next to the bed. "I wasn't sure, didn't want to take liberties."

"No problem, Tom, try to close your eyes for a bit," said the nurse gently as she closed the door.

Tom leant forward and took hold of Joanne's hand, something a few hours earlier he wasn't sure that he would ever do again; all he wanted was to hold her tight, but for now he had to be satisfied with sitting next to her bed and knowing that she was still alive. Moving his chair again, he positioned it so that he could rest his head on the bed. He felt strange as he recalled the last few weeks and how the roles had changed between the two of them. Joanne had been sitting in a similar chair only recently, wondering if *he* would be alright, and now it was him who was in that same situation. Tom could no longer stall the tiredness he was feeling, and it was in that position, holding Joanne's hand with his head resting on the bed beside her, that he fell asleep.

Tom felt the light touch of a hand on his head. He turned, expecting to see a nurse standing there trying to wake him up, but he was mistaken – there was no one there. Maybe he had imagined it or maybe he was dreaming. He looked towards Joanne, but she was still in the same position; she hadn't moved. It was still dark outside, so he lay his head back on the bed again and closed his eyes momentarily before he heard a faint voice.

"I love you."

He was frightened to open his eyes, then he felt a light touch on his head. He looked up at Joanne's face; she was trying to keep her eyes open, but they kept closing. He jumped up out of his chair and ran to the door. Opening it, he shouted: "Nurse, nurse, she's awake!" and then rushed back to the bed and took hold of Joanne's hand.

"I love you too, Miss Webster," he said as the nurses rushed in.

"Sorry, Tom, could we ask you to wait outside for a few minutes please, we won't be long."

"I love you so much, Miss Webster," said Tom as he squeezed her hand and then left the room.

He took out his phone and went straight to fast-dial for Warren; it only rang a few times.

"Tom! What's wrong?" he asked.

"She's awake, but only just. I'll ring you back when I know more," said Tom as he ended the call. He just had time to ring Aunt Matilda before the nurse called him to go back in.

"She is very weak, so you will probably find that she will drift in and out of sleep, but that is quite normal. We have taken a blood sample and we have called the doctor to come and check her over. You can sit with her until he gets here."

"Thank you very much," replied Tom as he once again moved the chair over to the bed and held Joanne's hand; she was sleeping again but he held it tight and didn't let go. He kept a close watch on her, waiting for signs that she might be waking again. There was so much he wanted to say to her. So much he had realised in the few days that she was missing and how the effect of that had impacted on him, but he knew now what he had to do.

There was a knock on the door and the doctor walked in with the ward sister.

"Mr Maddox?" asked the doctor.

"Yes, that's correct, Tom Maddox," replied Tom.

"I'm Alan Coutts, one of the doctors here, and this is Sister Clarke. So, how are we doing? What's been happening with Joanne?" he asked.

"Basically, she was missing for more than forty-eight hours when we found her. She was tied up in a beach chalet, but I have no idea if she had been there the whole time although the probability is that she was," replied Tom.

"So, she could have been without water for the whole time?" he asked.

"I am really not sure, but yes, that is possible" commented Tom.

"Okay, well what we found was that she was severely dehydrated on arrival even though the paramedics had administered saline intravenously. She was obviously unconscious and she does have a slight bruising and graze on the side of her temple which may have caused her to temporarily collapse but apart from that, there were no outward signs to suggest she has suffered a considerable blow that would account for being in that state. Her white blood cell count was extremely high but that was probably due to stress and the trauma that she has been under. We have just received her latest blood results and the white count is coming down nicely. What position was she in when you found her?"

"It looked as though she had been sitting propped up against an internal wall, but she was actually lying on her left side on the floor," replied Tom.

"Okay, that's fine, I think that would account for the bruise and graze that she has on her left temple because if, as you say, she had been sitting up, she would most likely have fallen on her left side when she collapsed; the X-rays came back clear, so we don't need to worry too much about that. What we need now is for her to re-establish her bodily functions. So, when she wakes properly and is coherent, we need you to encourage her to eat and drink as much as possible. She will of course be hungry, but she may also feel sick inside with nerves, a reaction to what she has been through. Although we want her to eat, gorging herself will not be the answer; what we need is a gentle, structured intake of food. However, with regards fluids, she needs to drink as often as possible and as much as she can. You also need to encourage her to talk about what happened to her; psychological damage can be worse than physical injury. Okay, if you would just like to wait outside for a few minutes, I just want to give her a quick check over."

"Thank you, doctor," replied Tom.

Tom stood outside the room and sent a quick message to Warren and Aunt Matilda.

'Joanne doing okay, doctor in with her, no other problems only the dehydration so she should recover fine, contact you later, Tom'

Then he rang Susan, not sure if she would be awake or not.

"Hello?" she answered.

"Susan, it's Tom, just want to let you know that it looks as though Joanne will be okay. She woke up but then went back to sleep. There is a doctor checking her over now, but all indications are that there aren't any other injuries so as long as she gets over the dehydration, she should be okay," explained Tom.

"Oh, Tom, that is great news! Thank you so much and please let her know I send my love and hope she recovers soon. I can't wait to see her."

"I will certainly tell her that, Susan, and I will try to update you later. The doctor is coming out now I have to go. Bye," said Tom as he ended the call.

"Doctor, how is she?" asked Tom.

"She will be fine, I am quite sure. Just make sure you talk to her; she is awake now and was asking for you," he replied.

"Doctor, it is possible that the person who kidnapped her and held her captive is now dead. Should I let her know that?" he asked.

"After what she has been through, she may still be feeling somewhat frightened, so yes, I think that could well help with her frame of mind and, ultimately, her recovery," he replied.

"Okay, thank you," said Tom as he opened the door and went back inside to see Joanne.

"Hi beautiful, I'm here now. I was just waiting outside while the doctor was with you. How are you feeling?" he said as he leant over to kiss her.

"Thank you, Tom. I thought you had gone," she said.

"No, never again will I walk away from you. I love you and I am sorry for what I did. I blame myself for what happened to you and I'm so sorry," replied Tom.

Joanne took hold of his hand. "No Tom, don't do that, it's not your fault. But what if he comes back, whoever did this to me? I don't even know who it was."

"Joanne, listen to me. Warren, Susan and I think it was Jefferey, in fact, we could almost say for certain it was him," said Tom.

"But how can you? You weren't there," replied Joanne.

"Come on, this is too much for you now, but we do have proof that ties Jefferey to where you were found. Tell me, what is the last thing you can remember when you and Warren were looking for me?" asked Tom.

"I had gone to Holywell and I had just spoken to Warren, and we were going to head back towards the pier and meet there. Warren was in the town; I think he said he was near the railway station, but I am not sure. As I was walking along the pathway, I thought I heard someone call to me. I think they said 'Hi beautiful' or something like that. I called out, asking if it was you, but there was no answer, so I continued walking. Then I heard it again, but I couldn't see anyone. The voice seemed to be coming from a pathway further up, back towards the road, but my view was obscured by trees and bushes. Anyway, thinking it might be you, I walked up to where the voice came from but I couldn't see anyone. The pathway opened out on to the lane that leads down to the tea chalet, so I started walking down … and that's it. The next thing I remember is being tied up, sitting on a floor with a hood or blindfold over my eyes and tape over my mouth," recalled Joanne.

"Okay, that's enough, just rest now. What I can say, though, is that you were found in one of the beach huts just down from the Hollywell Tea Chalet. That hut had been rented from Eastbourne council by Jefferey. Susan took the key from his house when she went to see Lucy Saunders. So, it could have been Jefferey, or Lucy, or indeed both, who kidnapped you," explained Tom.

"Okay, so the police will find that out when they interview them?"

said Joanne.

Tom looked into Joanne's eyes and wondered if she was strong enough for this. He held her hand tightly, leant forward and kissed her, then as he sat back, he gave her the news.

"They can't interview Jefferey now, because his car was found at the bottom of Beachy Head with him in it," said Tom. He watched Joanne closely, but there was no reaction.

"There was a woman in the car, too. Detective Sergeant Field, the detective on your case, seemed to think that the woman in the car was you, that you had run off with Jefferey, but we always thought it was Lucy Saunders. Whether they were both involved in your kidnap or not, it would seem as though something went wrong with the plan," explained Tom.

"Thank you, Tom. What would I have done without you? At least I know now that that freak will not bother me again," replied Joanne.

Tom leant forward and kissed her again, and then said to her.

"Just remember that Field doesn't know the extra bits yet about how we got the key and found out about the chalet, so when he asks you, just tell him what you know, which isn't a lot," added Tom.

"Thank you, Tom. Left to the police, I would probably still be in that chalet and almost certainly dead by now," said Joanne as she took Tom's hand in hers.

"Hey, come on, let's not think too much about it. You need to relax and get your strength back so that you can be released from here," replied Tom.

"Did the doctor tell you how long I am likely to be in here for when you spoke to him earlier?" asked Joanne.

"No, he didn't but don't worry too much about that as you are safe in here," he said.

Joanne sat upright in the bed. "But I don't want to be in here, Tom. I want to go home with you, to our house," she replied.

They were interrupted by a tap on the door and in walked a group of doctors and nurses.

"Good morning, I am Doctor Annette Franklin. Are you happy for your partner to be here while we chat?" she asked.

"Yes, Doctor, no problem. I feel quite good, but still a little weak maybe," replied Joanne.

"Okay, well the good news is you do not have any broken ribs from the resuscitation attempts, though you do have a noticeable bruise on your forehead, probably caused when you passed out, but the X-ray is clear on that too. However, you were seriously dehydrated which is why you were awfully close to being in a coma. I am sure you would love to be going home now but for the moment I am going to suggest you remain here, and there are a few reasons for that decision. Firstly, you haven't yet been out of bed, so we need to make sure you have recovered sufficiently and are able to move about freely before we let you out. You also need to up your water in-take, but not too much in one go – it is much better to take sips of water more often, rather than a glass of water in one go. The last reason is that a Detective Sergeant Field is waiting outside to speak to you. I would rather he speaks to you while you are still here, so that I can monitor your reaction to his questions and to make sure he is not putting you under too much pressure," explained Doctor Franklin.

"Thank you," replied Joanne.

The doctor looked at Tom. "Mr Maddox, do you have any questions?" she asked.

"Errmm, yes, Joanne is a workaholic and I was just wondering if you would recommend that she rests for a few days between getting out of hospital and before going back to work," asked Tom.

"Very good point, Mr Maddox. Yes, you should rest for at least a week Joanne. You may feel physically fit, but in cases such as yours there can often be a mental reaction, or a delayed reaction if you prefer that term," replied Doctor Franklin. "I think we are finished here, then. I have two more patients to see, so I will be back in about fifteen minutes, that should give you time to take in more fluid, preferably water, but you may also drink tea and try to eat some food too. When I return, I will bring Detective Sergeant Field in with me," she added.

"Thank you, Doctor, I will be ready," replied Joanne.

Tom leant over the bed and kissed Joanne on her forehead. "I'll be back in a few minutes; just going to get a drink," he said.

Tom followed the doctor out of the room and went to get a tea and some more water, and then went straight back to Joanne. As he approached her room, he could see Field sitting further down the corridor, so he carried on walking towards him. He thought it would be an opportunity to see if he had gathered any more added information.

"Good morning, Detective. I didn't expect to see you here. Are you waiting for someone," he asked.

"Ah, Mr Maddox, we keep bumping into each other. I am beginning to wonder if there is a reason for that," replied Field.

"Not one that I can readily think of," replied Tom.

"No, that's strange because I am here to see Miss Webster," replied Field.

"Indeed … that's rather strange as you believed that Miss Webster was dead," replied Tom.

"Yes, well, we can all make mistakes, Mr Maddox," said Field.

"So, it would appear Detective, some more than others, and in your line of work mistakes like that could be quite costly to someone's wellbeing, maybe even resulting in their actual death, wouldn't you agree?" asked Tom, to which the detective failed to respond.

"I really would love to chat more, Detective," continued Tom. "However, I have to get back to Miss Webster. I do hope you are not intending to pressure her too much; she has been through a lot the last few days and I don't think she is up to needless questioning at this moment in time," said Tom, slightly raising his tone.

"I think you should let me decide on whether Miss Webster is up to answering my questions, Mr Maddox. She is relevant to a criminal investigation" replied Field.

Tom looked enquiringly at him as he took a sip from the tea he was holding. "That may be so, Sergeant, but it is something that she knows hardly anything about! As for you deciding if she is up to your questions, I am sorry to disappoint you, but I think it will be the doctor who will decide on whether she has recovered enough to be able to answer them," said Tom in a stern voice.

"We'll see," replied Field with a smirk on his face.

"We certainly will, Sergeant, and we won't have long to wait to find out because here comes the doctor now. I'll see you in a minute, then," said Tom as he walked away and back to Joanne's room.

"Hi beautiful. Sorry I was so long. I saw the detective in the corridor and went to speak to him. Just stay calm and don't let him pressure you. If you think he is getting the better of you, then just interrupt him, tell him if it were up to him, you'd be dead, that should shut him up. Oh, and here's your water," said Tom as he handed it to her.

"Thank you, Tom. I want to go home today. What do you think?" asked Joanne.

"There is nothing I would like more love, but we have to make sure you are well enough," he replied.

Joanne started laughing to herself. Tom turned back from the window and noticed the grin on Joanne's face.

"Something funny?" he asked her.

"Yes," she replied. "You called me 'love'. I do believe that is the first time that you have ever addressed me as your love."

"I'm sorry," replied Tom.

"What! Sorry for calling me 'love'?" she asked.

"No, definitely not! I am sorry for being such a fool; the last three days have been absolutely awful," admitted Tom as he walked over to the bed, placed his hands on her shoulders and pulling her towards him, he gave her a lingering kiss on her lips, to which Joanne responded in kind.

"Joanne, the last three days have taught me a lot. They have taught me how much I missed you and how much I love you and it frightens me to think that had things turned out differently, I would never have told you exactly how I felt about you. That is what I am sorry for, but at least I can say to you in all sincerity that I love you and I know I really mean it," he added as he leant forward and kissed her again.

They were interrupted by a knock on the door and in walked Doctor Franklin and Detective Sergeant Field.

"Miss Webster, sorry to bother you again when you are recovering from your terrible ordeal and you are desperately trying to rest, but Detective Sergeant Field here would like to ask you a few questions regarding your kidnapping. Do you feel you are up to answering his questions?" asked the doctor.

"As long as you are nearby, Doctor, just in case," replied Joanne.

The detective took a few steps towards Joanne and then stopped. "Miss Webster, what can you tell me about the afternoon you disappeared?" he asked.

Joanne thought about it, trying to remember what Tom had said to her, then she replied, "I think you are asking the wrong person because all I remember is a bang on the head, then being alone and cold and being tied, hands and feet, with a blindfold over my eyes and tape or something over my mouth. I couldn't move or scream or do anything."

"Do you remember anything else, Miss Webster?" asked Field.

"While I was there, someone came in. I heard keys in a lock or turning a lock, and then they were near me. I thought they were going to kill me but they made a hole in the covering over my mouth and made me drink, just a few sips of water ,and then they were gone," she replied.

"Do you remember anything else after that, Miss Webster?" asked Field.

"Yes, of course, waking up in this place," she replied.

"Nothing else at all, Miss Webster? It is really very important to our investigation," said Field.

"No, nothing else, but it doesn't make much difference anyway, does it? Had I have waited for you to find me, I would have been dead," replied Joanne in a rather rattled voice.

"Okay, Sergeant, enough questions for now, Miss Webster needs to rest," said Doctor Franklin as she took hold of Field's arm and led him to the door.

Tom waited for the doctor to close the door behind them.

"How do you feel now?" he asked Joanne.

"I feel okay. I had to take your advice, he was beginning to annoy me," replied Joanne.

"Don't worry, you're not the only one. He has the same effect on me. When Aunt Matilda reported you as missing, he came to the house and tried to tell us that you had run off with Jefferey who he thought was your lover! The man is an idiot," said Tom.

The conversation between Joanne and Tom was interrupted by the sound of raised voices coming from outside the room. Detective Sergeant Field was not at all happy with the way that the doctor had so abruptly ended his questioning of Joanne.

"Doctor, I realise that Miss Webster is your patient and is under your care, but I am trying to carry out an investigation here and to do that I have to interview people and ask them questions. That is the way it works, and whether you like it or not, I need to speak to Miss Webster and to ask her detailed questions," explained Field.

Doctor Franklin was annoyed at the detective's manner, and not only was she not prepared to be spoken to in that manner, she certainly had no intention of accepting the detective's argument. As far as the doctor was concerned, her patient was of her utmost concern, and she would not let her recovery be compromised.

"Detective, I appreciate your concerns, but you must understand fully that my first duty is to my patient and your questioning wasn't conducive to Miss Webster's progress and recovery. I am afraid you will just have to wait to question her again until she is discharged from hospital," stated the doctor.

"And when might that be?" asked Field.

The doctor looked at him. "Well, generally when I believe that she has recovered sufficiently and it's the results of tests that help me to make that decision."

Field shook his head and with raised voice he replied, "Well, I am afraid that is of no help to me, Doctor, and if you will not let me see Miss Webster later, then I will be back here tomorrow with an order that will allow me to speak to her, whether you like it or not."

"I am sorry, Detective, you will be wasting your time. But if that is what you want to do, then so be it," replied Doctor Franklin.

Field shouted, "Pillock!" then he spun on his heels and walked off down the corridor.

Doctor Franklin stood and watched as the detective walked off to the exit door. She was shocked by his attitude, but she would not be pressured into a corner by him. She waited to make sure Field had left the ward, then she turned and made her way back into Joanne's room.

"I am so sorry for that, Miss Webster, but I wasn't prepared for the detective's line of questioning to continue. I would expect he would like to continue tomorrow but at least you will have Mr Maddox at home with you to keep things in order."

Joanne's face lit up on hearing those words. "Does that mean I will be going home tomorrow?" she asked.

The doctor looked at her and picked up the chart from the end of her bed. "I am waiting for one more set of results, but if they are okay, you can go home tonight," she replied.

Joanne nearly leapt out of her bed with excitement. "Oh yes, please Doctor, I would like that very much," replied Joanne, hardly able to contain herself.

Doctor Franklin replaced the chart and, turning to Tom, she said, "Mr. Maddox you will need to get Miss Webster some clothes as the ones she was wearing have been taken by the police so they can run tests on them."

"That's not a problem," replied Tom. "I can go and pick up some clothes now."

"No, Tom," interrupted Joanne, "please don't leave me, you can ring Aunty and ask her to bring me some clothes; tell her to get a taxi, please."

Tom picked up his phone and rang Matilda. "Hi, could you choose a top and a pair of jeans from Joanne's wardrobe and fetch them to the hospital for Joanne to wear on the way home?" he asked.

"Oh, that sounds very encouraging, Tom," she replied. "I'll ring for a taxi now and then get her clothes. Hopefully I won't have to wait long," she added.

"I told Joanne that I would come and get her clothes, but she didn't want me to leave her alone in the hospital," explained Tom.

"No, you stay there with her, Tom. I can bring her clothes and I won't be long. See you soon, bye," replied Matilda as she ended the call.

While Tom was on the phone to Matilda, Doctor Franklin explained to Joanne what she could and could not do over the next few days; she impressed on her the fact that apart from food, she needed to keep up her regular intake of water.

"Now, Miss Webster, we need to get you out of bed, but I must see other patients too, so I will get a nurse to come and make sure you are stable on your feet. When you first swing your legs around out of the bed, just rest your feet on the floor for a minute or two, then gradually put weight on your feet until you feel comfortable to try standing. I know it has only been three days since you were last on your feet, but it is quite strange how dehydration can affect your sense of balance, so don't rush it," explained the doctor.

"Thank you, Doctor, and thank you for the advice," replied Joanne.

Tom walked over to the bed and picked up the water jug from the cabinet.

"Here, you need to drink some more water," he said as he poured the water into the empty glass.

"If I drink any more, I will want to pee again," she replied.

"Well, the choice is yours, my love, to pee or not to pee, or to spend an extra night in here. Of course, if you'd rather spend another night in here, rather than tucked up in our bed with me, then so be it," replied Tom jovially.

Joanne looked at him for a moment, as though she was struggling with her decision, eventually holding her hand out.

"I guess there is only one answer to your question. Give me the water, and then help me to the toilet," said Joanne with a smile on her face.

They were just coming out of the bathroom when the nurse walked in. she seemed surprised to see that Joanne was out of bed.

"Oh, Joanne, you are up? Dr Franklin just asked me to come in and see how you'd manage to get out of bed. I think you were meant to wait for me to help you so I could monitor your reaction," said the nurse with an air of consternation in her voice.

"Yes, I am sorry for that, but Tom forced me to drink more water and unfortunately I just had to use the toilet. I couldn't wait a minute longer, but he helped me, I promise I didn't go there on my own," replied Joanne.

"Okay, so let me see you walk on your own," said the nurse.

Joanne obliged by walking the length of the room unaided.

"How was that?" asked Joanne as she looked enquiringly at the nurse.

"I'd say that is just what the doctor ordered," replied the nurse. "Well done! I'll let Doctor Franklin know straight away," added the nurse as she left the room.

Joanne didn't have to wait long before there was a knock on the door and the ward sister entered the room with one of the junior doctors.

"Joanne, Doctor Franklin has been called away, but having seen your updated test results she is happy to discharge you, under the care of Tom, as long as you keep strictly to the set of rules the doctor laid down when she spoke to you earlier," explained the sister.

"Thank you. I am just waiting for my aunt to turn up with my clothes," replied Joanne.

CHAPTER THIRTY

Coming to Terms

Joanne was ecstatic to know that she would shortly be leaving the hospital and going home, something that had seemed impossible to contemplate just a few days ago. She considered herself extremely lucky: she had people around her that cared for her and the most important of those to her was not her aunt, it was Tom. The more she thought about what had happened to her over her weekend, she knew that had it not been for Tom she probably wouldn't even have been found, let alone be leaving the hospital. It was more likely that she would have been lying on a stone-cold slab in the morgue.

What Joanne now struggled to comprehend was not only how it all happened, but probably more importantly *why* had it happened. What had gone wrong that left her locked up like that? What was the intention of whoever had taken her? The more she thought about it, the more she became frightened of what the outcome might have been. If it was proven that it had been Jefferey who had kidnapped her and put her in the chalet, then *why?* She just could not understand why anyone would go to all that trouble to kidnap her, only to leave her locked up to die – it terrified her. What was just as frightening to her was that if it wasn't Jefferey who kidnapped her, then who was it and for what reason? If it had been their intention to leave her there to die, then why would they have come back to give her a drink? Joanne was just so confused, and she was trying to figure it all out in her head when she was interrupted by the sound of Tom calling her.

"Hey, are you getting in the car or are you just going to stand there?" asked Tom as he stood by the taxi with the door open.

"Sorry, I was miles away," she replied.

"You mean you wish you were miles away, but for now let's just get you home," commented Aunt Matilda.

The taxi pulled up outside the house and the three of them got out. Joanne stood there, for the moment stuck to the spot. Tom took hold of her hand and led her towards the open door.

"Thank you, Matilda," said Tom as she held the door open for them to enter. "Could you look after Joanne please while I go to run a bath for her?" he added as he went up the stairs.

Aunt Matilda took Joanne into the lounge and as they sat down on the sofa, Joanne burst into tears.

"Come on, dear, you're home now. You have Tom and me to look after you and we are not going to let anyone hurt you," she said as she placed am arm around Joanne's shoulder and gave her a hug. They were still sitting in the same position when Tom came into the room to get Joanne for her bath.

"Come on, love, the bath is ready for you, and I have steamed up the bathroom so it's really hot and you can lie there, relax and try to unwind," said Tom as he took hold of Joanne's hand and led her up to the bathroom.

Joanne stood there in the middle of the bathroom, doing nothing except looking at the walls. Tom was beginning to think it might have been better if she had stayed in the hospital for another night but then he was not a doctor, so he had to trust their opinion.

"Come on, love, step out of your clothes and relax in the bathtub. It will do you good. If you need me, just give me a shout," said Tom.

"Where are you going?" she asked.

"I will just be downstairs with Aunt Matilda," he replied.

"No, Tom, please don't go! I want you to stay here with me, I don't want to be alone," pleaded Joanne.

"Okay, I'll stay" said Tom as he stood behind her and placed his hands on her shoulders.

"Come on, now," he said as he started to remove the jumper she was wearing. "Let's take off your clothes or the water will be cold, and you'll lose any benefit of taking a bath."

Joanne didn't reply and she made no attempt to stop Tom from undressing her either; she stood there naked for a while and then she turned around to face him. Raising her hands to his shoulders, she moved forward and kissed him passionately.

"Hold me, please, Tom, I just want to feel you close to me," she uttered softly.

He placed his arms around her waist and pulled her to him, returning the kiss which she had bestowed on him.

"Come on, step into the bath now, you need to relax while I wash you."

Tom helped Joanne, washing her body and her hair while she sat there hardly moving of her own free will; it was as if she was in a trance. She could hear him talking to her, but his words were just a jumble that she could not decode. Once he was finished washing her, he sat on a stool by the side of the bath and just let Joanne drift off to sleep, leaving her like that until the water cooled, at which point he got her out of the bath and dried her. Tom led Joanne into the bedroom, took out a gown for her to wear and placed it around her before they both went back down the stairs to re-join her aunt in the lounge. As they entered the room, Tom could see that Aunt Matilda was already asleep on the sofa; he picked up a cover, placing it gently over her so as not to wake her, then he took Joanne into the kitchen, sitting her down on a stool at the breakfast bar.

"Thank you, Tom," said Joanne quietly.

"For what?" he asked.

She didn't reply, but just sat there staring at him. He took out a glass from the cabinet and opened the fridge door. He filled the glass with ice cold water from the dispenser and turning around, he placed it on the breakfast bar in front of her.

"Enjoy! Doctor's orders," he said with a smile on his face.

"You are so thoughtful, Tom. I have been missing for a few days and all I get is a glass of cold water," replied Joanne as she picked up the glass and took a sip. "Argh!" she shrieked. "You know, I am not sure which is colder, this water or your heart?"

Tom looked at her; the smile had gone and he now wore a serious frown. "There is a fundamental difference between the two, though," he replied.

"And what might that difference be, Mr Maddox?" she asked.

"Well, if you leave the water out of the fridge, it will become warm," replied Tom.

Joanne turned around and getting off the stool, she stood in front of him. Raising her hands to her gown, she undid the tie and slid it over her shoulders, allowing it to fall to the floor, revealing her naked body.

"Maybe I should try to warm that heart up for you, then. What do you think?" she asked as she took his hand and placed it on her breast.

"I think you need to sit in the fridge for a while to cool down," he replied. "Are you forgetting that Aunt Matilda is in the lounge?"

Joanne pulled away from him as she walked towards the kitchen door, before turning to him and saying in a raised voice.

"Are you for real? I am standing naked in front of you and all you can think of is my aunt Matilda, you weirdo," she said and then continued into the lounge.

Tom picked up her gown from the floor and followed her into the lounge.

"I think you forgot something," he said quietly as he held out the gown towards her. "Put it on, please."

"I just do not understand you, Mr Maddox. I thought you might have missed me but obviously not," said Joanne as she put her gown on and then sat down on the sofa.

"Look, of course I have missed you. I was so worried, I thought I had lost you forever, but there is a time and a place for everything. Do you not remember when I came out of hospital, we had to take things easy? Well, this is no different and I don't want you to end up back in the hospital again!"

"Tom, that's different, you had serious injuries," replied Joanne.

"Oh, so the fact that you nearly died out there is not serious enough for you? How much more serious do you want it to be? I need to sleep, and so do you. I am going to bed and if you want to join me, it's up to you. Goodnight," he said, leaving her sitting there.

When Tom woke up, Joanne was lying in the bed beside him. He turned to look at her; she was so beautiful. Beautiful body, beautiful mind, he thought to himself. He leant over and kissed her naked breast, then got out of bed and covered her over with the sheet before going to the bathroom and then down to the kitchen to get something to eat. He checked the lounge on the way. Aunt Matilda was still asleep, so he made himself a tea and put some bread in the toaster. He was just about to sit down and eat his toast when there was a knock at the front door.

"Detective Sergeant Field, Detective Green! What a lovely surprise! And to what do we owe this visit?" asked Tom.

"I am sure you are well aware why we are here, Mr Maddox; I would like speak to Miss Webster. May we come in please?"

"Is it really that necessary to come here so early in the morning?" asked Tom.

Field looked at him as he pushed his way past into the hall followd by Detective Green, answering as he did so.

"Yes, it is, Mr Maddox. Crime waits for no man or woman," replied Field.

"Well, Miss Webster is still sleeping, but go straight through to the kitchen, Detective, I am sure you can remember where it is," replied Tom.

Tom quickly went into the lounge to wake Aunt Matilda before going to wake up Joanne.

"Joanne, Joanne, come on, wake up, Detective Field is here and he wants to speak to you."

"Oh no, not again. I could really do without him pestering me. I get rid of one jerk and end up with another one pestering me; just my luck," she replied.

"Come on, just tell him everything you know or can remember and then maybe he will leave you alone, leave *us* alone. I've got to go back downstairs. I left him and Detective Green in the kitchen," said Tom as he turned and walked towards the bedroom door.

"Okay, tell him I will be down in a few minutes," replied Joanne.

Aunt Matilda was already in the kitchen when Tom walked in and the two detectives were sat at the breakfast bar. Tom couldn't help but notice that Field was eating toast.

"Are you enjoying your toast, Detective?" asked Tom.

"Oh, yes, thank you," he replied.

"It's not yours, it's mine, and in your line of work, wouldn't that be classed as theft?" asked Tom.

Field stopped just as he was about to place the last bite of toast in his mouth. He looked up at Tom and added, "It's only a slice of toast."

"So, is that what you say to the shoplifter who has just stolen a loaf of bread; don't worry, it's only bread?" asked Tom.

Joanne's entry to the kitchen seemed to stifle the conversation and she guessed from the looks on the faces of those present that things had not been going too well.

"Oh, did I interrupt something?" she asked.

"Not really, Miss Webster," said Detective Field. "So nice to see again and to see that you are on the road to recovery," he added.

"I think the detective has a truly short memory span, my love. We were actually just discussing whether or not the detective stole my toast. What do you think – guilty or not guilty?" asked Tom.

Joanne looked across at the table and saw Detective Field sitting in front of a plate with a half-eaten slice of toast on it.

"Oh, definitely guilty," she replied.

"Miss Webster, I think we have some unfinished business," said Field.

"Detective, be careful: I seem to remember that they were the same last words that Jefferey Philips uttered to me; the next thing, I knew he was dead," replied Joanne.

"Do you know anything about that, Miss Webster?" asked Detective Green.

Joanne gave Detective Green a darting look. "Hardly, seeing that I was tied, hand and feet, blindfolded and locked in a beach chalet at the time of his death. Unless of course you are suggesting that I tied myself up and locked and bolted the chalet from the outside when I was on the inside," said Joanne.

"You could have had an accomplice," said Field.

"This is crazy. I can't be dealing with this trash. You two had my partner wake me up to hear this load of crap! I suggest that before you want to interview me again, you try putting your brains in gear to match what comes out of your mouths. I told you what happened, and if you won't accept that, it is not my fault, it's yours. What you do expect?" she asked, to which they sat there dumfounded, probably just as well as she had by nowhere finished. "Did you expect to come here with some misguided idea that I could possibly change my account of what happened, so that it tied in with your make-believe version of events? Oh yes, I nearly forgot! According to you, I wasn't actually in the chalet, was I? Why would I be? I had run off with Jefferey Philips because according to you he was my secret lover; well, you were so wrong about that and you are so wrong about coming here today. You people make me sick," ranted Joanne.

The two detectives were motionless. They sat there transfixed, speechless, their mouths hanging open in total shock.

"Tom, please show these two muppets out. I am going back to bed," added Joanne as she walked out of the kitchen and went back to bed.

Detectives Field and Green sat there not knowing what to say. They looked at each other before Green took the plunge.

"So, what do we do now, Sir?" she asked Field.

Tom interrupted any thoughts or plans they may have had. "Excuse me, but whatever you are going to do next, can you do it somewhere else because you are no longer welcome here, and you need to leave, now! I'll show you out."

Tom closed the door and went back into the kitchen.
"Tea, Matilda?" he asked.
"What? After that? Are you kidding? I need a strong coffee with plenty of sugar!"
They sat there quietly drinking until Tom found he was staring into an empty cup.
"Your niece certainly has a way with words," he said as he placed the cup back on the table.
"Yes, she always has had. I guess that was why she wanted to be a solicitor, to stand up for people who were not like her, people who had no voice," replied Aunt Matilda.
Tom got up from the stool and turned to Aunt Matilda.
"I need to go into town to find Joanne's car. I also need to speak to Warren to let him know what has been happening and to arrange delivery of the other photos that I had enlarged on canvas; will it be okay with you if I leave you here to take care of Joanne?" he asked.
"Of course it will, you go and do what you need to do, and yes, Joanne will need her car, so you have to find that for her," she replied.

Tom went up to the bedroom to check on Joanne. She was lying on top of the bed asleep; it looked to him as though she had just flung herself down and there she'd stayed. He covered her over so she would not get cold. He picked up the spare set of car keys from the drawer in the bedroom and then went back downstairs to wait for a taxi to take him to the town.

Tom was confused. Joanne was adamant that she parked her car by the Lifeboat Museum, but he could not see it there anywhere. He began to think that maybe the police had found it and moved it, but then, if that was the case, why wouldn't Detective Field have told them earlier? Tom reached into his pocket and took out the card that Field had given him; he was reluctant to contact him, but he knew that was the only way to find out if the police had indeed found the car and moved it. Tom waited patiently for his call to be answered.

"Field's office, Green speaking, how can I help you?" asked the detective.

"Hi, it's Tom Maddox. Is Field there, please?" he replied.

"Ah, Mr Maddox, no, sorry, he is not in the office at the moment. Can I help?" replied Green.

"Maybe. I have been looking for Joanne's car, but it's not where she told me she'd parked it, so I was wondering if it had been found by your team and removed for investigation?" he asked.

There was quite a pause and Tom was thinking that maybe the call had been cut off or something like that.

"Hello, are you still there?" he enquired.

"Yes, sorry," replied the detective. "I am still here."

"So, do you know if you have the car or not?" he repeated his previous question.

"No, I am sorry. We don't have her car," she replied as she tried to think how best to explain a tricky situation. "Unfortunately, at the time Miss Webster was reported as missing and the details of her car were also reported to us, there was a conflict of opinion, so no time was allocated to searching for her car. I am sorry," she replied.

"Thank you, that is all I needed to know. So now, Joanne has been found but her car is not where she said she parked it, and if you haven't got it, then who has?" asked Tom. His reply was more of a statement rather than a question.

"Do you think that I now need to re-report the car as being stolen?" he asked.

"I think that would be a good idea, Mr Maddox. I will check the details from the original report and make sure that Miss Webster's car is now listed as stolen," replied Green.

"Thank you, that would be a great help," replied Tom before ending the call.

Tom stood there, staring at the screen of his phone. What could he do now? He was becoming even more angry at the actions of Detective Field, whom he felt had not taken Joanne's disappearance seriously when she was first reported as missing. Although he knew there was nothing he could do about that now, he still found it very annoying. Apart from that, the other problem he had was he now didn't have a car, and in situations such as the one that he and Joanne were in, they needed a car. The best thing to do was to call a friend. With that in mind, he decided to call Warren to find out if he was in his office.

Warren was busy reading through case notes when he heard the buzz from his mobile phone which was on the desk in front of him; looking at the screen as he picked it up, he answered the call.

"Hi Tom, how is Joanne?" asked Warren.

"She is okay, thank you Warren. She slept well last night. I am in town at the moment and was wondering if you were in the office and not too busy, could I pop in for a quick chat?" enquired Tom.

"No problem at all, Tom, and yes I am in the office. I have just been reading through some case notes but almost finished now, so yes, please do pop in," replied Warren.

Tom hurriedly made his way to Warren's office and pressed the buzzer to gain entry.

"Oh, Tom, come straight up, please," came the reply.

As he reached the top of the stairs, he was met with more questions that he could answer, everyone wanting to know how Joanne was. He was truly shocked by their support.

"Hi, thank you all so much, but sorry, I just need to speak to Mr Fredericks and then I will come back and answer all your questions," said Tom as he walked past them all and continued to Warren's office.

"Warren," he said as he held out his hand to greet him.

"Sit down, Tom. How is Joanne? What has been happening, we're all eager to know?" he asked.

"It looks as though she will be okay, obviously she needs to get over the psychological effects of what she has been through and although it may not be nice, I get the impression that she is relieved that Jefferey Philips won't be troubling her anymore. The reports from the hospital were good, and they believe she will make a full recovery, she just needs to keep drinking fluids to re-stabilise her body and in that respect, she is doing very well; she is almost there. However, I am not so sure about how she is going to cope mentally with all that has happened to her, and it's her mental well-being that I'm really worried about," explained Tom.

"So, some good news but some worrying news, too," replied Warren. "However, about her mental well-being – that is something that I can help with. The health plan that we have in place here also incorporates a mental awareness program, something that is very necessary in our business. As I am sure you are aware, some cases can be quite harrowing and they can have a profound effect on mental health. Obviously, we are all looking forward to seeing Joanne back in the office; personally, I miss her professionalism as do all the staff. I will make sure that she is referred to one of our mental awareness therapists before she comes back. In fact, I will tell her that myself, so that she knows she will have to comply."

"Thank you, Warren. I'm very relieved about that."

"That's really good news, Tom, about her recovery. We are all looking forward to seeing her and having her back here where she belongs. Please tell her we all miss her."

"I will certainly tell her that, Warren, but you and Patricia are more than welcome to pop in and see her whenever you want to," said Tom.

"Thank you, Tom, maybe later in the week. I'll let you both get settled in again first," replied Warren.

"Any time. Joanne's Aunt Matilda is still with us for now as I thought it might help having her there. We do all need to sit down and discuss what has happened, I think with Susan, too. The police called this morning, Detectives Field and Green, and Joanne wasn't happy at all. Field totally messed up with his questioning and it all ended very acrimoniously, with Joanne ordering him to leave," said Tom.

"You know you are right, Tom. Maybe if Field wants to speak to her again, just put him off, tell him she is not well enough and struggling to cope with what happened to her. I will try to get around to see her along with Susan, although I think it might be better if you could bring her here on Friday afternoon, as everyone will be in the office then. They'd all love to see her and we can have our chat, sort of kills two birds with one stone," explained Warren.

"Okay, we'll work towards that then and I will confirm on Friday morning. I have to go now, I have been out quite a while. I really came down to find Joanne's car, but I just cannot see it anywhere. I thought maybe the police might have found it, so I rang them, but they haven't got it. I just don't know where it is, unless of course it has been stolen," remarked Tom.

"That's always a possibility, Tom. You may need to report it as stolen to the police and the insurance company."

"I think you are right, but I need a car now and I don't want to bother Joanne with all of this just now, not while she is recovering. Do you have any contacts in the car business?" asked Tom.

"Not really," replied Warren. "Are you thinking of buying a new or used one?"

"I just want something for a week or so until we find out what has happened to Joanne's. I don't know, maybe I will have to buy a new one but that will take a few days to sort out. I think hiring a car might be complicated as my address still shows that of my old house, but I haven't lived there for five years, and I don't have any confirmation of my address at Joanne's house," replied Tom.

"That does cause a bit of a problem, then," replied Warren.

"Tell me about it," commented Tom. "I have been so stupid! I really should have sorted my life out before now," he added.

"But then you wouldn't have met Joanne," replied Warren, "and I am a firm believer that everything we do is done for a reason," he continued. He opened the draw of his desk and took out some keys. Warren held them in his hand, placed them on the desk in front of him then slid them across the desk towards Tom.

"What's that?" asked Tom.

"Keys to a car that is sitting in my garage at home. It's yours for as long as you need it; I'll ring the insurance company now and add you as a named driver while you go and get the coffee," replied Warren.

"Thank you, thank you *so* much!" replied Tom as he left Warren's office to get the coffee.

.

Warren was just ending the call when Tom walked back into his office.

"There, that's all done – it's insured for you to drive straight away," said Warren as he beckoned to Tom to take a seat.

"Thanks, Warren. So, what do we do now about Joanne's missing car?" asked Tom.

Warren leant back in his chair and placed his hand on his head as if he was stuck for a response.

"I'm not sure, but something's not right. I remember Joanne telling me that she had parked near to the Lifeboat Museum, and if she told you the same thing, then why would it not be there?" questioned Warren.

"I'm not sure," replied Tom. "All I do know though is that the police don't have it, or at least that is what they are telling me."

Warren sat there for a while thinking things through, before continuing. "So, if what the police are saying is correct, then the car must have been stolen."

Although Tom was inclined to agree, he was not one hundred per cent sure. that was the case.

"But what if it was Jefferey? What if he meant to kill Joanne all along or maybe keep her kidnapped? He could have spotted her car there and moved it himself after he had shut her in the chalet; remember there were no car keys found on Joanne when she was found," explained Tom.

"That is gruesome, Tom, and if you are right, it just shows how warped Jefferey's mind was, and by moving Joanne's car, maybe even concealing it somewhere, it would have added credence to Field's argument that they had run off together," replied Warren.

Tom picked up the cup from the desk and took a long slow drink of coffee while he was collecting his thoughts.

"We know that none of *us* moved Joanne's car, and the police say they didn't move it either, so it really only leaves two possibilities. Either Jefferey moved it, or it has been stolen, and whichever it might be we need to tell the police, but I think I know what Field's reply will be," said Tom.

Warren picked up his phone and, looking at Tom, said, "I think you would have made a good copper; you have an open mind."

"Who are you calling?" asked Tom.

"I am going to contact Field and give him your thoughts on the disappearance of Joanne's car," replied Warren.

"Do you really think that we should do that? Do you not think I should check with Joanne one last time before contacting him? I mean, I don't want to give him any excuse to think that we are playing with him as I get the impression that is what he feels now. What if I got it wrong? What if *near to the Lifeboat Museum* was just a figure of speech … don't you think I should check with Joanne first? Just in case she was mistaken?"

Warren replaced the phone on the receiver and looked up at Tom. "Well, okay, you win, but only until you have checked with Joanne. Should she confirm that she did leave her car where she said, then we must inform the police at once," he replied.

"Thank you," replied Tom as he held out his hand towards. "I think we make a good team."

"It would appear so, young man," replied Warren as he accepted Tom's handshake.

Warren got up from his chair, placed some papers in his case and, picking up his jacket, turned towards Tom.

"We should be going now. You have to come with me to pick up the car and then get home to your lovely lady. She will be wondering where you are," he said.

Tom followed Warren out of his office only to be confronted by some of Joanne's work colleagues who were waiting to find out the latest news on her recovery. Tom explained that she was now recovering at home and that if she felt okay by the end of the week he would bring her into the office on Friday so they could all see her. While he was explaining all this to them, Susan was standing next to him; when he had finished, he took her to one side.

"Susan, I know how much Joanne wanted to see you to thank you for your help, but she also has work related questions to ask you. However, the doctor has said she doesn't want her doing anything connected with work until next week. I would appreciate it if you could wait until then to chat to her as I really want her to make sure she honours the doctor's request," explained Tom.

"No problem at all, Tom, the thing we all want is to see Joanne back in the office and ready for work. I wouldn't want my actions to cause a delay to her return."

"Thank you, Susan. I've agreed with Warren that if Joanne is feeling better later in the week, then you and he could come to the house to see her. I feel we need to chat about what happened," explained Tom as he turned to leave.

Tom left Joanne's office feeling very at ease with himself and the situation. He had been wondering how her colleagues would have felt after hearing of the death of Jefferey Philips; after all, they had worked with him for years. He was surprised that their only concern now was for the speedy recovery of Joanne, and he was relieved to know that they were all rooting for her and looking forward to seeing her back in the office.

Tom got into Warren's car with him, where he sat quietly during the short journey to his house. Warren pulled up next to the garage, got out of the car and opened the doors.

"There she is," said Warren as he placed a hand on the wing of the car. "She should start okay. I start her up every week and keep her polished as you can see."

Tom looks at the car. "She is immaculate – are you want to lend her to me?" he asked.

"Yes, of course," replied Warren.

"I will take good care of her for you," said Tom.

"I know you will, Tom, which is why I am lending her to you," said Warren as he opened the driver's door for Tom to get in. He stood there and watched as Tom got onto the car and started the engine up.

"She was my daughter's car," explained Warren as he wiped a tear from his eye. "I couldn't bear to sell her, hanging onto the past, a bit like yourself Tom," he added.

"Thank you so much. I so appreciate what you are doing for me, and I will take extra good care of her for you," replied Tom as he placed his hand over Warren's.

"You had better be going or Joanne will be wondering where you are. Call me and let me know how she's doing, and if there is anything you need, don't hesitate to call me," said Warren. He stood there watching as Tom placed his foot on the accelerator and drove slowly out of the garage and down the drive.

CHAPTER THIRTY-ONE

Pulling Together

Before heading back to the house to see Joanne and Aunt Matilda, Tom visited the shop to check on the canvas prints he had ordered and to ask for them to be delivered as soon as possible. As he drove up to the house, he could see the van was already there and the driver was just getting out of his cab.

"Ah, Mr Maddox. Where would you like me to fix these for you?" asked the driver.

"Oh, are you offering to put them on the wall for me as well?" enquired Tom.

"It's an optional service we now offer. It will only take me fifteen minutes to put them up if you show me exactly where you want them," replied the driver.

"That would be great. I would really appreciate that. They are going in the back lounge, on the long wall. Would you do me another big favour and leave the covering on but just lightly pin it at the top so that I can pull the cover off when I'm ready to show my partner?" asked Tom.

"No problem," replied the driver as Tom showed him to the back lounge and explained exactly where he wanted the pictures hung.

Tom left the man there and went into the kitchen to make himself a drink. When he went back into the lounge, the three canvas portraits were already up on the wall.

"There, I've finished," said the man. "All I have done is just tuck the covering between the wall and the canvas, so you only need to give it a slight tug and the cover will fall away. Okay, if you are happy with them, I will get home," he continued.

"That's perfect," replied Tom as he took some notes out of his pocket, folded them up and placed them in the driver's top pocket. "Here, that's for you, thank you very much," said Tom.

"Thank you, Mr Maddox, and enjoy your evening. Good night."

After seeing the man out, Tom went in search of Joanne and Aunt Matilda. He found them both in the main bedroom, but he was so surprised as what he saw. Joanne was lying on the bed shaking, and Aunt Matilda was lying next to her, trying to comfort her. Tom walked around to the side of the bed where Joanne was. He knelt next to her and placed his hand on her shoulder.

"Hey, beautiful, come on, don't pressure yourself, just relax," said Tom as he leant forward and kissed her gently on the forehead.

Joanne opened her eyes. "Where have you been? I thought you had left me," she said.

"Don't even think that because it's not going to happen. I am here with you forever, or until you kick me out, but even then, I would still be in the barn," replied Tom.

Tom looked over towards Aunt Matilda. "How long has she been like this?" he asked.

"Maybe two hours or more. I just could not get her to calm down, sorry Tom," she replied.

"Sorry? What for? You have nothing to be sorry about, I'm the one who is sorry. I shouldn't have stayed out so long. I'll stay with her now and try to get her to sleep; you can order yourself something to eat if you want to – you must be hungry," said Tom

"I was just going to get myself something when I heard her screaming; it was awful, I thought someone had broken in and was trying to kill her," replied Aunt Matilda.

"I am so sorry, I should never have left you all that time," replied Tom.

"Can I get you something to eat at the same time Tom?" she asked.

"No, I'm fine thanks, I'll get something later. Oh, go on then, maybe just a tea would be great. I did make myself a drink, but I think it may be cold by now," he replied.

"No problem," she said. "I'll bring it up to you."

Tom sat there on the floor with his back resting up against the side of the bed. He found himself closing his eyes until Aunt Matilda woke him up when she placed his tea on the dressing table.

"Thank you. Have you decided yet what you are going to order?" he asked.

"Well, I was thinking about ordering barbecued chicken, but I didn't want to order it just for me," she replied.

"Okay, order some for me too, please. Just chicken and fries, please," requested Tom.

Just as Matilda turned to leave the bedroom, there was a faint voice in the background.

"What about me? Do I get to eat or am I still being held against my wishes?" asked Joanne.

Tom leapt up and turned around. "Oh baby, you are awake! You should be sleeping," he said.

"Yes, I know, but I'm hungry, and chicken sounds good," she replied.

"I think that will be chicken for the three of us then!" said Tom.

"Okay, you two can stay there for a while and I will call you once it has been delivered," replied Aunt Matilda as she turned and left the room.

Tom got up off the floor and laid down on the bed beside Joanne. As he cuddled up to her, he whispered something in her ear.

"I'm not sure I heard you correctly – can you repeat that a little louder please, Tom?" she asked.

Tom did as he was asked and repeated himself a little louder, but once again Joanne asked Tom to repeat himself a little louder.

"You know, when you go back to the hospital for a check-up, I think they need to check out your hearing," said Tom.

"No!" exclaimed Joanne. "There is nothing wrong with my hearing, you just need to speak up properly so that you can be heard!"

Tom sat up on the bed and leant over Joanne and in a loud voice, almost shouting, he repeated what he'd been saying.

"Miss Webster, I love you so much," he said and he lowered his head towards hers and kissed her on the lips.

"I thought that was what you said, but I just wanted to check. I love you too, very much, Mr Maddox," she replied as she pulled him towards her and gave him a lingering kiss.

Tom, broke away and looking down at her. "No excitement – remember what the doctor ordered," he said with a smile on his face.

"But it's only a kiss," replied Joanne.

"Sure, and kisses can very often lead to something else," said Tom as he lay back down beside her, placing his arm over her body to cuddle her. As he looked at her face, he noticed that tears were forming in the corner of her eye and seconds later they had broken free and were running down the side of her face towards her ear.

"Hey, come on, you're safe now," he said as he squeezed her waist, pulling her closer towards him; then pulling a tissue from the box at the side of the bed he wiped her tears away and kissed her ear. Joanne responded by turning on her side to face him, resting her hand on his chest as she did so.

"I know, but that's not what caused my tears," she explained.

"What then?" he asked.

"When I was in that place, alone, sometimes cold, sometimes hot, and very thirsty, unable to see anything, all I could really think about was you and how I might never see you again. Although it was hard, because at times I felt like just giving up because I was frightened of what might happen to me, I couldn't because I wanted to see you again," she elaborated as she opened up to him for the first time since being rescued.

"I am so sorry," he replied. "I just can't imagine what it must have been like for you, being in a situation like that."

Joanne looked him in the eye. "I felt so alone, discarded, but now I am here with you, which is what I have longed for and you won't even give me what I need," she replied.

"So, will sex change that for you?" he asked.

"No!" she almost shouted as she leapt on top of him again. "I don't just want sex, I want you to make love to me," she added.

Before Tom had a chance to answer, they were interrupted by the sound of Aunt Matilda calling to them from downstairs.

"Come on, you two, our food has arrived," she called.

"Saved by the bell, or more precisely by Aunt Matilda. Aren't you the lucky one, Mr Maddox," said Joanne.

"So it would seem," he replied.

Joanne got up from the bed, took some clothes out of the wardrobe and went to the bathroom to get dressed.

"I'll be downstairs when you're ready," he called out as he passed the bathroom on the way to the stairs.

"Please yourself," replied Joanne.

Tom continued down to the kitchen expecting to see Aunt Matilda waiting there for them, but the room was empty.

"Where are you?" he called.

"I'm here in the back lounge," came the reply.

Tom walked into the lounge and seeing Aunt Matilda sitting there on the sofa, he sat in the single chair opposite her.

"I hope you don't mind me bringing the food in here, Tom?" she asked. "But I was kind of intrigued by what those sheets are hiding on the wall?" she inquired.

"Eating in here is fine, but as for the sheets, you will have to wait until your niece joins us to find out what they are hiding," replied Tom.

They were interrupted by Joanne standing in the doorway of the lounge. She noticed the food on the table. "So why are we eating food in here and not in the kitchen?"

"I just thought we weren't making use of all the rooms and fancied a change of scenery," replied Tom with a giggle.

"Is that so?" she replied. "Then why did I hear Aunty enquire about what those sheets are doing there? Are they hiding more of your photos?"

"Obviously the distress you suffered has not interfered with your hearing and they are not photos – they are *canvas prints*," he replied.

"Can we see them then, or are you going to leave them like that?" she asked.

Tom took hold of the strings that were attached to each of the sheets and handed them to Joanne.

"When you are ready, just give the strings a sharp tug and the sheets will fall to the ground, leaving you to view the prints," he said as he sat down on the sofa next to her.

Tom looked at Joanne; he had expected that she would tug on the strings straight away, but there was no movement from her.

"Come on, then. I thought you wanted to see the prints! what are you waiting for?" he asked.

Joanne looked at him, and then replied, "You've taken so many photos of me. I'm not sure what I will see."

"There is only one way to find out, dear," commented Aunt Matilda as she placed her hand on Joanne's shoulder, offering her some encouragement.

With that, Joanne took a deep breath, closed her eyes and gave a sharp tug on the strings; sure enough, all three prints were revealed before them. There was a deadly silence in the room. Tom looked at the prints and thought they looked better than he could have imagined.

"Well, what do you think?" he asked.

Joanne opened her eyes and gasped while Aunt Matilda just sat there open-mouthed with delight at what she was looking at.

"I think they look quite beautiful, a little revealing, maybe, but beautiful all the same," said Tom.

Joanne looked at him. "Tom, they are so lovely! You make me look as though I am the most beautiful woman in the world," she replied.

"That's because to me, Miss Webster, you are," he replied as he took the string from her hands.

Joanne turned to her aunt, who was still sitting there just staring at the prints. "What do you think, Aunty?" she asked her.

"I don't know what to say, dear, they are just so …" Then she stopped.

"So *what*, Aunty?" asked Tom.

"So much flesh, I think I'm trying to say," replied Aunt Matilda.

"Do you think they expose too much flesh?" he asked as he looked at Joanne and her aunt.

"No," replied Joanne. "I love them, Tom, they are breath-taking, thank you so much."

"What do you think, Aunty, are you still shocked?" asked Tom.

"A little," she replied, "but if my niece likes them, then I like them too."

"Thank you, thank you both," replied Tom, and looking at Joanne he added, "I just wanted to show you as the beautiful woman you are, the woman that I see every time I look at you, the woman that I love."

"You have certainly done that," said Joanne and she turned towards Tom and gave him a lingering kiss, before adding, "Thank you. I love you so much, Mr Maddox."

"Does that mean you will listen to what I say and do as the doctors have asked for the next few days, until you have fully recovered?" he asked.

"Yes, I guess I will have to now," she replied.

"I think we should eat, our food is getting cold," remarked Aunt Matilda as she leant forward and took a piece of chicken from the box.

"Let me re-heat it," said Tom as he picked up the box from the table. "Who wants a drink

"Could I have a coffee, please?" asked Joanne.

"A tea for me please, Tom, thank you," added Aunt Matilda.

Aunt Matilda sat motionless as she watched her niece, who at first just sat there looking at the photos on the wall before getting up and walking towards them to get a closer look.

"Do you think he really loves me?" asked Joanne as she turned towards her aunt.

"I would have thought that was obvious," replied Aunt Matilda.

"Well, yes, it is I suppose, but does he really love me? I keep thinking about when I first met Andrew and how similar that feeling is now, but I soon found out that things weren't right between us," replied Joanne.

Matilda just sat there, waiting for further comment from her niece as she didn't really want to get involved in her love affairs.

"Aunty, help me here, please, I have no one else to turn to. What do you think?" pleaded Joanne.

"You know, I never really liked him. From our first meeting, there was just something about him, something I couldn't explain, but just a feeling," replied Aunt Matilda.

"What?" exclaimed Joanne.

"Well, you asked me, dear, and I am just being honest with you, maybe a bit late in the day, but nevertheless it's the truth," commented Matilda.

"But I thought you liked him, Aunty! That was the impression I got, that's the impression you gave. You always seem so comfortable around Tom," replied Joanne.

"Tom?" queried Aunt Matilda. "I was talking about Andrew! But Tom is different, oh, he's such a darling," added Matilda.

"Who's a darling?" asked Tom as he entered the room, interrupting them.

"Oh, I didn't realise you were there, Tom," replied Matilda. "I was just commenting on you being a darling, taking such lovely photos of my niece."

"Well, the secret is, taking the photos was easy, it was your niece who had the hard part by being such a good subject," replied Tom.

They sat there quietly eating their food, with Joanne and Matilda glancing regularly at the photos.

Aunt Matilda looked at her watch. "I should be going; could you get me a taxi please?" she asked.

"Do you have to go?" asked Tom. "I was hoping you would stay to keep an eye on your niece as I need to do some work around the house, catch up on some decorating, things like that," he added.

"Please, Aunty, Tom is right, please stay. I'm going to need you to talk to and keep me sane," said Joanne.

"Okay, you've persuaded me, but I have to pick up some more clothes, so if you could run me home, Tom?" asked Matilda.

"I would do but I don't want to drag Joanne out, she has to rest, and we can't leave her here alone, I will get a taxi for you. They can wait while you sort some clothes out and then bring you back," replied Tom.

"That's sorted then. You're coming back. That will also give us chance to continue our discussion," added Joanne.

"What discussion is that, then?" asked Tom enquiringly.

"Nothing for you to worry about, Tom, just girl talk," replied Joanne.

They were all aware that Joanne needed time to recuperate from her ordeal and Tom was pleased that Aunt Matilda would be there to keep an eye on her. There was also an interview booked with Detective Field and although Warren had arranged to be present when it was conducted, Tom was pleased that Aunt Matilda would also be there as he didn't want to be anywhere near when the detective was in the house again.

Joanne wasn't looking forward to Field's interview, but Warren had pleaded with her that it was the only way to get him off her back. When there was a knock at the door, knowing it was Field, Joanne broke out in a hot sweat.

"So, Miss Webster, would you mind going over your statement again? From the last time you spoke to Mr Fredericks when you were near the Hollywell Tea Chalet?" asked the detective.

Joanne was beginning to feel uneasy; she had already recounted that part of her statement two or three times.

"Is that really necessary, Detective?" asked Warren. "Miss Webster has already been over that several times."

"I'm sorry, Miss Webster, but it is really important that I understand completely the chronological order in which everything happened to you that evening," replied Detective Field.

Joanne took a deep breath and, giving a big sigh, she started to re-tell her account of what had happened to her.

"I had walked down as far as the Hollywell Tea Chalet and I was hoping to have got a drink there, but it was closed. I turned and started to walk back but thought I should ring Warren first, just to let him know where I was. It was just after that when I thought I heard someone call me; I didn't take much notice at first; I did slow down but I kept walking. Then I heard the voice again, so I stopped and looked around, but I couldn't see anyone, the light was fading fast," said Joanne as her voice began to break up with the emotion of re-telling the next part of her story.

"Sorry to interrupt you, Miss Webster, but how far had you walked back at that point?" asked the detective.

"Not far at all. I had just passed the second row of chalets. There is a pathway that leads up behind the chalets to the Italian Garden, and that is where the voice appeared to be coming from," she replied.

"So, you walked up the pathway in the dark?" asked Field.

"Well, yes, but not immediately. I waited a minute of two and then heard the voice again. I asked if it was Tom but there was no answer so—"

The detective interrupted her once again. "Sorry, Miss Webster, you asked if the person calling you was Mr Maddox? Did it sound like him to you, then?" asked Field.

"Well, I wasn't sure. I was just asking the question, but there was no reply, so I walked up the pathway to where the voice appeared to come from, but I couldn't see anyone. I turned to walk down the path leading back to the Tea Chalet and that's when something or someone hit me and covered my mouth. The next thing I knew, I was waking up with a blindfold over my eyes, tape over my mouth with my hands and feet bound," recounted Joanne.

"Did you see anyone, Miss Webster?" asked Field.

"What was I meant to see exactly? I had a blindfold covering my eyes! Did you not listen to what I said?" she asked sarcastically.

It was at that point that Detective Green, who had sat there quietly all the time, jumped in.

"Miss Webster, you said previously that a person returned to where you were held. Did they say anything at all?" she asked.

"*Drink*," replied Joanne.

"Oh, thank you, tea, please," replied Field.

"That wasn't a question," replied Joanne, "it was the answer to Detective Green's question."

"And was that all they said?" asked Green.

"I heard someone entering, keys jangling, and a lock being turned, the shuffling of feet getting closer. I had no idea of what was about to happen to me; I was panicking. Then I felt pressure on my mouth, and cold metal on my lips; I thought I was going to die. Then they were pushing something into my mouth, it was a straw. *Drink*, that was all they said," replied Joanne.

"Before you were attacked, when you heard someone calling you, you thought it was Tom. Did you get the same feeling when the person told you to drink?" asked Field.

"No, definitely not, and I never said that I thought the person calling me was Tom. I didn't know who it was; the voice sounded strange. I was asking a question when I asked if it was Tom, I wasn't stating a fact," replied Joanne.

"So, at that point, the only people who knew where you were, were Mr Maddox and Mr Fredericks?" said Green.

"Well, not really," replied Joanne. "I hadn't spoken to Tom so he couldn't have known where I was, and Warren was in town, but yes, he knew I had gone to the Tea Chalet, but I had told him I was walking back so he would have expected me to have left the Tea Chalet area," she continued.

"Is there anything else about the incident that you can remember, Miss Webster?" asked Green.

"Apart from feeling hungry and thirsty and sick all at the same time, as well as thinking I was going to die before anyone found me, no, not really," replied Joanne.

"Okay, thank you Miss Webster, I think we are done here for the moment. Thank you for your time; it's good to see you are recovering well," replied Field as he got up from the chair.

"I'll show you both out," said Warren.

Detective Field stopped at the doorway to the lounge and turned back towards Joanne.

"Tell me, Miss Webster, how sure are you that Mr Maddox was not your kidnapper?" he asked.

Joanne wasn't sure how to respond. She looked towards her boss, but he just shook his head, hoping she would ignore the detective's comment, but she despised him so much she couldn't let it go.

"Tell me, Field, have you always been a dumb-arsed prick?" she said staring straight at him.

Warren had heard enough; he ushered the two detectives out of the house before anymore insults could be exchanged.

After seeing the two detectives out of the house, Warren returned to the lounge where Joanne was still sitting.

"So, I think that went reasonably well," he said as he sat down opposite her.

"You really think so?" she asked.

"Well, apart from the final five minutes or so, yes. I thought you stayed remarkably composed."

"It wasn't easy. I really don't know what he was trying to get at with that line of questioning," said Joanne.

Aunt Matilda had been sat quietly listening to the conversation when suddenly she let out a barrage of expletives, culminating in, "The more I see of that man, the more he disgusts me. He really is the vilest person I have ever had the misfortune to meet," she said.

Joanne and Warren sat there, open-mouthed with shock.

"Well, where did that come from, Aunty?" asked Joanne.

"I'm sorry, but I just had to get that off my chest," replied Aunt Matilda.

"Get what off your chest?" asked Tom as he entered the lounge.

"Matilda just told us exactly what she thought of Detective Field, and she didn't leave anything out," explained Warren.

"Sorry I missed it," replied Tom. "So how was Field, anyway?"

"He asked me if I thought it was you who kidnapped me," replied Joanne.

"You are joking, aren't you?"

The three of them sat there, looking at him. Just the look on their faces told him everything.

Their silence was interrupted by a mobile phone ringing. It was Warren's. He answered it while they sat there patiently waiting for him to finish.

"Susan sends her apologies, she was hoping to join us but something important cropped up at work and she won't be able to make it," explained Warren.

"Did she say what it was? Does she need my help?" asked Joanne.

"No, she has it all under control, thank you. She said she hopes you will understand and looks forward to seeing you on Friday."

"She works too hard," replied Joanne.

"I wonder who she gets that from," remarked Tom.

It was then that Warren announced he had to be going back home. He had promised Patricia that he would not be late. A promise that he would be in danger of breaking if he didn't make a move soon.

"I hope to see you all on Friday," he said as he turned and walked toward the front door.

Tom followed him, taking his hand and giving him a quick hug before releasing him and waving goodbye. He stood watching as Warren drove off before re-joining Joanne and Aunt Matilda in the lounge.

Joanne spent the next few days relaxing as she tried to regain both her physical strength and mental fitness under the watchful eye of Aunt Matilda. As much as she loved her aunt dearly, it took Joanne just a couple of hours to remember why she chose the hotel rather than stay with her aunt when she first moved from London to Eastbourne. She could not do anything or go anywhere in the house without Aunt Matilda being two steps behind her.

Unfortunately for Tom, there was no such thing as relaxing, not that Joanne was pushing him to complete jobs around the house, it was more he had decided when Joanne and Aunt Matilda were together for more than a few hours, it was best to be somewhere else. He soon realised he had made the right decision as he once again amazed himself at the speed which he could work when left to do so uninterrupted. He had finished the exterior fencing and completed the decking which he knew would please Joanne as she wanted to put a hot tub there.

Tom walked into the kitchen just as Aunt Matilda was making another cup of tea for him.

"You know, Tom, my niece can predict you like clockwork. She said you would be in for another cup of tea and here you are, right on cue," she remarked as she handed Tom the cup.

"Thank you, Matilda, where are you sitting?" asked Tom.

"In the front lounge," she replied. "It's much quieter in there."

"Yes, sorry about the noise, but you'll be glad to know I've finished the decking now, so you'll be able to sit out there once the varnish dries," replied Tom.

Joanne walked into the kitchen while Tom was still drinking his tea.

"I thought I heard voices, but I wasn't sure if it was you, or if aunty was talking to herself," she joked.

"You'll be pleased to know as well that I've finished the decking outside the back lounge so you can order the hot tub you want now," said Tom as he took a sip of tea.

"Really? Oh, that's just perfect, thank you Tom!" replied Joanne as she moved towards him and gave him a big hug followed by a long kiss. This time, Tom didn't pull away or try to cut her kiss short, but he responded with a long, tender kiss of his own.

"Would you two like to be left alone?" asked Aunt Matilda in a loud voice as she thought they might have forgotten she was there.

"Sorry, Aunty, Tom's fault," replied Joanne as she moved away from him.

Tom looked towards Joanne whom he was still holding in his arms, then to Aunt Matilda. "Not me aunty, your niece started it."

"I know very well whose fault it was, don't I, Joanne?" replied Matilda.

"You know, I just don't believe you two! Why do I always get the blame?" said Joanne.

"Well, I could hardly fault Tom now, could I? I mean, he is just so *lovely*," replied Aunt Matilda, to which the three of them burst out laughing.

After they had finished dinner, Tom cleared away the dirty dishes and then announced that he was going to have a shower before going to bed. Joanne sat for a while talking to her aunt and then casually added that she felt tired and thought she would have an early night too.

"Okay," replied her aunt. "I'm going to watch telly for a while."

"No problem, goodnight, Aunty," said Joanne as she leant over and kissed her on the cheek, before turning and walking towards the stairs.

"Joanne!" called Aunt Matilda.

"Yes, Aunty," replied Joanne inquiringly.

"Don't forget you are still recovering so make sure you get some sleep."

"But of course," replied Joanne as she turned and disappeared up the stairs.

Joanne went straight to the bedroom but as Tom wasn't there, she picked up a towel and went into the bathroom. He was still in the shower, so she discarded her clothes on the bathroom floor and crept into the shower behind him.

"Would you like me to wash your back?" she whispered.

"What took you so long? I thought you were never coming," replied Tom.

"Sorry, I was chatting with aunty and I didn't want to make things too obvious," she replied.

"What things might they be then?" asked Tom.

"Well, you coming to have a shower and me following you straight away would have been too obvious," she replied.

"And did you succeed in making your actions less obvious?" asked Tom.

"Not really," replied Joanne. "Aunty has reminded me I am still recovering and to make sure I get some sleep,"

"How do you feel about the sleep bit, then?" he asked.

"Why? Do you have something else in mind?" questioned Joanne.

Tom turned off the shower and, turning towards Joanne, he lifted her up in his arms, carried her still wet-through to the bedroom and gently placed her on the bed. Leaning over her, he held both her hands in his and spread them out wide on the bed. He softly kissed her lips, then her neck and then moving slowly down her body, over her chest, placing kisses on the mounds of her breasts and moving ever so slowly down to her abdomen. Joanne could feel the tension rising in her body, and freeing her hands from his grasp, she placed them on his buttocks and swiftly pulled him towards her. The feeling was electric; it was what she had been waiting for, longing for, and now she didn't want it to stop.

Joanne opened her eyes and turned her head towards Tom. He was still asleep; she lay there for a short while just watching him and replaying in her head the memories of the hours before and the satisfaction she had felt with their lovemaking. She rested her hand on his chest and then moved it slowly down his body, tracing the contours with the tip of her fingers. She paused momentarily as he stirred, but he was still asleep; she continued with the movement of her hand, slowly across his abdomen, down to his hip and then down across his thigh to his knee. She circled the tip of her finger around his knee a couple of times before moving it slowly up the inside of his leg, across his thigh muscle to his groin. Her efforts showed signs of having the desired effect as she noticed a flickering of his eyelids as he began to wake up. As she continued with the movement of her fingertips over his groin, she soon detected more movement, so she positioned herself over him.

"You are completely insatiable, Miss Webster," he said softly before raising his head off the pillow and kissing her lips.

"You think so now," she replied. "Just you wait until I have completely recovered."

"I thought we were going to your office today?" asked Tom.

"We are, but they can wait, and this can't. Just lie back and enjoy it," she replied softly as she continued her movement.

It was almost five o'clock when they pulled into the car park at her office; Joanne couldn't believe it, there was barely room to park, every space and more was taken apart from hers, where Tom was now parking Warren's borrowed car. As they approached the top of the stairs, her colleagues were stood in line, just like a guard of honour, lining the way to Warren's office. Joanne knocked on the door which swung open – Warren was clearly waiting for her.

"Joanne, it is really great to see you! Welcome back. We can't all fit in here, so let's adjourn to the meeting room," he said.

Joanne was shocked as she followed Warren into the meeting room: it was evident to her that they had probably spent all morning blowing up balloons and decorating.

"What is all this in aid of?" she said to Warren.

"Well, we just wanted to show you how much we have missed you and that you have the support of every one of us. We are so sorry for what happened to you."

"Thank you, everyone," replied Joanne. "I would just like to thank you all for your support and to say that I am so sorry how things ended up with Jefferey. Even after what I have been through, I can honestly say I passionately believe he never meant me any harm. Thank you all for a terrific welcome back."

Tom, who had been standing by Joanne's side, noticed two people in the doorway.

"It would appear we have intruders. Someone call the police ... oh hang on, they *are* the police," he remarked sarcastically.

Detective Field walked towards them. "I'm sorry to interrupt your celebrations. I hadn't expected to see everyone in such a jovial mood after the loss of one of your colleagues. I would just like to update you all on the case and I can now confirm that the occupants of the car were, in fact, Jefferey Philips and a Mrs Lucy Saunders."

The detective paused momentarily, allowing Warren Fredericks to intervene.

"Thank you for that, Detective Field. I hope we can all move on now, which is what we are trying to do here; maybe you would like to join us in our celebrations?"

"Not quite," said Field. "In fact, I am here to *complete* my investigation. Not only have I been trying to piece together the kidnapping of Miss Webster, but also the incident with Mr Philips and Mrs Saunders. What appeared to be a case of suicide is now a murder case as both occupants of the car were already dead before the car was propelled over the edge of the cliff."

The room fell silent.

"I'm here with Detective Green and some uniformed officers to make an arrest," continued Field.

Warren could not believe what he had just heard. He looked around the room and then, raising his hands as though to encompass everyone in the room, he said, "I hope that is a bad joke detective. Who could you possibly have reason to suspect here?" he replied.

Field stepped forward and, approaching Tom, he said, "Mr Maddox, I am arresting you on suspicion of the involvement of the kidnapping of Miss Joanne Webster and of the murder of Mr Jefferey Philips and Mrs Lucy Saunders. You are not obliged to say anything, but anything you do say will be taken down and may be used in evidence against you."

Field was interrupted by Joanne as she let out a loud scream before collapsing on the floor in front of him. The elation she had felt the previous night had come crashing down in front of her; she was inconsolable.

"You will pay for this, Field! You have totally lost the plot, you daft prick!" shouted Tom as he was led away in handcuffs by the uniformed officers.

To be continued

ABOUT THE AUTHOR

After writing several short stories for fun, I decided to adapt one to novel length. But why this one? Why *Joanne*? I guess I could see an intriguing development which I was looking forward to expanding.

I have thoroughly enjoyed writing my first novel and I hope you get just as much enjoyment from reading it.

www.ingramcontent.com/pod-product-compliance
Lightning Source LLC
Chambersburg PA
CBHW030225100526
44585CB00012BA/223